FOREWORD

This is a book about channeling, for those who may not have guessed from the title. It could have been simply titled, "Mediumship," but then the name medium has fallen into disrepute in recent times due to several publicized investigations into activities at some spiritualist camps involving fraud and trickery.

Something flows through a channel, be it water, wind, or, in this case, wisdom. With such information or revelation, the more readily accepted term channeling is popular in today's vernacular. It avoids the taint of the term "medium," and allows for something good and positive, flowing from whatever source, to irrigate and fertilize the mind in dimensions unlimited by any ordinary standards.

Therefore, I suggest the reader approach this book with an open mind, and also with levity. Both are recommended to help keep one's feet on the ground and at the same time allow the senses to take wing into the world of the "known," but frequently questioned and denied.

Arthur Ford, author of Unknown but Known, is one of a handful of channelers for whom the channeled information has been so evidential that even die-hard skeptics have a hard time ignoring it. He was profoundly startled by the sudden onset of his "gift" during World War I, when, as a young man, he saw in his dreams the lists of men killed in battle which would be posted the next day. Checking out the names the following day, he was shocked to find his dreams were accurate. But Ford's most noted feat was his reception of a coded message that the deceased magician, Harry Houdini, had left with his wife to test whether discarnate communication was possible. Sir Arthur Conan Doyle called Ford's demonstration "one of the most amazing things I have seen in 41 years of psychic experience." (The Washington Post Book Review, by James McC. Truitt, November 12, 1968.)

I, too, knew Arthur Ford, not only personally, but closely. I was privy to and present for several uncanny events with him, including trance sessions with his guide, "Fletcher," and sermons from a church pulpit, for Ford was an ordained minister. He continued to be puzzled by his abilities and questioned the reason and meaning of it all to the time of his passing.

There is no proof, no irrefutable and conclusive evidence, to completely and appropriately define this area of centuries-old reported phenomena and make it a commonly accepted everyday reality for all. Yet for those who have had the experience, there is no question or doubt. All attempts to explain it satisfactorily have gone begging for centuries. Even hard-nosed critics and cynics, and many "doubting Thomases," have had life-changing experiences when confronted by their own moment of entry into this unexplainable and uncharted realm.

For example, Edgar Cayce, one of the best known channelers, was once studied by a Dr. Hugo Münsterberg, a well-known Harvard University professor. Münsterberg was a very critical man, out to expose Cayce as a fake. After interviewing Cayce and several of his clients, the professor's perspective began to change. Several times Cayce had invited Münsterberg to witness a reading. He finally accepted, and it was *following this reading that Münsterberg became fully impressed with Cayce's simplicity and sincerity.*

During the reading Cayce described a young man's physical ailments. Having read about Cayce in a Cincinnati newspaper article, the man had requested an appointment without revealing why he wanted the reading. When the man, upon questioning, confirmed the accuracy of his reading, Münsterberg advised him to follow Cayce's advice precisely, and to do exactly as he recommended. (The Story of Edgar Cayce [There Is A River] by Thomas Sugrue, Dell Publishers, 1942, page 32.)

Arthur Hastings has performed a monumental task in this book, gathering together a wide range of channeling history and personalities. Many of these insights may already be familiar, having been covered in other books, both old and new. But, I assure, he presents many others that will be entirely new and surprising. As he worked, his own interest and enthusiasm for this subject grew and expanded, as did the manuscript. It took him deeper and deeper into the research of materials, and further afield in his inquiry, than he himself had envisioned when beginning this book.

As I sit here by the window, looking out across the water channeled by the Lake Worth inlet near my home, I cannot see the turbulent currents deep beneath the surface. But I know they are there. I observe fronds on the palm trees being tossed about by winds channeled from the latest tropical storm in the Caribbean, but I cannot see the wind. The effects of both are all the proof I need that wind and wave, properly understood, can be put to use for good. As I think on these things, a comparison with consciousness rises in my mind. I believe it is the effect that determines the value and usefulness of channeling.

If I were to determine what one particular thing most influenced my life, and was most meaningful to me in my overall life experience, I would have to eliminate all of the most usual criteria cited. I would narrow it down to the increased awareness of the meaning of life made possible by my introduction to, and immersion in, matters of spiritual and psychic phenomena.

My sincere hope is that Arthur Hastings' superb efforts to serve up this most tantalizing menu of "channeling" happenings and theories will make this an adventure and reading pleasure not soon forgotten. A last word of caution. It may change your thinking—for life!

> Henry J. Rolfs
> Palm Beach, Florida
> October 12, 1990
> Director, Institute of Noetic Sciences

PREFACE

What is currently called channeling has existed since the beginning of recorded human history. The process is one in which information, ideas, creative works, and personal guidance come to our minds from a source outside our own selves. The individual's mind seems to act as a receiver for another communicator. This book uses the term channeling because it is current, but the process has been called prophecy, oracle, revelation, spirit communication, possession, and the inspiration of the muses. The Biblical tradition in Judaism and Christianity says that the prophets received and spoke the words of God. Today, there are many individuals who speak words that are said to come from disembodied teachers on other levels of reality. The process, though not necessarily the content, appears to be the same.

This book is a study of these phenomena, from ancient times to now, from the content of the messages to the psychology of the process. It asks the questions:

What is the nature of channeling?

What is the significance of channeling for us?

When I began, I assumed that topics such as these should not be dismissed without investigation. My intention was to study channeling with as few presuppositions as possible and to base any conclusions on what I found. I wanted to look at the evidence and its implications. I hoped neither to idealize channeling nor to discount it.

Frankly, I was not sure of what I would find. I interviewed many people who channel. I located cases and experiences throughout history and read thousands of pages of books, poems, sermons, and teachings that have been channeled. Much of this material is abysmal, and I would not recommend it except as a remedy for insomnia. But I was surprised and impressed to find that the best of it is interesting, practical, provocative, insightful, and inspirational. Channeled communication, under many names, has played a significant role in human history. The best channeled material is worth knowing about for its own sake. Further, it shows that there are exceptional levels of creativity and wisdom that are accessible to us, regardless of where we believe they originate.

Several of my interests and studies influenced how I investigated channeling. My original academic training was in communication and rhetoric, so I am interested in channeled messages as communications. What is their content and what are their purposes? My involvement with the field of parapsychology (psychical research) gave methods to study psychic information in channeling and to evaluate the possibility that the sources are nonphysical beings or spirits. My study of transpersonal psychology provided ways to understand the psychological, creative, and spiritual aspects of channeling. Many other disciplines have contributed useful information and approaches: anthropology, social studies, history, philosophy, classical studies, and religion. The answers to our questions are not going to come from any one discipline, but from an understanding that draws on many fields of thought.

This is not an academic book, but I have tried to be accurate in presenting information and points of view. Names of authors and dates in the text will guide interested readers to the references. The appendix gives sources for further investigation of channeling.

The title comes from the first letter to the Corinthians in the New Testament, where Paul writes about the gifts of the Holy Spirit, including prophecy. "If I speak with the tongues of men and of angels, but have not love, I am become sounding brass or a clanging gong." This means that regardless of the source of the message, we need to add our own qualities of love and wisdom for channeling to be used wisely and with discernment.

While I was writing this book, several people asked me if I was channeling it. My answer was yes. I channeled a fellow named Arthur Hastings. I hope he has done a good job, and that you will find the book interesting, informative, and provocative.

ACKNOWLEDGMENTS

The idea for this book came from Henry Rolfs, who also provided financial support to give me the time to carry out the research and writing. An additional grant came from Lucy Waletzsky, M.D. The Institute of Noetic Sciences sponsored the project and provided support in staff time and assistance. The Institute of Transpersonal Psychology contributed resources, library, and administrative support. I am grateful to all of them.

Sandy, my wife, managed the rearrangements of family time and activities that made the work possible. She also read every page, often several times, and helped me with many substantive comments.

The many illustrations and graphics were tracked down and assembled by Carol Guion, of the Institute of Noetic Sciences.

I received helpful ideas, materials, and assistance from many people and organizations. My special thanks go to Willis Harman and Charles Tart for their encouragement and insights throughout my investigation of channeling. Appreciation for many kinds of assistance goes to: Ina Adams, Dan Alford, Alfred Alschuler, Joel Andrews, the Association for the Anthropological Study of Consciousness, Carole Austen, Richard Bach, the board and staff of the Institute of Noetic Sciences, Stephen Braude, Gwen Briscoe, Matthew Bronson, Roger Brown, Goodrun Cable, Don Campbell, Charles Thomas Cayce, Margaret Chandley, Lisette Coly, Eileen Coly, Tom Condon, Arthur Deikman, Etta Deikman, Patricia Drury, East-West Bookshop, Hoyt Edge, Kenneth Eyer, James Fadiman, Jon Fox, Robert Frager, Winston O. Franklin, Geri-Ann Galanti, Luiz Gasparetto, June Gordon, Sandy Gordon, Stanislav Grof, Catherine Heath, Robert Hoffman, Leona Jamison, William Kautz, Nicola Kester, Sange Khendro, H. J. Kramer, Sue Lanier, Love and Light Research, James R. MacMahon, William A. McGarey, Barbara McNeill, Nari Mayo, Jean MiLay, Minerva Books, the Missouri Historical Society, Ernest Moore, Tam Mossman, Dio Neff, Tina Oldham, Richard Page, Helen Palmer, John Palmer, Ira Progoff, Debra Reynolds, Thomas B. Roberts, Scott Rogo, Samantha St. Julian, C. Norman Shealy, Charles Spaegel, Dennis Stillings, Judy Tart, Liz Thacker, Justine Toms, Michael Toms, Marcello Truzzi, Paul Tuttle, Janis Tyrone, Walter Uphoff, Jacques Vallee, Frances Vaughan, Roger Walsh, Rita Warren, Julian White, William Whitson, Colin Wilson, and Peggy Joy Young.

WITH THE TONGUES OF MEN AND ANGELS

A Study of Channeling

CHAPTER 1

CHANNELING

In recent years there has been an increase in an activity called "channeling." In channeling, a person claims to communicate messages that come to him or her from supernatural beings, spirits, or other nonphysical intelligences.

In the most dramatic form of channeling, a person goes into a trance or dreamlike state and another being speaks through him or her. This new personality claims to be an advanced spirit from a nonphysical reality, temporarily occupying the body of the person. This entity gives advice, information, and teaching. The person whose body is involved usually has little memory of the experience.

There are other, less dramatic, forms of channeling—of receiving information from some source outside the ordinary mind. At least 15 percent of the population has heard at one time or another an inner voice giving them information or guidance. Whole books have been written, some good, some not so good, based on the words of inner dictation. Some people experience automatic writing, in which the person's hand writes messages including poetry, inspirational ideas, and psychological information, without conscious effort.

Regardless of the validity of the claims of supernatural agency, the fact remains that mentally healthy individuals experience these phenomena. Moreover, a large number of these messages contain meaningful information and exhibit knowledge and talents of which the channeler is completely unaware.

Whatever one's view of the origin of the messages, the phenomenon itself merits serious examination.

OTHER BEINGS OR PART OF THE MIND?

Channeling raises many intriguing questions. Is there really another entity communicating from outside our physical reality? How do we know? If this is another being, does it provide a wider perspective on our human condition or offer greater wisdom in solving our problems? What can be learned from these beings?

On the other hand, perhaps we are not hearing spirits from a higher realm, but parts of the person's mind that have been separated from con-·scious awareness, and these parts are presenting themselves as other entities or spirit guides. Channeling might be a nonpathological form of multiple personality or dissociated subpersonalities. If so, then perhaps we can learn how complex ideas and skills can originate outside the conscious part of the mind. Channeling may throw some light on how another part of the self can obtain knowledge not known to the primary personality. Perhaps the process of channeling gives a person options he or she would not have with only a single self. How this might occur is a puzzle of the mind that should be explored. Does this possibility mean that creative and active intelligence can be independent of the conscious personality?

What are the answers? In the words of Saint Paul in his letter to the Corinthians, do these channels speak with the tongues of men or of angels? Do they bring love, wisdom, and knowledge, or is it rambling nonsense?

What is the nature of channeling? What is its meaning and significance? What implications does it have for our self-knowledge and our view of the universe? This book will explore these questions as well as others.

SOME VARIETIES OF CHANNELING

Channeling is a recent word, but the phenomenon has a long history. It is found in almost every culture from ancient times to the present. Let us begin with some examples, giving them as they have been reported.

Perhaps six centuries before the birth of Christ, a priestess of the oracle at Delphi in Greece goes into a trance to meet a delegation from the Liparians. Her voice becomes deeper; her face changes as she is possessed by the God Apollo. Responding to a question about battle strategy, the oracle tells the Liparians to defend themselves against the attacking Etruscans with as few ships as possible. They send out five ships against a full fleet. The Etruscans, not to be called unfair, send out only five ships, which are sunk. They send out five more, which are also destroyed. This continues. Eventually, the Liparians sink twenty ships and the Etruscans retreat, defeated.

In the sixth century A.D., the Arabic prophet Muhammad begins to perspire and shake, even though the evening is cool. In a trance, he speaks words of the angel Gabriel; Muhammad's companions take down the phrases. The words later become a chapter of the Koran, the holy scripture of the Moslems.

Edgar Cayce, a professional photographer in Hopkinsville, Kentucky, in the 1920s, lies down and goes into a self-induced hypnotic sleep. In this state, his subconscious self describes a woman several hundred miles away and gives accurate information about her health problems and how to treat them.

Alice A. Bailey, an Englishwoman, agrees to telepathically receive information on spiritual training and service. From 1922 to 1949 she writes twenty books mentally dictated to her by an advanced master who says he is living in a monastery in Tibet.

A woman in Michigan, Dorothy Martin, begins to receive messages through automatic writing from crews of unidentified flying objects (UFOs). They tell her and her group of followers that flooding and cataclysmic destruction will strike the world on December 20, 1954. The group prepares for the worst. Nothing happens. The UFO occupants say that the cataclysm was called off because of the faith of the members.

Jane Roberts, in Elmira, New York, contacts an entity named Seth through the use of a Ouija Board. Within a few sessions, Seth is able to use Jane's voice and body to communicate. In the 1970s, he begins to dictate books and teach personal growth classes with Roberts.

In the 1980s, thousands of people, intentionally or not, begin to hear voices, write automatically, trance-speak, and in other ways receive and transmit communications from a source outside their conscious mind. Some keep it secret; others go public. Many build large groups of followers and attract media attention.

As these examples show, there is no one way that channeling occurs; but the process is one in which information from outside the conscious mind is communicated through the person. The messages may seem to come from an outside being such as an angel or spirit, from another part of the self as a voice or writing, from extraterrestrials, or from entities claiming to be in other dimensions of the mind. Some messages are of social and personal value, some are trivial, some are dramatically wrong.

DEFINITIONS

We know not the mysterious . . . Things
of God but as they have been channel'd
to us by God himself in divine
Revelation.

—R. Carpenter, 1657
Oxford English Dictionary

I have heard the word "channeling" used in many ways. One person will say "another entity took over and was speaking through me." Another will say "I just opened my mouth and channeled whatever came through." To begin, we need to have a definition of channeling that will identify what we are talking about. The quotation from Carpenter is the earliest reference I have found to channeling in the sense that is current: messages coming from the world of deities and supernatural beings. Earlier in this century, the word "channel" was used to refer to spirit mediums by their spirit guides. The word was in use in England in the 1930s, perhaps earlier in seances and spiritualist literature. The *Oxford English Dictionary* defines this sense of channel as "that through which information, news . . . passes; a medium of transmission, conveyance, or communication." This definition even uses the term "medium," which shows the close similarity between the two words.

The implication intended by using the word "channel" is that the person simply transmits the messages from spirits, as an instrument or vehicle, without adding anything of his or her own material (though careful research on mediumship shows that the medium's personality and knowledge often affect the message). In modern usage, the connotation is the same: the individual ego mind steps out of the way, and the message comes through unimpeded and unchanged.

In his comprehensive survey, *Channeling: Investigations on Receiving Information from Paranormal Sources,* Jon Klimo (1987) defines channeling on a continuum. At one end is "classic channeling," with an external, identified source such as a spirit, independent of the individual. At the other end, he places "open channeling." This refers to information originating from beyond the individual's self and beyond ordinary reality, but which is not identifiable and does not identify itself. As examples of open channeling, Klimo mentions intuition, inspiration, and creativity. His full definition of channeling is "the communication of information to or through a physically embodied human being from a source that is said to exist on some other level or dimension of reality than the physical as we know it, and that is not from the normal mind (or self) of the channel" (p. 2).

The popular use of the term, and what most practitioners claim, is that channeling is the transmission through a human being of messages from a discarnate being using telepathy or bodily possession. Of course, this definition assumes the source is a separate, discarnate entity. The existence of discarnate beings in channeling remains to be proved. The fact that automatic writing claims to be from a spirit guide or a channeled personality who gives a name and address on the seventh etheric plane is not sufficient reason to accept the source as an outside entity. We can only say that the source *claims* to be a separate being or is *experienced* by the person in that way; however, another part of the mind may be forming a secondary personality, as with people who have multiple personalities, or there may be a dramatization of another aspect of the self. One of the purposes of this book will be to explore the evidence for the possibilities of outside beings in channeling.

Because the phenomenon has many variations, I'll start with a description rather than a strict definition. This description identifies several aspects of "mainstream" channeling cases:

Channeling refers to a process in which a person transmits information or artistic expression that he or she receives mentally or physically and which appears to come from a personality source outside the conscious mind. The message is directed toward an audience and is purposeful.

This definition has several elements which will distinguish a fundamental type of channeling from the many variants that may or may not be similar; if we can get some understanding of the central issues related to this fundamental type, then perhaps the nature of the less obvious forms can be better understood. Some basic characteristics of this kind of channeling are as follows.

1 *The message must be coherent and intelligible.* The transmission is "information" in the sense that it has meaning; it is not random words or phrases. It is not speaking in unknown languages or writing in unknown and unrecognizable script. One of my friends spoke with a woman who said that she channeled the spirits of the dolphins. "What do they say," he asked. "We don't know," she said, "They just go boop, boop, beep, queep, toot." She was apparently serious in her belief, but such a message would not meet this standard for channeling.

2 *The source must be perceived as coming from outside the conscious self.* This may occur in several ways. Some messages just appear in the mind as fully formed thoughts in words, but without having been constructed or processed by the individual and without the identifying feel of it being one's own. It is as though one is listening to a mental telephone.

The message may come through automatic writing or drawing, with the person's hand moving "by itself"; the person is not consciously controlling it. Sometimes the "writer" as differentiated from the "author" can be talking with a friend, drinking coffee, or even reading something else while this is happening. Whole books, stories, drawings, and poems have been written through this form of channeling.

The channeler may also feel some other "person" physically influencing or controlling the body and speech from the inside. Usually, the channeler "steps back" to let the other take over. In extreme cases, the other personality completely controls the body, and the individual is in a trance state. The channeler's memories of the experience are vague or nonexistent. The common point is that the person experiences the messages or actions as being alien, different from his or her own self-identity.

3. *The origin of the message is perceived or identified as a definite source—that is, it has an existence of its own.* The origin may be from God or a celestial being. It may be a strong personality with a name, with writing or speaking mannerisms, emotions, and other personality characteristics. There may be minimal nuances, with only a feeling on the part of the human being that the messages come from an "entity." Sometimes the source may seem to be a principle such as "creativity" or "limitless love and light," or the planetary logos. The person may speak under the inspiration of the Holy Spirit. If the person senses another presence communicating, this would fit within our definition.

This third characteristic excludes "open channeling" in which people receive inner information without an identifiable source. It is more specific than William Kautz's description of channeling as "a means of access to intuition" (Kautz and Branon, 1987). Poets such as A. E. Housman and Rainer Maria Rilke (1939) reported that verses simply appeared in their minds, fully written. Mozart and other composers heard inner music playing spontaneously as they composed. These, along with intuitions and creativity, are not channeling according to this criterion. Studies in philosophy and psychology have illuminated many characteristics of intuition and creativity. It is not clear that the process of spontaneous creativity or intuitive thinking is the same process as one in which there appears to be an outside personality or entity. This book will focus primarily on the "definite source" type of channeling. The three characteristics described above define classic channeling. There are some further aspects that are essential components of channeling in human affairs.

4. *There is an audience for the channeled message.* This may seem obvious, but it is important to point out that the message is directed to someone: the channel himself, a questioner, therapists, business persons, listeners in an auditorium, even a nation or society. Messages are always directed and adapted to listeners. The audience is an essential part of any communication relationship, whether it is sympathetic to the speaker or not. This means that we must note how responsive channels are to their audience, and how the channels respond to the needs and circumstances of the times in which they speak.

5. *The channeled message has a purpose.* Every message in communication conveys a meaning for a particular purpose. The purpose may be to inform, to persuade for a point of view, to evoke feelings, or to inspire. It may be intended to change a person or society. All channeled communication is purposeful; by looking at the purposes, we may learn the role channeling plays in society and culture and the function it serves for individuals who listen.

This book will also consider cases of channeling that vary from these central elements and, through comparisons, analyze the range of the process that we call channeling.

A BRIEF HISTORY OF CHANNELING

There is no new thing under the sun.

Ecclesiastes 1:9

A brief look at history will show that channeling has occurred in many forms in many cultures. In early tribal cultures, there were priests, shamans (tribal medicine men or women), and others who would transmit messages from spirits and gods for healing, advice, and group rituals. These forms continue even today in similar societies.

In Greece, Egypt, and the Near East, as far back as the fourteenth century B.C., oracles of Ishtar, Apollo, Hercules, Zeus, Amon, and other gods were established and were consulted by everyone from ordinary citizens to generals and heads of state. Usually a priest or priestess would go into a trance and speak the words of the god.

In many early societies, the messages communicated through trances and inspiration were taken as divine instructions for the people. Some fell on fertile ground and became religious teachings. The words of the Biblical prophets such as Jeremiah, Isaiah, and Micah; the Koran; some Taoist scriptures; and transmitted books of Tibetan Buddhism are examples. The early Christian churches considered prophecy and inspired speaking to be gifts from the Holy Spirit; they can be viewed as a form of channeling. In medieval Jewish practice, many rabbis had a maggid, a spirit teacher who mentally spoke to them and even through them.

Channeling later fell on hard times, even in religion. The voices of Joan of Arc were discounted; prophecy was relegated to the Old Testament. Religions are now reluctant to compare their origins with current forms of channeling; antiquity lends authenticity to the revelations of faiths. Nevertheless, the process appears to be much the same. Other chapters of this book will consider the role of channeling in prophecy and in traditional and contemporary religious teachings.

In the 1800s, spirit mediums in Western society replaced the oracles and medicine men in their social role of communicating with the "other side." Mediums said they could contact the spirits of the departed to give advice and reassure the living of the survival of death. Mediums clearly held a role outside the mainstream of social beliefs. They spoke mostly to unquestioning or gullible followers. The few psychic researchers who sat through sessions found mostly messages of emotional reassurance, vague generalities, and much fraudulent phenomena.

As scientific materialism increased in influence in the nineteenth century, it rejected the concept of the existence of supernatural beings along with the astral plane they were supposed to inhabit. In the twentieth century, proponents of psychoanalysis decided the messages came from dissociated repressions that should be cured.

A few researchers began to investigate the questions raised by mediumship with scientific methods, such as testing the validity of information given under controlled conditions, developing methods for objective tests, and conducting psychological analysis of the medium. Among all the unpromising material, there appeared some evidence to suggest the existence of spirit beings and consciousness after death. The Society for Psychical Research in Britain and the American Society for Psychical Research compiled studies of confirmed information, apparitions, and cases of complex messages that apparently could come only from the other side. These studies were not credible to the vast majority of Western intellectuals and scientists because of the high number of fraudulent mediums and the inconsistent quality of the evidence.

The investigative efforts of the researchers soon turned to studies of human psychic ability and led to naming the field "parapsychology" in the 1930s. Psychic ability was called extrasensory perception and now is usually termed *psi*. Many of these scholars believed that any valid information from mediums actually came from the medium's own ESP rather than the presence of spirits. Skeptics also rejected the existence of ESP, arguing that it did not fit with laws of physical reality and had not been established with satisfactory evidence.

The studies of psi and research findings are well documented in parapsychological literature and will not be discussed in detail here. The controversy continues in the scientific world as to the validity of this work, and readers can find discussions of it in popular and professional publications. However, some channeled messages give valid information that was not known to the channel, and we need to consider where that information comes from. Later chapters will look at possible instances of psi (ESP) in channeling.

Currently we find the phenomenon of channeling to be increasing. According to sociologists Earl and Sheila Babbie there are thousands of individuals claiming to be channels. The sources of the information claim to be higher beings, spiritual masters, extraterrestrials, or some other impressive personality. This is a new development. In ancient times they were considered to be gods and goddesses, nature spirits, and angels. A century ago, in the era of the mediums, they were Native Americans, Orientals, spirits of the deceased, and other spirit guides.

Whoever they are now, they are being listened to. Channels and channeled teachings have many devoted followers from isolated readers and their clients to small local groups and nationwide study groups. Channeled books have sold millions of copies. We may soon begin to see some influences of their ideas on cultural attitudes and social change.

The increase in those who channel has also brought critiques from skeptics and observers who fear channeling is a combination of fraud, irrationalism, and gullibility. They believe it is a development which does not speak well for education, scientific attitudes, and rationality. Generally, the controversy has been polarized between naive believers and rigid skeptics. Very few of the endorsements or critiques are based upon knowledge of the phenomena, serious research, or an open-minded scientific belief system. In this book, the attempt will be to look at channeling without presuppositions and to let the data of channeling itself suggest the various points of view.

The effects of current channeling are amplified by the media. Television and radio programs have presented channeling to millions of people. Audio and video cassettes make the messages available for anyone to experience. Newspapers run feature stories on cults around channels or how businesspeople seek channeled financial advice. If there is good in the messages, then perhaps it will get communicated; however, the media tends to emphasize the sensational, the conflictual, and the problematic, so significant ideas may be lost in media "noise."

Some of the channelings are messages to society, directed toward change and transformation of our collective condition and calling for governmental and planetary responsibility. Some messages consist of philosophical, metaphysical, and spiritual teachings. Channelers also give personal advice, technical information, and counseling on love, marriage, and the many ills of the human condition. Unfortunately, the quality varies and is not always as high as the credentials the sources give. There are some profound ideas and much trivia, some pertinent counseling insights and much ordinary motherly advice (depending on what kind of mother one has). New Age platitudes rub shoulders with perennial wisdom. As with any advice we are given, we need to learn how to appraise the quality of these messages without assuming they are either nonsense to be dismissed or transcendent wisdom to be embraced.

WHAT CAN WE LEARN?

What can we learn from all this, and what are the values and dangers of channeling? First, we can look at the significant accomplishments of channeling. As you will see, there have been exceptional cases of writing, art, mathematics, spiritual teaching, and psychological insight derived through channeling. These have made contributions to individuals and to society. If people can access or transmit worthwhile material through the channeling process, then it deserves study as a "technology" of information and human potential. If these materials are coming from transhuman sources, then a vast resource may be available for our understanding.

Second, there are thousands of people who go to channels for personal help. What is it that they receive? How can it be evaluated by them and by those of us who are concerned with the quality of people's personal growth? Therapeutic advice and problem solving are also sought from channels. How valid are their responses? Is this a source of understanding that can be tapped?

Third, there are instances of psi (ESP) that appear to occur in channeling. Channeled messages often predict events such as natural catastrophes. What is their track record? Understanding this will add to our information about both channeling and psi and will tell us how to evaluate such messages.

Fourth, many messages from channels are spiritual, philosophical, or religious in nature. They are teachings on attitudes, beliefs, and the nature of reality. Some channeled messages are generalities, others are sophisticated psychological and spiritual systems. This may be part of a new spiritual awakening in our time. If so, it will affect more than just those who listen to the channels. We should ask what values they contribute and how their doctrines are to be judged.

Fifth, the problematic aspects of channeling are many. Socially, many of the channels encourage emotional dependency among their followers, though often enough the listeners are willing to supply it on their own. The "other world" status of entities often causes people to give them authority and power. The temptations of fame and money can deteriorate channels and sources alike, regardless of the entity's claim to be nonmaterial (if not nonmaterialistic). From the channel's point of view, the inner process can be demanding and intrusive. Even with good ego strength, there is often difficulty in dealing with fear, doubt, confusion, and the adulation of others. There are perhaps ways that channels themselves can improve the quality, accuracy, and literacy of the messages. An understanding of the psychology of these processes may be a protection for all concerned.

Finally, we have much to learn about consciousness, the self, personal identity, and our relation to other realities. If these processes point the way toward the existence of other intelligences, then we have access to other domains that are probably beyond our imagination. Whatever the source, the models that we develop to describe the channeling process will tell us more about ourselves and our capabilities, as well as illuminate our connections to the universe within and without.

In the following chapters, there are studies of cases of channeling, samples of channeled communication, the conclusions that emerge from them, and a discussion of the significance of channeling for us and our times.

CHAPTER 2

EXAMPLES OF EXCEPTIONAL CHANNELING

We will begin by looking at several contemporary cases with exceptional features. In some of these cases, the material is exceptional in quality or content. In others, the skills involved go well beyond the talents of the individual doing the channeling (Hastings, 1988). These cases will illustrate some of the ways in which channeling has been used and the level of messages that are possible.

TECHNIQUES

First, we will review some of the processes through which this material is actually received. The Ouija Board, now manufactured by Parker Brothers, has been around since the late 1800s. It is a well-known parlor entertainment and is sold only as a game, according to the manufacturer. In 1967, the board actually outsold the game of Monopoly. The participants place their hands on a sliding pointer which, apparently by itself, moves to letters and numbers on the board to spell out messages. The actual movement of the pointer comes from subconscious movements of the operators' hands, but the question is where the messages come from. Often they claim to come from spirits.

Messages may also come through automatic writing or, in modern times, typing or computer word processing. The individual experiences a slight dissociation, and the message is written or typed without conscious volition.

Another mode of the channeling process could be called an inner voice. Messages, teaching, poetry, information, profound (or trivial) thoughts are spoken in a mental voice.

While in a light trance, the individual may feel inspired by another presence and speak words that come spontaneously. The early Christians called this prophecy, a gift of the Holy Spirit. As the channel moves into a deeper trance, similar to hypnosis, the individual's personality moves aside and another begins to appear until the other is predominant. This is similar to possession states found in tribal societies and to divination and oracular ceremonies in which a deity is presumed to possess the speaker.

HEALTH DIAGNOSIS AND TREATMENT

We will now turn to abilities and skills that have manifested in a channeling mode, beginning with advice on health. The most famous psychic in America is probably Edgar Cayce, who was born in 1877 and died in 1943 (H. L. Cayce, 1964; Sugrue, 1945). He is best known for his clairvoyant readings on health. During his life, he gave about sixteen thousand readings for individuals, speaking while his conscious mind was in a trance state. Most of these readings were about health problems, diagnosing the person's physical state and giving instructions for treatments (E. Cayce, 1970). Cayce would be told the name of the individual, and he would describe what the individual's health conditions were. This might include heart and circulation problems, nerve disorders, organ malfunctions, spinal misalignments (in the language of chiropractic), and nutritional needs. Cayce often referred to stress, exhaustion, overexertion, poor mental attitude, and the individual's spiritual state, and so has been referred to as holistic. After his diagnosis, he would give recommendations for treatment. These were generally oriented toward natural remedies such as folk medicine, over-the-counter remedies, herbal preparations, formulas for colds and eye disorders, and castor oil packs for skin and circulation problems. He would also recommend exercise, diet, and attitude change. We should note that he did not hesitate to recommend surgery in certain cases, including one recommendation for himself.

Edgar Cayce, America's most famous psychic, channeled health readings in a hypnotic trance.

The diagnosis and treatment were remarkable in that Cayce performed them at a distance. Sometimes the patients were in the room or the same house; usually, however, they were miles away, often thousands of miles. According to records, many of the diagnoses were confirmed, either by physicians or the individuals involved, and the remedies were reported to be effective, including some in which medical treatment up to that time had not been successful. Some recent clinical work has attempted to confirm several of Cayce's remedies, with some success (McGarey, 1970, 1983). A recent experimental study suggests that Cayce's often-prescribed remedy of castor oil packs may have value in stimulating the immune system (Grady, 1988). Unfortunately, there were no objective investigations of his work; current study remains based on case transcripts and correspondence kept at the time. A study of 150 cases, selected randomly from the files, found that correspondence from patients and physicians reported good results in 43 percent of the cases and negative results in 7 percent. For the remainder, there was no follow-up data (E. E. Cayce and H. L. Cayce, 1971). As the authors point out, however, some of the subjects of the readings were present, and one cannot exclude the role of unconscious perception of some symptoms.

Edgar Cayce was referred to by his own entranced self as a channel for higher consciousness. He said that the information was received by his subconscious mind from the subconscious minds of other people or from the Akashic Records. (In occult terminology, the impressions of all actions and events on the skein of space-time are called the Akashic Records.)

Occasionally, an entity spoke through Cayce—the Archangel Michael, an angel named Halaliel, and some spirits of the deceased. However, Cayce consistently chose to use his own mind for the channeling state, rather than allow other entities to speak. He said it was his own subconscious that did the speaking.

Other channels have given health diagnoses. Mrs. Eileen J. Garrett's guide Abdul Latif claimed to be the spirit of a twelfth-century Arab physician and often would diagnose physical and mental illness. In contemporary times, neurosurgeon C. Norman Shealey has called upon intuitive diagnosticians, including channels, for information on physical, emotional, and spiritual aspects of illness (Shealy and Myss, 1988). The best ones, he says, are more than 90 percent correct, even at a distance. I asked Shealey if there was a difference in accuracy between a channeled diagnosis and one that was simply psychic, without an outside entity. Shealey said that the accuracy depends on the individual, not the method used.

In recent years there has been much discussion of psychic surgeons. The best known of these are located in the Philippines and Brazil. These individuals claim to be possessed by spirits of doctors and carry out procedures in which they seem to make incisions in a patient's body with their bare hands, producing blood and tissue, or they perform minor operations without usual medical procedures. Careful observation of these practices has found them to be based on sleight of hand, with no paranormal aspects (Randi, 1982).

LITERARY CREATION

The channeling mode stands out as a source of creative literature. The British poet and artist William Blake was highly responsive to what he termed spiritual perception. His major prophetic work, a long poem titled *Jerusalem*, apparently came to him entirely through the dictation of an inner voice. He said he had written "from immediate Dictation, twelve or sometimes twenty or thirty lines at a time, without Premeditation & even against my Will; the time it has taken in writing was thus render'd Non Existent, & an immense Poem Exists which seems to be the Labour of a long Life, all produc'd without Labour or Study" (Wilson, 1971, p. 78). The authors of it, he said, were in eternity. It was as though the material had been prepared somewhere else and was being read off to Blake, a characteristic that has been reported by most channels who are given written compositions.

At the beginning of his poem *Milton,* Blake deliberately cultivated inspiration from the Daughters of Beulah, muses on the third plane, for his writing. "Come into my hand," he wrote, "By your mild power descending down the Nerves of my right arm From out the Portals of my brain, where by your ministry The Great Eternal Humanity Divine planted his Paradise" (p. 78).

Other authors have incorporated material from channeling into their writing. William Butler Yeats (1938) based his mystic work, *A Vision*, on channeled messages from his wife, who was a medium. James Merrill (1982), a contemporary American poet, has used messages channeled through a Ouija Board as an integral part of his works, including the *Book of Ephraim* and *Mirabell's Books of Number*. His writings have received a Bollingen Prize and a National Book Award.

The finest literary works produced by channeling came through Mrs. Pearl Curran, a St. Louis, Missouri, housewife (Prince, 1927; Litvag, 1972). She and some friends were experimenting with a Ouija Board in 1913, and a spirit came through claiming to be Patience Worth, an Englishwoman of the seventeenth century.

Soon Mrs. Curran found the words coming directly into her mind, rather than being spelled out on the board. Over the next twenty years, Patience (as she came to be known) dictated award-winning poems, short stories, and novels that were well reviewed. Her poetry was ranked with that of Amy Lowell, Edgar Lee Masters, and others who are still widely known today, though Patience is largely forgotten. The poetry was blank verse, generally romantic, and would not be in style today. But there are still some nice pieces. Patience usually composed spontaneously, being given a topic by one of the people in the room and beginning dictation within a few

Pearl Curran of St. Louis received messages from the spirit of Patience Worth who dictated novels, stories, poems, and plays.

seconds. Here are two examples, the second one regarding people who considered her not to be real.

ON FEAR

The shadow of valor,
The sheath of every sword.
And yet he who fears may plunge
Him headlong to the fray
If he but love.
He who fears
Must love over his fearing,
For love be the sun
That dispels that shadow.

(Worth, January 22, 1925, p. 1913)

PATIENCE WORTH

A phantom? Weel enough,
Prove thyself to me!
I say, behold, here I be.
Buskins, kirtle, cap and pettyskirts,
And much tongue!
Weel, what hast thou to prove thee?

(Braude, 1980, p. 159)

Once she was asked for a poem for children to say at night, one more cheerful than "Now I lay me down to sleep," with its images of falling and dying. She took a month to consider this, then composed the following.

A CHILD'S PRAYER
I, Thy child forever, play
About Thy knees at close of day.
Within Thy arms I now shall creep
And learn Thy wisdom while I sleep.

Amen.

(Worth, July 31, 1919, p. 1913)

Mrs. Curran wrote impressive novels and plays from dictation by Patience Worth. *The Sorry Tale,* published in 1916, was a 325,000-word epic story set in the time of Christ and was favorably reviewed by *The New York Times.* The novel *Telka,* a medieval idyll, was a 60,000-word play written in archaic dialect, with 90 percent of the words said to have Anglo-Saxon roots. This is a remarkable feat because the words in the works of Shakespeare are only 59 percent Anglo-Saxon in origin, and the King James Bible is 77 percent Anglo-Saxon in origin. Knowing which words have Anglo-Saxon roots is a scholarly task, yet Patience did it without research, at least on this side. Not only that, most of the prose of *Telka* is in iambic pentameter verse (like the plays of Shakespeare). A third novel was *Hope Trueblood,* a novel about Victorian England, written, the dust jacket noted, "by a Pre-Victorian writer." The reviews in Great Britain were favorable; most of the reviewers assumed the book was written by an English author rather than a spirit on the other side of the Atlantic. Patience wrote in a dialect that was both archaic and peculiar. Some of her obscure seventeenth-century words were identified by scholars only after research.

Patience carried on lively conversations with the Currans and their friends. She had a sharp tongue and did not hesitate to put people in their place. Once, when the seance group tried to hurry her, she observed, "Beat the hound and lose the hare." Another time, when the company returned from a refreshment break, she commented, "Swilled enough, and still they grunt for more!"

On the theme "Patient God," she said "Ah, God, I have drunk unto the dregs, and flung the cup at Thee! The dust of crumbled righteousness hath dried and soaked unto itself, e'en the drop I spilled to Bacchus, whilst Thou, all-patient, sendest purple vintage for a later harvest" (Slightly edited, from Worth, February 8, 1914, p. 62). When the group discussed this, Patience said, "Tish, tish, Ye driveleth!"

In these examples of written composition, there was usually nonstop dictation without any obvious composition process. Patience could also dictate chapters for each of two or three on-going novels plus poems and table talk in the same evening. There were rarely any changes or corrections; the material came through in final form. The dictation was notable for its rapidity. In one evening session, Patience dictated 5,000 words for *The Sorry Tale*. (Another example of this process is the English automatic writer Geraldine Cummins, who could write 2000 words in an hour and a half.) The Patience Worth writing was of good quality. However, as is true for ordinary writing, not all channeled works meet the standard of a William Blake. I have read many poems, parables, and essays that appeared to be expressive of feelings and ideas relevant to the channel, but which either did not have the universal qualities that we expect of literature or whose composition was simply deficient.

MATHEMATICS: SRINIVASA RAMANUJAN

One of the major contributors to modern number theory in mathematics received formulas through a channeling process. Srinivasa Ramanujan (1887–1920) was a mathematical genius (Harman and Rheingold, 1984).

He grew up in a small village in India, poor and uneducated. At the age of sixteen, given an out-of-date mathematics book, he learned all of the theorems, then went forward on his own. Eventually, he sent some of his work to mathematicians in England and was recognized as an outstanding mathematical theorist.

Srinivasa Ramanujan, a brillant mathematician, received number theorems from Indian goddesses.

Ramanujan said that he received many of his mathematical concepts from the Indian goddess Namagiri, a local deity, and from Saraswati, the deity of language, song, and logic. The formulas given to Ramanujan were acknowledged to be brilliant. When Cambridge mathematician Godfrey Hardy saw Ramanujan's formulas, he said, "They must be true, because if they were not true nobody could have had the imagination to invent them." Interestingly, not all were correct when the proofs were worked out; some were wrong.

Regarding the rest of science, I have reviewed channeled materials in astronomy, physics, evolution, geology, and various technical subjects. There are rare correct predictions, but much discussion of scientific theories, mostly appearing to be extrapolations of ideas of the time. *Oahspe*, published in 1882, discusses cosmic vortexes, the planets, creation of races, space ships, angels, and other topics. A description of one vortex in the 990-page volume has been taken to describe the Van Allen radiation belt around the earth. Jacob Lorber (1800–1864), a German prophet (Eggenstein, 1973), wrote of what we would call galaxies and supergalaxies, revolving around central suns. He gave the lifespan of elementary particles to be one trillionth of a second, reasonably correct. Andrew Jackson Davis (1875) predicted in *The Principles of Nature*, first written in March 1846, the discovery of an eighth planet. The eighth planet, Neptune, was discovered in September 1846, but its presence had been hypothesized for several years. Other data about Neptune, such as its satellites, diameter, and composition were off the mark. Davis also described a ninth planet, and Pluto was discovered in 1933. *The Urantia Book* (1955) includes extensive descriptions of the creation of our solar system, evolution of life, human races, social institutions, and history. These are described as if from the vantage point of outside entities helping the Earth to develop. More recently, Andrija Puharich (1974) received messages from the Nine, which included one or two theoretical formulae in physics. However, they do not appear to have scientific meaning. Stuart Edward White (1940) in *The Unobstructed Universe* received reconceptualizations of the principles of the universe such as, "The essence of Time is Receptivity . . . the essence of Space is Conductivity . . . the essence of Motion is Frequency" (p. 107). These appeared to be thought experiments designed to expand the thinking of the recipients. Messages purporting to come telepathically from UFO occupants often have scientific information, but, to my knowledge, none of these have proved to be technically or theoretically useful.

Overall, in the scientific areas, channels have provided very little useful information. The material seems to emerge from the point of progress of science at the time of writing, perhaps with some extrapolation or modification. Creativity in science is more frequently reported to come from hunches, intuitions, and dreams, rather than channeling. If it occurs, it is not publicly discussed, perhaps understandably. It also seems to be the case that the communicator, whoever it is, must draw on the knowledge of the individual doing the channeling, and most persons channeling now and in the past, including UFO contactees, are not scientifically sophisticated.

MUSIC

A number of respected musical compositions have come through the channeling process. The most famous is Giuseppi Tartini's "Sonata in D for Violin," named "The Devil's Sonata." Tartini dreamed that the Devil was his slave. He gave him the violin, and reported: "How great was my astonishment when I heard him play with consummate skill a sonata of such exquisite beauty as surpassed the boldest flights of my imagination. I felt enraptured, transported, enchanted: my breath was taken away and I awoke. Seizing my violin I tried to retain the sounds I had heard. But it was all in vain. The piece I then composed, 'The Devil's Sonata,' was the best I ever wrote, but how far below the one I had heard in my dream" (Harman and Rheingold, 1984). This is not exactly the same as direct channeling, but seems quite close to the process.

We can now turn to Rosemary Brown, an English psychic, who one day in the 1960s discovered Franz Liszt standing by her piano in spirit form (Brown, 1971, 1974). Since then, Liszt, Chopin, Beethoven, Schumann, and other composers have dictated musical compositions to her which have been put in print by recognized music publishers (Brown, 1977, 1978, 1980). One phonograph album (Brown, 1970) has been recorded. Mrs. Brown has minimal musical training, and the compositions are often dictated an element at a time, which musicians tell me is tedious and difficult. The style and form are very much like those of the composers. As musical pieces, they are short and usually not complex, but some have been judged quite good. Musicologists have studied these pieces, and there is a case to be made that these are genuine transmissions (Parrott, 1978). Such compositions could be written by musicians trained in composition, but they are beyond Mrs. Brown's capability in terms of her experience, training, and knowledge of the technicalities of composition. Why are the composers' spirits doing this? They say that they are trying to show that they still exist and that life continues after death. This case will be discussed more in Chapter 16.

Another example of channeled music is that of contemporary American harpist Joel Andrews, who performs music said to come from Saint Germain, the Elohim, and other advanced masters (Andrews, 1989). When I visited him, Andrews told me that the skill and composition of the music is beyond what he could do himself. He says that he receives the music in four ways: auditorily, he may hear chords or notes; visually, he may find his eyes focusing on particular strings; kinesthetically, his hands may automatically move toward certain strings; and verbally, he may hear words telling him the key signature or other information.

There have been several cases of musical mediums who played improvised piano music, presumably under the control of spirits who included Liszt, Thalberg, and Chopin. These are described in the *Encyclopædia of Psychic Science*, edited by Fodor (1966), and the similar encyclopedia by Leslie Shepherd (1984). Listeners who had actually heard some of the performers while living were impressed with the performances.

ART

Turning to painting, William Blake said that he drew upon his spiritual vision to see angels and spirits, and his notebooks are filled with heads and figures of these visions. To a critic who said that these came from his own mind, Blake commented, "How very Anxious Reynolds is to Disprove & Contemn [*sic*] Spiritual Perception!" (Wilson, 1971, p. 79). The contemporary Brazilian medium Luiz Gasparetto channels paintings said to come from deceased artists Degas, Picasso, van Gogh, Monet, Manet, Toulouse-Lautrec, and others (Dubugras, Gasparetto, and Espiritos Diversos, 1979; Gaetani, 1986). Gasparetto goes into a light trance, takes pastels or acrylics, then sketches very rapidly, doing some pictures in three to five minutes, others in an hour. He often does this in a darkened room, sometimes with the paper upside down, sometimes with both hands working on drawings simultaneously, and even with his feet.

Luiz Gasparetto, Brazilian medium, channels paintings and sketches from well-known, deceased artists.

A Degas painting channeled by Gasparetto.

   The drawings certainly reflect the style of the painters, though they have
not been judged by experts for the more subtle characteristics of the artists.
The ability to paint this rapidly and under difficult conditions is striking. As
with Mrs. Brown's music, the painters say that through Gasparetto, their
intent is to prove that there is survival of death.

A van Gogh still life transmitted through Gasparetto.

There have been other mediums who have produced paintings and drawings credited to spirits. As with Gasparetto, these were often produced very rapidly, in darkness, sometimes with both hands, and so on. (See Fodor, 1966, and Shepherd, 1984, for examples.)

RELIGION AND PSYCHOLOGY

Many messages from the channeling process can be categorized as spiritual teachings. Generic New Age platitudes are frequent, but a few communications are quite sophisticated systems of psychological or spiritual development. There is ample precedent for channeled religious teaching, since this process of receiving information and teaching from sources outside the self is a form of revelation found in many traditions.

An example of a current channeled spiritual teaching is *A Course in Miracles* (1985a, 1985b, 1985c). The material was dictated by an inner voice to Dr. Helen Schucman, an academic psychologist. The speaker eventually identified himself as Jesus, much to the embarrassment of the recipient, who considered herself to be an atheistic Jew. The dictation could stop in mid-sentence and begin at the same point days or weeks later. The Course has a complex, interlocking structure that leads one to believe that it was composed with the entire scheme in mind. It is sophisticated psychologically and is a system of concepts and practices that are intended to transform perception and personality. Since its publication in 1975, 700,000 copies have been published. Interestingly, like some of the writing by Patience Worth, many pages of the prose are in subtle iambic pentameter, as though whoever wrote it did not have enough to do, so they put it into verse also.

The material is in three volumes, a text, a set of lessons, and a manual for teachers. The text deals with salvation, guilt, love, fear, judgment, atonement, and other elements of spiritual life, usually with a psychological flavor. Here is a sample on "change."

> Many stand guard over their ideas because they want to protect their thought systems as they are, and learning means change. Change is always fearful to the separated, because they cannot conceive of it as a move toward healing the separation. They always perceive it as a move toward further separation, because the separation was their first experience of change. You believe that if you allow no change to enter into your ego you will find peace (1985a, p. 45).

An excerpt from lesson 188, "The Peace of God is Shining in Me Now," which is a guided meditation, reads: "Why wait for heaven? Those who seek the light are merely covering their eyes. The light is in them now. Enlightenment is but a recognition, not a change at all" (1985b, p. 347). This excerpt is in rough iambic pentameter, though the verses are not tied to the sentences.

The Course is the most systematic spiritual system that has come through a channeling mode. There are many who study its teachings individually or in small groups. A recent survey of readers of *Common Boundary,* a publication oriented toward psychotherapists interested in spirituality, listed the volumes of the Course as the most influential book they have read.

There are other modern channeled teachings that present spiritual and psychological teachings. The material channeled by Jane Roberts from a personality named Seth is well known (Roberts, 1970). It emphasizes that the mind is not limited to the conscious ego. Exercises and techniques are given to expand the consciousness of the self into a larger reality. Another spiritual program was presented by Alice A. Bailey, an Englishwoman who wrote twenty volumes of esoteric material said to be inner dictation from a Tibetan master (A. Bailey, 1922). Both the Seth writings and the Bailey teachings have a following of study groups and institutions that are devoted to the material. Later chapters will examine channeled spiritual and psychological systems more fully.

GARDENING AND COMMUNITY

Messages on both practical and spiritual matters have come through the channeling process to members of a small community at Findhorn, in northern Scotland (Hawken, 1975). In the early 1960s, Peter and Eileen Caddy and Dorothy MacLean began hearing inner guidance coming from the devas, or angels of the forces of nature. These devas gave instructions on gardening and growing plants in the cold, inhospitable subarctic climate. Composting, time of planting, thinning, fertilization, landscaping, and other practices were explained to the group, who knew little about these subjects. Under the instructions of the devas and nature spirits, they learned to be sensitive to the energies of plants, to talk to them, and to develop a relationship to the needs of nature. The astonishing results were crops of fruit and vegetables and beds of flowers and herbs that were large, healthy, and exceptionally productive for the sandy soil and location.

Along with the horticultural advice, there were messages of spiritual inspiration emphasizing the oneness of nature and humanity and the qualities of attunement and alignment with these values (Caddy, 1976). There was more to cultivate than just the plants; the group gradually increased in size, as other seekers joined it. It became a spiritually based community, with the members individually and as a group receiving inner guidance on community organization and decisions. The original founders eventually left, but the community continues, attempting to provide a model for living and working together in harmony with each other and with nature (Findhorn Community, 1976; Popenoe and Popenoe, 1984). Here is a case in which the channeling process has contributed to a social institution, one which considers itself a center of light in the world.

COMMENTS

In these channeling cases, we can observe several characteristics worthy of consideration. First, there are a variety of skills demonstrated that come from outside the conscious mind of the person, including musical composition, health diagnosis, mathematics, painting, literary composition, and religious teaching. These are specific and organized, purposeful, and directed toward an audience. These communications usually come from a personality or source of consciousness. They may come only as an inner voice, or the source may give a name or identification.

Second, the creation of the material is effortless, immediate, and spontaneous, with no apparent conscious construction of the material. The individual appears to be a recipient, rather than a participant, in the production, though the person may be very active in using the information or developing the material. For example, Jane Roberts wrote several books herself expanding on the channeled material from Seth.

A third characteristic is that some of the skills are at the level of exceptional human capabilities, such as complex literary composition, the multiple evening dictations of Patience Worth, and the clairvoyant perception of Cayce. They can be at the level of prodigies or gifted individuals, though the persons channeling do not appear to have these qualities.

Fourth, there is accessing of information and concepts of an ethical and spiritual nature, such as the messages of religious prophets and religious teachings.

Finally, it is notable that the channels themselves in these cases are not abnormal or dysfunctional. They are usually normal, healthy individuals.

Other cases could be cited where this process has provided information, ideas, and guidance. The cases discussed have been contemporary, but historical cases also show a variety of ability, cultural contribution, and social impact. Whatever the origin, it is evident that this process of channeling has the capability of making important contributions to our knowledge and experience.

CHAPTER 3

CHANNELED ADVICE:
Practical, Therapeutic, and Psychological

Many people go to channels for private consultations on conducting their lives. Usually this is a one-on-one meeting, but it is sometimes a group session. A fee is usually charged. The clients ask for advice regarding their health, job, emotional issues, romantic and other relationships, finances, and spiritual matters. The questions range from worldly events (Should I buy this house? What is causing my infertility?) to psychological issues (How can I change my fear of assertiveness?) to existential and spiritual concerns (Am I on the right spiritual path? What were my past lives?). Often these are the same issues that impel us to seek the advice of financial experts, counselors and therapists, physicians, and other experts. However, the channel is not seen as a narrow specialist, but a source of "cosmic" truth, or all-knowing wisdom. I have listened to many consultations and reports of them in which the inquirer evidently accepted the answer as relevant and drawn from a consciousness that was more all-knowing than his or her own. A matchmaker might ask an individual to describe his or her ideal partner before attempting to give romantic advice; the channeled entity is expected to give advice without asking any preliminary questions. The answers I have heard are sometimes specific, sometimes general. Some come from no more than common sense, but at other times they appear to draw on paranormal levels of information; then, there are other answers that are, as we say technically, "off the wall." I will give examples that show the range of channeled counsel, from personal decisions to therapeutic systems.

SPIRIT ADVICE TO LINCOLN

We will begin with a famous person who received advice channeled by a medium that affected his public role: Abraham Lincoln is reported to have had sessions with a medium, Nettie Colburn Maynard (Ebon, 1971).

In her memoirs, Maynard reports that in a session in December, 1862, Lincoln was advised by a spirit coming through her to resist pressure to defer enforcement of the Emancipation Proclamation, but to "fearlessly perform the work and fulfill the mission for which he had been raised up by an overruling Providence" (Maynard, in D. Knight, 1969, p. 36). In February, 1863, a spirit named Dr. Bamford said that the Union army was demoralized and threatening to retreat. Lincoln acknowledged the terrible state of affairs and asked for a remedy. Dr. Bamford recommended that Lincoln visit the troops at the front immediately, taking his wife and family, inquire into the grievances, and demonstrate his awareness of their many trials. The president heeded this advice and went to the front, which resulted in bolstering the spirits (there seems to be a pun there) of the Army of the Potomac. Though we have only the report of Mrs. Maynard as to the events of these seances, it is agreed by biographers that Lincoln attended spiritualist sessions during his terms of office.

PRACTICAL ADVICE

Sometimes advice is specific and practical. David Kahn reports that Edgar Cayce often gave him what I would call predictive advice (Kahn, 1970). Cayce recommended that he sell his stocks shortly before the 1929 stock market crash. He recommended that Kahn go into a business involving woods and metals (which he did very successfully) and predicted the success of specific business negotiations. Comments of this sort obviously require combining several causal chains and may also involve self-fulfilling elements. I have looked at many personal readings by channels in which statements are made regarding future events such as jobs, health, travel, romance, and other life events. I know of no follow-up studies of these by channels or researchers to find out what their accuracy is.

A personal example will illustrate an example of helpful advice from a channel. After eight years of administration at the Institute of Transpersonal Psychology, where I am on the faculty, I resigned as Dean of Faculty. I asked Pleiades, a source channeled by Debra Reynolds, to comment on this change. Pleiades said that being in the administrative role had given me emotional experience I would otherwise not have received nor solicited (true indeed!) and that this helped my ability to confront such situations with balance. Further, being in that position had provided contact with many persons, and this would be beneficial in the future. These comments were very helpful in reviewing what that job had contributed to my life. I felt they were in fact quite correct, and others who knew me agreed. They did not provide facts ("you will resign on August 30") but rather a valuable way of organizing and perceiving the experiences.

There are examples of less useful advice. A journalist told me that she asked a channel about whether she should buy a particular house. "You can't go wrong in real estate," was the blanket answer. In another case, a student of mine named Sarah asked a source identified as Madame if she should move. Sarah was told that Madame never told people what to do (admirable, that) and that Sarah should follow what she really felt in her heart. Motherly advice, as one of my associates commented, but that depends on the kind of mother you have. If you paid an expert consultant to answer such questions, you would not be getting your money's worth with those answers. But on the other end, that question shows a giving over of power to the channeled entity, a turning of the decision over to an outside authority. Perhaps the answer rightly turned it back to the questioner.

SOULMATE

When the questions get into personal and metaphysical affairs, all stops are out. I have heard channels tell inquirers that their problems come from past life conflicts with their current lover or spouse, that visualizations will change their attitudes, that a disease will clear up in three months, and a variety of pronouncements about motives and personality issues. Generally they appear to be at the level of projection and fantasy. Unfortunately, they are accepted by people with strong emotional needs to believe and who have no experience in evaluating pertinent information, feelings, and ideas. If some correct information is mixed with these projections, then credibility is often given to the whole message.

I recall one channeled being who was personified as a twelve-year-old girl. A young man asked if the girlfriend he was seeing was the "right one" for him. (Such naive questions must drive channels crazy, though for a twelve-year-old girl it is probably terrific.) The answer was that, no, he "had not found his soulmate yet." The young man later told me that the answer was particularly significant for him, first because he suspected she was not his soulmate, but second because the young woman's actual name was Soal! One may suspect that this answer involved telepathic reading of his feelings and feeding his opinion back to him, confirming it with the name itself. The girlfriend later married another person.

However, this same entity also was asked about a recent airplane disaster involving hundreds of deaths. She blithely commented that all those people chose to die like that. This is an irresponsible metaphysical statement, in my opinion. If an entity has just given some accurate personal information, the tendency to believe everything else is very strong, and unverifiable assertions such as that one are assumed to be equally correct.

PAST LIVES

Besides answering questions and giving advice, channeling sessions can go into religious or metaphysical issues such as the purpose of life, karma, past lives, paths of growth, and so on, with the entity giving authoritative pronouncements on these matters. Cayce often gave such information in his life readings. Gina Cerminara reports one case in which an individual named by Cayce in a past-life reading was verified as having historically existed (Cerminara, 1950). Statements about past lives and karmic forces are impossible to verify with any certainty. Stevenson (1974) and others have researched memories of past lives in children and it is clear that some can be supported with excellent evidence. However, most cases of past-life memories have not been confirmed, regardless of their realism or therapeutic value. Channeled messages on past lives are usually simply assertions, not memories or historical data, and they must be accepted on faith. Few inquirers are interested in checking out the historical verification. Some claims of past lives presented in channeling seem to be metaphors or scenarios that fit the emotional needs or personality of the individual. They may provide emotional pleasure or facilitate therapeutic processes.

An interesting approach to past-life work is taken by a group in Southern California, the Unarius Foundation. The channels provide past-life information to the group as a whole. The people in the group are told of their past lives when they were together before, for example, as centurions and disciples during the time of Jesus or as Spanish soldiers in conquest of the New World. Then they conduct psychodramas exploring the problems arising from their experiences at that time (Norman and Spaegel, 1987).

PSYCHOLOGICAL INSIGHT

Channeled messages may also be oriented toward therapy, for example in uncovering traumatic experiences in this life (or a previous one), identifying conflicts, pointing to issues, and reframing situations. The psychologically oriented messages often serve therapeutic ends or are seen by the individuals as assisting in personal development. I know some psychologists and therapists who use channeled advice as input in their work with patients.

There have been no investigations to evaluate objectively how effective these therapeutic communications are. Even regular psychotherapy is difficult to evaluate by either therapist or client. Therapy in a channeled setting is even more difficult to appraise. I have heard many channeled readings that seemed to me to be generalities and platitudes and lacking in any psychological insight. I could not believe that they would be of any assistance in personal understanding or change, though sometimes the person claimed to have gained. I have heard a few that I felt hit the nail on the head and would be of value if the person incorporated the information and used it.

In a group setting I observed a channel, Debra Reynolds, doing individual readings of people she had not met previously. The source was identified as Pleiades, an energy rather than an individual. Some of what was said for one person was this: "Partnership does not dance to any music put on by another. . . . Would indeed that what you are seeking, what you are craving is the melody within. . . . Do not place your trust in another to have it dashed again. Set your commitment to trust yourself" (Author's file, 1988). Pleiades also identified three facets to the lady's personality: a girl in a blue cornflower dress, a barefooted girl in jeans, and a robed figure with cropped hair. The individual felt the description was an accurate characterization. She said that her trust had been dashed over and over again. She recognized the three figures as subpersonalities—a feminine self, a tomboy, and a nun—and she felt that she needed to learn to trust herself to get those three selves together. This kind of commentary is hard to evaluate, even though it is meaningful to the individual. I do find that when a characterization is felt to be accurate at a deep emotional level, the effect is often moving and transformative. In this case, the lady commented that the material in the reading helped her decide to end a relationship that had been troubling her.

THE MICHAEL PERSONALITY MODEL

Another approach to personal advice has been developed by Michael, who claims to be an entity of 1000 beings. Michael was channeled through the Ouija Board and automatic writing by a private group in Oakland, California (Yarbro, 1979, 1986; Stevens and Warwick-Smith, 1986). He communicated a complex personality theory in which people are identified as one of seven roles: slave, artisan, warrior, scholar, priest, sage, and king. Each person within the role goes through seven soul stages over several lifetimes. Those are infant, baby, young, mature, old, transcendental, and infinite. To illustrate, baby souls are agreeable, accept and hold consensual beliefs (for example, fundamentalism), are embarrassed by sexuality, and are not venturesome. Young souls are aggressive, achieving, adventuresome, and learning. Mature souls are more troubled, reflecting on lessons learned, and seeking meaning and truth. (These descriptions are all very brief excerpts.) There are also aspects such as goals, overlays, body types, and other features that affect the individual. The Michael messages identified the types of people in the group and classified famous people (Freud, Marx, Adler, Perls, Kant, Aristotle, and Einstein were mature souls). These identifications are intended to assist in self-knowledge and a framing of the issues that help or hinder an individual. My guess is that they are potentially as informative as many of the other typologies found in clinical psychology. However, they do not come from a system which provides ways of working clinically or therapeutically with the information, and this limits their usefulness. Further, the placing of a person in role, soul level, and goal is dependent on the word of Michael and his channels. This is susceptible to inconsistency, projection, and accident, since accuracy is not guaranteed by channeling. The original group is no longer in existence, and there are dozens of people and groups who now claim to channel the Michael teachings (Clifton, 1987; Pope, 1987). It is an easy system to present, and may serve as a vehicle for psychic or counseling advice. However, as with most other channeled therapeutic systems, there is no assurance of therapeutic judgment from those who use it.

THE HOFFMAN QUADRINITY PROCESS

One systematic therapeutic approach that has come from a channeling process is the Hoffman Quadrinity process. Businessman Bob Hoffman of Oakland, California, had been learning psychic development as an interesting hobby. One night in 1967, he was awakened by what seemed to be the spirit of Dr. Siegfried Fischer, an orthodox psychiatrist and friend who had died six months earlier. Dr. Fischer communicated to him that he had access to new sources of wisdom on the other side and had developed a technique for resolving emotional problems and neuroses, particularly, as it turned

Robert Hoffman, founder of the Quadrinity process.

out, those coming from feelings of unlovability and lack of self-love. He proposed to teach this approach to Hoffman. After protesting that he was no therapist and no one would listen to him, Hoffman finally suggested that Fischer demonstrate on him, since he felt that he needed emotional healing as much as anyone. Fischer agreed and that night took him through processes that persuaded Hoffman of the validity of the method. The method involved re-experiencing childhood traumas and negative love attachments to mother and father, recognizing attitudes and behaviors that identified with or reacted against parents, and then reliving the childhoods of his own parents to experience how they had been programmed to be unloving and neurotic. Hoffman reports that at the end of the five-hour session, his anger had turned to compassion and love for his parents (Hoffman, 1979; St. Clair, 1974).

Hoffman taught the process to personal development groups and began to counsel individuals, using his psychic skills to identify childhood events and provide information about the parents' childhood. Later, he taught his clients to psychically perceive these events themselves, which engaged the clients more fully in the experiences. In the early 1970s, psychiatrist Claudio Naranjo restructured the technique, which he named the Fischer-Hoffman process, for use in a group setting. Hoffman took the ideas of Naranjo and others, added further suggestions from Fischer, and created a format of group lectures, experiential sessions, and individual consultation. Hoffman renamed it the Quadrinity process and offers it for groups in a seven-day residential setting (Ridall, 1990). Testimonials for its effectiveness have come from therapists as well as clients, though I know of no research on long-term outcomes. The original methods are described in *No One Is to Blame* (Hoffman, 1979). In an interview, Hoffman told me that he continues to channel intuitive information and ideas on improving the techniques used in the process. Obviously, the approach can be analyzed in terms of Freudian theory and developmental models, but the method itself is an active intervention process using imagery, experiential reliving, and inner dialog (Naranjo, 1985). This is a case in which insights from channeling have been connected with human knowledge and management to create an innovative therapeutic program.

EVALUATING ADVICE FROM A CHANNEL

There often appears to be paranormal (ESP) information in channeled messages, and the types of personal readings by channels sound much the same as those done by psychics. We know that these are not always accurate (and sometimes totally inaccurate). We know that often the apparent validity of the information is based on astute psychological inferences about the questioner, ambiguity, common-sense answers, self-fulfilling prophecies, and the desire of the questioner to believe. On this, see the excellent chapter "How to Use a Psychic Reading" by Charles Tart (1989) in his book *Open Mind, Discriminating Mind*. Certainly, all of these factors can lend plausibility to channeled advice, and belief is amplified when the source is seen as an entity beyond human bias or limitations. It would be very useful to have reliable studies of channeled advice, but, for the present, this is an area for individual education and judgment. If someone is going to inquire seriously of a channel, they should consider the following suggestions.

The first step in seeking advice on a question, whether from a "conventional" counselor or a channeled source, is to do your homework. Review the question and its issues deeply, including your own state of need. Tart recommends beginning with an honest and accurate self-appraisal. Discuss the situation with others and draw upon your own inner resources. Refer to *At a Journal Workshop*, by Progoff (1975), for journal writing; *Living Your Dreams*, by Delaney (1988), for dream incubation techniques; Vaughan (1979), *Awakening Intuition*, for intuitive development. Examine your motives. Go as far as you can in understanding and resolving the issue. Try to identify the missing element, obstacle, or area of uncertainty. What is it you need to move you to the next step of the decision process? What specifically do you want from the channel? Then, phrase your question or concern in the most informative and communicative way. This may include giving the channel full background information. Unless there is the need for a validation of the entity's psychic abilities, I believe it is better to give all the information necessary for the context of the issue. Approaching it in this way activates your own responsibility in the situation, stimulates your own conscious and unconscious work, and will help focus the response.

Tart further suggests that you not evade your own responsibility in facing issues in your own development. Information from channeling may give you a new perspective, but it will not do your life work for you.

In choosing which channel to consult, exercise some judgment. References are useful and best when you can read what has been said for another or listen to a tape. Listen for clarity and responsiveness to the individual, rather than generalities. Get a sense of the level of spiritual awareness. You might ask whether you would listen to this channel if he or she were giving you advice without channeling someone else, suggests Corinne McLaughlin (1987). Extravagent fees often lend impressiveness, but do not correlate with validity or the value of the information. It is also a warning sign if a reading takes power away from the individual and creates dependency on the entity or channel.

In the reading itself, if it is verbal, tape record or take notes on the channeled response and ask questions for explanations and clarification. Single-sentence answers leave much unsaid. Take your time and, if necessary, repeat questions which appear not to have been answered. On the other hand, do not expect perfection.

Afterward, review the answers or information in terms of your own understanding of the issue. Does it clarify, organize, or assist your understanding? Does it point out choices or consequences. Does it move you to the next step in the decision, insight, or action? Discuss the response with friends. Compare the answers with other sources of information. Review the response after a period of time has elapsed and especially look at the consequences of following it. All these are rational considerations, so it is also important to ask your heart how it feels about the situation. I have given much the same advice regarding readings from psychics (Hastings, 1983), and it is applicable to almost any kind of counsel.

In my experience, there are few channels who provide counsel that is equal to that of an experienced therapist, an insightful and honest friend, a high quality psychic, or a specialist in the field. However, it is often possible to get a key insight, a new perspective, or critical information, because the process of channeling can reach outside the framework or set of the mind that has led to being stuck. It may provide stimulation which leads to creative solutions. It may have an integrative point of view or call attention to something overlooked. In all cases, the individual should be the one to decide how much weight to put on the channeled message.

CHAPTER 4

ESP IN CHANNELING

In many cases of channeling, information is given that goes beyond the knowledge available to the channel. The message may mention some personal fact about an individual, unknown to the channel, or make a prediction that proves accurate. When the information given goes beyond the facts known to the person or entity, the process is termed extrasensory perception (ESP). Professional researchers use the general term *psi* (pronounced "sigh") to refer to the process or ability to know or perceive paranormally, what the public calls psychic ability.

EDGAR CAYCE

Many channeling cases on record suggest that psi is operating to provide the entity information about people or circumstances. The channel best known for psychic functioning is Edgar Cayce. He showed ESP in his readings and also in his everyday life. His health readings were usually given with the patient at a distance and unknown to Cayce or others in the room. Nevertheless, specific diagnostic accuracy was reported in many cases, according to letters in the files. On December 18, 1934, Cayce diagnosed children 3000 miles away as having "intestinal infections . . . from a form of worms" and prescribed medicine. A letter from the grandmother on March 30, 1935, reported "in three weeks' time we repeated the dose and got a quantity of pinworms." According to Hugh Lynn Cayce, the original letter gave no indication of the condition, saying only "I now have two little grandchildren who are needing medical attention badly, but we are unable to obtain a correct diagnosis for them" (H. L. Cayce, 1964, p. 55).

In another case cited by Hugh Lynn Cayce, a diagnosis was given for a 48-year-old woman several hundred miles away in North Carolina. There were fourteen checkable conditions stated: anemia, low blood pressure, dizziness brought on by the menstrual period, position of stomach, personality characteristics of determination and set opinions, excessive kidney activity, and others. Edgar Cayce suggested specific spinal adjustments, gave an herbal formula to prepare, and laid out a nutritional program. Hugh Lynn Cayce says that the woman "went to a prominent doctor in Raleigh.

He wisely refused to follow the suggestions until he had checked to confirm the conditions described. She was given a thorough examination including a series of X-rays. The reading was corroborated" (H. L. Cayce, 1964, p. 28). Other reports of confirmed diagnoses are found in the literature about Cayce. While these have not received thorough case studies that would meet professional standards, the descriptions suggest the occurrence of ESP.

Another aspect of Cayce's ESP is important to note. His friends and relatives reported that he often made statements, apparently coming from psychic awareness, in everyday life. David Kahn tells of Cayce giving him advice on business matters that seemed to involve psychic information, including recommendations to get out of the stock market prior to the 1929 crash and suggesting dollar amounts for business negotiations (Kahn, 1970). Harmon Bro, who also knew Cayce personally, tells how Cayce would occasionally make accurate comments to strangers, such as waitresses, about their lives, apparently with psychic perception. With his friends and relatives, his waking psi was apparently more frequent.

> It was not unlike the man awake to mention someone he thought would telephone soon or to observe that a certain letter or visitor was coming—and be correct. When several times he told his wife and the writer that he would never again see his two sons in the service, he refused to be consoled by encouragement—and his own death bore out his prediction. . . .
>
> . . . . Holding a letter in his hand as he dictated, he would pause to tell a secretary what the sender looked like, of whether there was hope for the case. Dictating to the writer's [Bro] secretary when his own was overloaded, he stopped to tell the girl she was pregnant, and to mention the sex of the coming child; he startled her, for while she had just been to the doctor and confirmed the pregnancy, she had not yet told her husband. Cayce had found years ago that he could send for others to come to him by concentrating on them, but had also decided not to play around with his ability (Bro, 1970, p. 23).

Cayce was said to be able to pick up the thoughts and feelings of people he was with. I remember asking Hugh Lynn Cayce in 1968 what it was like to live with his father. He said that it was difficult being the son of someone who always knew what you were doing. Bro reports the same experience.

> At the "natural" or spontaneous waking level of psi, or psychic ability, he seemed daily to pick up moods and thoughts of those around him, both in direct impressions and in casual glimpses of auras. Because of this, Cayce was not easy to live with, as the writer can testify; one could never be sure of privacy of thoughts, or whether Cayce might react to someone's ugly mood which nobody else had noticed (Bro, 1970, p. 22).

Unfortunately research studies were never made of Cayce's work, in or out of trance. The reports that we have are anecdotal accounts, voluntary follow-up reports in the files of the Association for Research and Enlightenment (ARE), a study of 150 cases in the ARE files (E. E. Cayce and H. L. Cayce, 1971), and some *ad hoc* investigations by writers (for example Stern, 1967). These are suggestive but not definitive. There have been no follow-up studies of the cases, with verification of the conditions of privacy of information about the patient or objective judging of the accuracy of the diagnosis. Nor were there any controlled tests of the waking ESP that Cayce exhibited. So, there is no way to evaluate how much psi Cayce was using or how much information was provided by previous knowledge, nonverbal communication, inference, and the benefit of years of experience.

Nevertheless, the incidents of psi reported about Cayce are similar to ones documented and verified in the scientific literature on parapsychology. The health readings are identical in form to many mediumship sessions, called proxy sittings, in which information is given about living individuals who are not present. The everyday life ESP, real time and precognitive, is well within the scope of verified ESP abilities. Thus, even given the informal nature of the evidence, I think there is a reasonable case for Cayce's psi abilities.

Cayce also gave life readings for individuals, a description of the person's personality, potentials, problems, and other aspects. These would be known today as clairvoyant or psychic readings. The feedback and informal documentation on these life readings show some to have given accurate statements and characterizations that go beyond generalizations and platitudes (H. L. Cayce, 1964; Cerminara, 1950).

What we have seen with Cayce is typical of many persons who do channeling: they seem to have elements of psychic ability in their everyday lives.

PSI IN PERSONAL READINGS

In channeled consultations for individuals, there is often concrete information that seems to be provided by psi—details of childhood, families, emotional reactions, everyday activities, traumatic events, and predictions of future events. If these are accurate, and there is no normal source for the information, then it is possible that the material came through extrasensory perception. Sometimes this information cannot be evaluated because it is so general that it is true of many people: "There were troubles in your childhood," and "You have some thoughts that you do not tell frankly to others." Other information may be ambiguous, a mixture of accurate and inaccurate information, or simply wrong. We will look at several examples.

In an interview with Mrs. Eileen J. Garrett, psychologist Ira Progoff asked Abdul Latif, one of Mrs. Garrett's spirit guides, to give a clairvoyant reading of one of Progoff's clients. Abdul Latif made such correct observations as these:

- The main part of the patient's problem is passivity.
- The problem began in the teens.
- He is unsure of his religious dogma.
- There is a loss of security with him.

Latif also suggested to Progoff that he should try to get the man to draw, particularly a plan of a room. In fact, the man had already shown Progoff a sketch of a house which had provided some fruitful work. Since it had not been mentioned verbally, Progoff felt certain that it was picked up telepathically by the guide. Progoff summarizes by saying that the reading was strikingly correct at several points, though some of these were quite general; it was not correct at other points, though these were not serious; and there were other points that arose in the session that could be said to be helpful suggestions for later work with the client (Progoff, 1964).

An interesting approach of some channeled readings is the characterization of a situation or personality issue. The following excerpt is from a characterization channeled for a woman, Glenna, who was present in a large gathering and not known to the channel.

> When you were born, the masculine and feminine entwined in equal balance therein. All this was shaken up and questioned by every other entity that tried to raise you. Is she a boy, is she a girl? Is she sweet, is she strong? She's everything! Leave her alone! . . . But indeed, what are parents to do when there is nothing to do for their child? Applaud them? . . . Could you write on her epitaph 'Here lies Glenna, men never understood her'? (Author's file, 1986).

The group burst out laughing, and Glenna said, "You got that right!" She said that the characterization captured her own issues and perceptions, and her friends agreed.

The poetry of Patience Worth, channeled by Mrs. Pearl Curran, was often directed toward a particular individual and seemed to incorporate information derived psychically. Once, a Miss B., alone with Mrs. Curran, was given the following by Patience:

> Tis echoed voices, love athrob, awaft through days and nights, ahang 'pon tilting leafy branch and hid 'mid wastes afar and near, come nestled like to a mother's song—a breath o' joy, to babe bemothered not, save by the songs and loves o' them along agone (Worth, 1915, p. 86).

When this puzzled Mrs. Curran, Miss B. explained "that she had never known her own parents and was an adopted child. She therefore understood what was said and was much touched." Mrs. Curran was apparently not aware of the circumstances, though Prince notes that this is not proven (Prince, 1927, p. 302).

Prince was most persuaded by several instances when he was the subject of apparent telepathic information. Once he had been thinking of an emotionally traumatic experience in his life and considered how to ask Patience to compose on it. He could not decide on a way of stating the topic without revealing the incident, so he gave up the idea, "mentally relinquished" it, in his words. Then, spontaneously, Mrs. Curran told him "Patience has something for you" and delivered a poem beginning:

O God, the sands!—the vasty waste of sand and scarce one palm!
O God, the heat!—the aching, wilting heat,
The fury and wrath of the blazing sun, and scarce one sup!
O God, the sands! the vasty, vasty sands; and night, the pitchy night!
(Prince, 1927, p. 310)

There was more, all elaborating on the image of the desert. Prince comments that the tone of the poem was exactly right for the experience he had been recalling. What was most impressive, he said, was:

. . . once, long ago, I wrote a set of verses about the matter to which I refer, and it contained exactly that metaphor of the blistering waste of the desert.
Prince: Why did you give that as for me?
Patience: Sirrah, I ken an errant spot athin thee.
Prince: I understand it (p. 310).

Patience demonstrated knowledge of the feeling or the "errant spot" of the experience and was able to give the exact metaphor and words Prince had once used to describe it.

As a note on the psi process, a telepathic transmission frequently is reported to occur at the point when an idea has been held in consciousness with the desire of communicating it and then is dropped or replaced by something else. It is often at that time, perhaps when it is in the preconscious, that it is accessible to another mind telepathically or is free to be transmitted. It is as though when the full attention of consciousness is on it, it is held too firmly and only by relinquishing the hold can it be perceived by another.

In another instance, Patience wrote a poem for Prince about a spaniel in which she captured his particular thoughts about his own dog.

Prince: Did you get these thoughts from your experience with dogs or did you divine my thought?
Patience: Well, ye skim milch, and ye hae milch AND cream (Worth, January 13, 1926, p. 3692).

Prince also carefully analyzed an instance in which Patience wrote a poem using specific words from a letter received by a friend, a letter Mrs. Curran had not seen but which had emotional significance for her. Prince concludes that the evidence for telepathy was clear.

Thus, even though this Mrs. Curran did not channel "readings" as such, the record says "Patience not only knew the inmost hearts of those at the board, but was willing to take a leaf from their lives as her subject. . . ." (Worth, November 8, 1919, p. 2051)

The evidence is neither extensive nor conclusive, but there is enough to indicate that some form of psi operates in the channeling mode and may give information that goes beyond the normal sources of knowledge (Hastings, 1990). It is important to realize, also, that many channeled messages may respond to questions or present ideas that do not need to draw upon paranormal sources of information or, as mentioned in the previous chapter, they may rely on inferences and cues for their information. I recall one channeling session in which each person asked a question and received what I considered a good answer. But as Sandy, my wife, remarked, the answers did not require an outside vantage point, such as ESP, but were simply good counsel.

SOURCES OF PSI IN CHANNELING

If an outside entity is the source of the channeling, then a natural assumption is that this entity, existing in a nonphysical realm, must have ESP. J. B. Rhine, discussing one of Mrs. Garrett's guides, commented, "I cannot understand how, were he a spirit, Uvani could get along without these extrasensory modes of perception, since presumably [regular] senses are a part of the body which he left on the sands of Arabia centuries ago" (Rhine, 1937, p. 224). However, it may not be the case that the ESP originates with the spirit. In several cases, there is data relevant to the psi abilities of the person in a normal state compared with the abilities shown in a channeling mode. The suggestion is that the abilities may come from the human being. We can refer again to Cayce, who exhibited psychic perception in both his waking life and also his channeling. These were clearly his human abilities, since there was no outside entity involved, and his own channeling said that he could be more clairvoyant in the waking state than when entranced.

Jane Roberts and Seth
Jane Roberts began her experience as a channel with the intention of developing her own ESP ability. She was doing this in preparation for

writing a book. Seth began to communicate first via the Ouija Board, then spoke mentally, and finally would take possession of Miss Robert's body. She continued to work with her ESP skills, and the Seth personality assisted with exercises and advice. The reports of her practice are detailed in the book *How To Develop Your ESP Power*, later republished as *The Coming of Seth* (Roberts, 1976). One exercise involved routinely making five predictions for the coming day—a word, a phrase, a sentence. Then the items were checked against daily events.

Here are some examples of her results. At 8 A.M. on a March 4, she wrote "stranger to the house." That evening, friends unexpectedly arrived bringing with them a complete stranger. Roberts notes that, at the time, she and her husband lived quietly and entertained strangers only once or twice a year, and she had made a similar prediction only two other times; in each case it proved true. She says that no strangers arrived when they were not predicted (Roberts, 1976, pp. 138–9).

On a January 27, she wrote "a secret told . . . a sharp tongue . . . a tease [ellipses in original]." That day, she was visited by the housekeeper of an elderly neighbor, who reported that the neighbor had "a very sharp tongue," and had taken to teasing the housekeeper. Then the housekeeper divulged a personal secret (p. 139). By Roberts' own evaluation, out of 741 predictions, 320 show significant results, ranging from precise hits to likely but not clearcut hits. (The word "significant" is used in an informal sense; researchers use it formally to indicate precise statistical levels of results.) Roberts reports her results with various other experiences in telepathy, clairvoyance, and precognition. Some of these involved exercises, others were via dream and trance states. Her ESP perceptions of events and activities are remarkably similar to those reported by others in more formal scientific research. They have the flavor of authenticity.

With the emergence of Seth as a channeled personality, Jane Roberts and her husband, Robert Butts, became interested in Seth's psychic abilities. In 1965, they met G. H. Estabrooks, a professor at Colgate University and a long-time researcher in hypnosis and spiritualism. Estabrooks suggested some clairvoyance tests in which Seth would attempt to perceive targets set up in Estabrooks' office. They performed seventy-five of these tests, sending Seth's responses twice weekly, but never hearing from Estabrooks about any results. According to Roberts, Estabrooks indicated he did not know how to evaluate the responses against the odds of guessing, and he did not have enough evidence to convince hard-nosed scientists (Roberts, 1970). To my knowledge, Estabrooks did not publish or present any results of these tests, positive or negative, before his death. This is unfortunate because there are ways of evaluating this kind of ESP response, even if the odds are not precisely calculable.

Roberts reports that she and her husband themselves carried out eighty-three tests of their own in which Mr. Butts would seal an object in bristol boards inside an envelope, and Seth would give verbal impressions. In one case, the target was a portion of a page from *The New York Times* torn by Butts without looking and, with his eyes closed, sealed in the envelope. They report these impressions by Seth:

> A paper item, rougher than smooth background (correct, rough newsprint)
>
> A gray view (correct, gray-toned illustrations)
>
> 'Liberal giving' and 'method of disposal' (It was a Macy's sale advertisement saying 'liberal discounts,' and 'generous discounts'.)
>
> Connection with a telephone or telephone call (One line says 'no mail or phone')

These impressions will be recognized by parapsychology researchers as similar to those that occur in laboratory experiments of remote viewing, perceiving drawings, or ESP imagery studies.

Seth also used the word "gubatorial," apparently meaning "gubernatorial." The target was a small piece from the bottom of a larger ad headed "Election Day Sales." Roberts took the gubernatorial allusion to refer to the ad headline, since the election included that of the New York state governor. What struck them was that the election headline was on the rest of the page back in the stack in Mr. Butts' art studio, not on the piece torn off.

Seth's comment was, "A portion is always connected to the whole of which it is part. . . . From the torn section, then, to me the whole can be read. With enough freedom on the one hand, and enough training on the other, Rubert [Jane], speaking for me, could give you the entire copy of *The New York Times* from a torn corner" (Roberts, 1970, pp. 80–83). Seth then makes a statement that I think may apply to all channeling: "Rubert's abilities are what I have to work with and through—besides, of course, my own" (p. 84).

In the case of Jane Roberts, both the channel and the entity show psi ability and to approximately the same degree. As with Cayce, this suggests that the psi ability comes from the same source.

ESP Tests of Eileen J. Garrett and Uvani

The studies of Eileen Garrett by J. B. Rhine (1934) and his colleagues point to the conclusion that the psi involved in channeling comes from the individual, not the entity. Rhine tested Mrs. Garrett using the well-known ESP cards. Six series of tests with clairvoyance and five with telepathy were conducted. In clairvoyance, the shuffled cards are not seen by anyone before they are guessed. In telepathy, another person, the sender, looks at each card. In three of the series, C, D, and E, Mrs. Garrett's spirit guide Uvani

Eileen J. Garrett, whose spirit guides included Uvani and Abdul Latif.

was also tested. In the clairvoyance series, Mrs. Garrett scored 2,433 correct hits in 10,900 cards, for an average of 5.7 per 25. The chance expectation for pure guessing is 5 per 25, and her score is statistically significant. Uvani hit 209 out of 1,000 cards for an average of 5.6, but because of the much lower number of cards this was not statistically beyond chance.

In the telepathy tests, the scores for both were much higher. Mrs. Garrett had an average of 10.1 and Uvani hit 9.1, which are exceptionally significant. The averages indicate a high level of psychic functioning in each state.

Mrs. Garrett said, "In the telepathy experiments I was freed from direct concentration on the cards themselves and was able to receive the symbols from the mind of the transmitter, where they acquired vitality and provided the energy stimulus necessary for my perception" (Garrett, 1949, p. 163).

The parallels between the scores of Mrs. Garrett and Uvani are striking. Charts 1 and 2 show that the averages varied proportionately. Statistically they were highly correlated, which implies that the psi ability is essentially the same for each (Hastings, 1990).

Uvani said that he had no ESP abilities of his own and that he used those of Mrs. Garrett. The tests bear this out in the similar overall averages within the two modes and also in the rise and fall of the daily scores during testing. Rhine commented, "Uvani would seem to be right; the gifts are the gifts of the medium, whatever Uvani himself may be" (Rhine, 1937, p. 225).

CLAIRVOYANCE

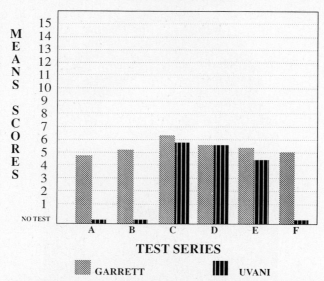

Chart 1. A comparison of scores on clairvoyance tests with Mrs. Garrett and her channeled guide Uvani. The chance average for pure guessing is five for each series. Mrs. Garrett's scores are significant. Uvani's are not.

TELEPATHY

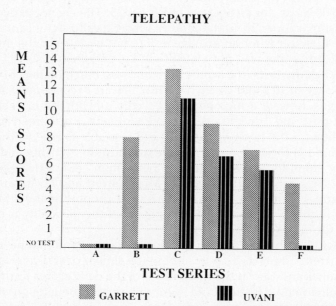

Chart 2. Mrs. Garrett and Uvani made much higher and exceptionally significant scores above chance on the telepathy series. Again, their scores parallel each other.

Cayce and Clairvoyance

Cayce's comments about his own abilities suggest the same conclusion. When asked in his hypnotic trance about his readings, he said that they came (1) from his subconscious mind which was in touch with other subconscious minds, or (2) that his subconscious made contact with the Akashic Records. In either case, these were his own capabilities. In one trance session, he said that he was "More [clairvoyant] in the normal or physical state than in the hypnotic state; though *all* are one when in perfect accord with the universal forces from which the records of all activities may be taken." When then asked if he could get the information in his waking state, he replied, "Not until there has been a more perfect cleansing of the carnal influences in the experience of the soul. . . . (E. Cayce, 1934).

The point made is that the influences of the material world must be reduced before Cayce could get the information in his waking state. This is similar to recommendations found in many systems of ESP and spiritual practice: to quiet the mind and reduce emotional reactions, desires, and external concerns.

There are other cases in which persons who are channels show evidence of ESP in their ordinary nonchanneling state. Helen Schucman, the scribe of *A Course in Miracles*, often had psychic impressions that proved correct, according to William Thetford, her colleague (*The Story of* A Course in Miracles, 1987). Alice A. Bailey, the telepathic receiver of a vast esoteric teaching from The Tibetan, reported several telepathic incidents in her day-to-day life. Many of the persons who are channeling now were originally interested in psychic functioning, and some originally considered themselves as psychics or intuitives before the channeling mode developed. There are other channels, however, who show no psychic ability in their waking state and may or may not function psychically in the channeling mode.

ESP from the Channel

Thus, there are good reasons for believing that psychic information is drawn from the abilities of the person doing the channeling. First, in formal and informal tests, the ordinary personality and the channeling entity seem to have about the same level of psi. Second, several entities indicate that it is the psi abilities of the host that they use. The fact that many persons who channel reportedly have psychic abilities is also suggestive of the conclusion.

A generally held opinion in parapsychology is that psi occurs in the unconscious part of the mind, then moves into conscious awareness, with clarity or distortion affected by the system. In the case of channeled entities, the same process could take place. That is, the ESP material could be obtained from the channel's unconscious mind by the personality of the entity.

If any psi ability in channeling is that of the individual doing the channeling, then the entity is probably drawing on the person's ESP at unconscious levels. Many, but not all, parapsychologists consider that psi is a general ability and almost everyone has it to some degree or another. For that reason, the occurrence of accurate ESP in channeling cannot be taken as proof of an independent spirit. We should also be aware that channeled ESP impressions, like ESP in the ordinary state, are subject to distortion, error, and mistakes. It probably also follows that channeled entities, like human ones, could learn to improve their ESP with training in the techniques that have proved useful for psychic functioning, such as mental relaxation, concentration, visualization, and learning to separate the psi signal from their personal overlay.

ESP in Mediumship and Hypnosis

Some of the relevant information from other fields can be noted here. First is that the early studies of mediums in England and the U.S. soon revealed that the paranormal information produced by the spirits could also originate in the psychic abilities of the medium. This possibility bore on the question of the existence of the spirits as separate entities (Myers, 1903). The controversy still continues as to whether psi can completely explain some or all mediumistic cases (Gauld, 1977; Cook, 1987). It seems unlikely that either side can be proven with satisfaction.

In the early days of hypnosis, the occurrence of clairvoyance of distant scenes and events in trances was an accepted and documented phenomenon. It rarely happens now, and modern hypnosis research takes no account of it. Another phenomenon was the "community of sensation or action" in which the hypnotized subject was apparently able to experience body sensations such as smells, pinches, and movements of the hypnotist. Early hypnotists also reported that the condition of hypnotic rapport enabled the subject to be aware of the hypnotist's thoughts. Contemporary studies of hypnotic trance and ESP have been performed with cards and other targets. They are consistent in showing that ESP scores are generally enhanced by the person being in hypnosis. Since the channeling state is often a trance of varying depth, we would expect that it would enhance ESP, even in persons who show no ability in their ordinary state.

In another area, that of multiple personality studies, I have been told by a Michigan therapist that a personality of one of the multiples that he worked with was able to read his thoughts—often embarrassing ones. (Roger Brown, personal communication, 1987). I corresponded with this part, which was referred to as Organizing Mind, who told me that she was able to have telepathic awareness of the Organizing Minds of other persons. I do not know if this is a common finding in clinical multiple personality or if many researchers would even be willing to notice if it occurs.

The idea that channeled psi abilities originate in the host was not a concept that I held originally, but one that emerged in the course of studying channels. My first question about this was to ask if the reverse position was not also tenable; that is, that the psychic abilities that people have are provided by nonphysical spirits who perceive psychically and then give the information to the person. There are some spiritualistic or spiritist models that maintain that position. From a purely logical position, there is no way to completely prove or disprove that alternative. However, it is not what the charneled beings themselves say, as I have indicated. Further, the forms of psi response—the words used, the way the impressions come—are the same as when humans make the responses, with all the earmarks of the human processing system and the ways it handles psi information. If the information is coming directly from a spirit in the channeling mode, perhaps it would be expected to be purer and more free of noise, because the physical components are reduced or eliminated. Yet, the psi information seems no different than that which comes though the mental processes of the ordinary personality. Thus, it seems more likely that the psi comes from the person and not from the channel.

CHAPTER 5

ANCIENT AND MODERN ORACLES

Looking at the early origins of channeling takes us back to the famous oracles of the gods in Greece and the Near East. Tradition holds that Ge, the earth goddess, gave oracles at Delphi in Greece in the second millennium B.C., and Babylonia had an oracle of Ishtar in the eleventh century B.C. After the goddess religion declined, there was a proliferation of local deities and more widely known gods who had oracles through which they spoke. Often this was through trance speaking, though there were other forms of divination that were used. The oracles were essential for cities, tribes, and individuals to provide authority and advice in conducting affairs of state, religious matters, and everyday lives.

At the oracle location was a shrine or temple and a priestess or priest who spoke for the god, or who would conduct a divination process. The questions asked of the oracles were concerned with personal questions as well as weighty matters of politics, war, worship, and philosophy. The following matters are some that were asked by common citizens of the oldest Greek oracle, that of Zeus at Dodona in Greece:

Would it be better for Onasimos to get married now, or should he avoid it?
Would it be advisable for Ariston to go to Syracuse?
Timodamus asks whether he should invest his money in a trading fleet or in a business.
Lysias wants to know if he will be successful in sea trade. (Vandenberg, 1982, p. 20f.)

The Dodona oracle was located in a grove of oak trees sacred to Zeus. The questions were written on thin lead plates, rolled, and put into a jar. The priestess would take one out, listen to the rustling of the trees in the wind, and pronounce the words she heard. These would be written down as the response of the god. For example, to the question of Timodamus, the oracle responded, "Stay in the town and open a business" (Vandenberg, 1982, p. 21). Later, the oak tree voices were replaced by a priestess who went into a trance state to speak the words of Zeus.

The oracles were consulted on all major political, economic, and military matters; their answers were kept on record, and their reputation for accuracy was high. The Roman senator Cicero observed that the reputation of the oracles could not have been so high had they not been correct over the centuries. In addition to divination of the future, requests to the gods, and judgments on controversies, the answers sought were often counsel or guidance on decisions. There were several instances of apparent psychic functioning on record. A Greek military leader named Cimon sent a delegation to the oracle of Amon in Egypt. The oracle sent the delegation home, saying that Cimon had already gone to Amon. The delegation left, not understanding the pronouncement, until they learned that Cimon had died the very day they spoke with the oracle (Vandenberg, 1982).

DELPHI

There were many oracles in the Near East, each the site of a deity, including Ishtar, Hercules, Apollo, Athena, Artemis, Areas, Zeus, Amun, and Leto. The best known by moderns is the oracle of Apollo at Delphi in Greece, which had the recommendation "Know Thyself" written on the temple (Parke and Wormell, 1956). Other oracles of Apollo were at Claros and Dydima. From the myths, it seems that the Apollo cult took Delphi over from Ge, the Earth goddess. The spokesperson for the god remained a woman, who paid homage to the Earth in her prayer of invocation before

Themis, an early priestess of the Delphic oracle, sits on the tripod of Apollo to answer an inquirer.

she prophesied. She was known as the Pythia, perhaps after the python, sacred to Ge.

Questions would be brought to the oracle by petitioners who ranged from the leaders of the country to the common populace. The Pythia would go into a trance and be possessed by the god to speak the answer. The process was one of receiving information from outside the conscious mind as in mediumship, channeling, and prophecy.

The Ritual

The priestess entered the prophetic state with a ritual. She would first bathe ritually, then be led into the temple. The Pythia was robed and had a wool strip placed around her forehead. A laurel crown was placed on her head. A young goat was sprinkled with water. If it began shivering (a propitious sign), it was sacrificed. The priestess went into the inner room where she drank from waters of the stream Cassotis, which was supposed to stimulate her powers. She was given bay laurel leaves (sacred to Apollo) to chew. More laurel leaves were burned as incense, and there were other perfumes and smoke in the air. Then the priestess sat on the tripod, a seat with three legs, to prophesy.

Pythia and the Tripod at Delphi

A dramatic portrayal of the priestess as she prophesies and her priests record her words.

We recognize this ritual as an altered-state induction procedure which would put the priestess into a trance state. Many religious and spiritual ceremonies embody ritual purification, incense, special clothing, and other evocative techniques to destabilize the normal state and create a trance state. The theory of this type of state change has been described by Charles Tart in his book *States of Consciousness* (1975). The state is created with the intention and expectation of being possessed by Apollo, and these expectations determine the nature of the trance and what happens in it, similar to the idea of demand characteristics in hypnosis, which are assumptions held by the individual that act like hypnotic suggestions.

According to a description by Apollonius of Tyana, the Pythia changed physically when she was possessed. Her chest swelled, she flushed then paled, and her limbs trembled convulsively more and more violently; her eyes flashed fire, she foamed at the mouth, and her hair stood on end. Then she tore off the strip of wool around her head and spoke a few words, which the attendant priests wrote down (Glass, 1969). Other sources say that the priestess spoke in a different voice when prophesying (Vandenberg, 1982). As the god Apollo, she spoke in first person. Also, she originally gave answers in hexameter and elegaic couplets. In later centuries, the versification stopped, and the priests were responsible for putting the answer into rhyme.

We see here familiar aspects of trance channeling: an induction ritual that leads to an altered state; the personality of the individual being replaced by that of the god; the changes in posture, behavior, and voice; speaking in verse.

The Case of Croesus

An illustration of oracular advice is a series of messages given to King Croesus of Lydia, about 550 B.C., by the oracle of Apollo at Delphi. First, the king tested all the famous oracles by sending delegations to ask each what he was doing on the hundredth day after the delegation left. On the hundredth day, in his capital of Sardis, Croesus cut up a lamb and a tortoise and boiled them in a brass pot. Of all the oracles, only the Pythia at Delphi was correct, saying:

Can I not number all the grains of sand,
And measure all the water in the sea?
Tho' a man speak not I can understand;
Nor are the thoughts of dumb men hid from me.
A tortoise boiling with a lamb I smell:
Bronze underlies and covers them as well.

(Herodotus, Carter trans., 1958, p. 17)

The temple at Delphi stands in ruins today.

Persuaded that Delphi was truly prophetic, Croesus asked his questions. First, should he attack Persia, an empire that was beginning to threaten his kingdom, and should he find an ally? Second, would he have a long reign?

The oracle answered "After crossing the Halys [a river], Croesus will destroy a great empire." And he was told to ally himself with the most powerful of the Greek states. On the second question, the prophecy was that he should flee when a mule became the king of the Medes. Croesus interpreted all these as favorable, but his interpretation was colored by his hopes. Croesus did ally himself successfully with Sparta but, when he attacked the Persians, he was defeated; the empire that was destroyed was his own. The ruler that conquered him was Cyrus, not an animal but a mule in the sense that he was of mixed parentage, Mede and Persian (Glass, 1969).

Croesus was wise to test the oracle before he posed his important questions. This is a practice that should be matter of fact with any psychic or prophetic claims. Indeed, channels themselves should be the first to test and evaluate the quality of their channeled messages.

PSYCHOLOGICAL FACTORS IN PROPHECIES

The answers that the oracle gave to Croesus were ambiguous, though this was not apparent to Croesus. Why were they phrased thus, when the oracle apparently had the capability for precise and matter of fact statements?

Perhaps because the oracle was facing a difficult situation. Here was one of the most powerful and wealthy rulers in the world, (hence the phrase "wealth of Croesus"). The correct answers to his questions were definitely against his interests and could incur his wrath. Remember that the Greeks had a propensity to kill the messenger who brought them bad news. On the other hand, if the oracle gave incorrect answers and predicted that Croesus would triumph when he would actually be defeated, the failure would be spectacular, with severe consequences for the Pythia's reputation. The resolution to the dilemma was to speak in a manner that gave the correct answer, but was semantically ambiguous. Croesus could interpret the answers in the framework of his desire for them to be favorable. Others would, in retrospect, see the true meanings and not blame the oracle. The responses were adapted to the complex needs of the "truth," the situation, and the audience.

This analysis is my speculation on the inner process of the oracle. I do not suggest that this situation was consciously analyzed at the time; analysis is not a job for ego consciousness, but is the sort of thing that is usually handled elsewhere in the mind (or perhaps outside the mind). It requires that the several needs, the conflicting points of view, and the consequences of alternatives are all taken into consideration, and the answers respond to whatever priorities are established among them.

Whether that is what happened with that prophecy or not, it is likely that messages of contemporary channels are processed in this way. I have listened to channeled messages that were arranged and phrased in terms that were most responsive to the particular audience in contrast to other audiences the entity had addressed. No messages from channels come through unadorned. All channeled information is modified by the channel and adapted to the audience, the circumstances, the purposes, and the consequences.

The part that Croesus played in the affair should not be overlooked. He was given a message that was not explicit. It was stated poetically, and the referent for "empire" was not clear. We have to say that it was his projection, no doubt unconscious, that the empire to be destroyed was Persian. It was an interpretation that linked with his hopes and so gained uncritical emotional confirmation. In the same manner, when channeled prophecies (or other messages) are ambiguous, they are likely to be interpreted to confirm a person's expectations, desires, or fears. This is also true of situations involving psychics, physicians, and others who are given authority, especially if the client's feelings about the situation have been suppressed or repressed.

THE ARK OF THE COVENANT AS AN ORACLE

The word "oracle" originally referred to the place where the gods spoke. By association, it became used for the person who spoke the words and even the messages themselves. In the original meaning, classical oracles were sites located in sacred groves, at springs, and at other locations in Greece, Africa, Babylonia, and other lands surrounding the Mediterranean. Rituals similar to those at Delphi and Dodona were used. People desiring answers would go to those sites, or send a representative, to ask their questions.

The Israelites, on the other hand, were a nomadic tribe and had no land of their own for oracles. Further, their deity had created a covenant with them that was exclusive; they could neither worship other gods nor make statues to take with them. Yet, their religion was one of revelation. How were they to receive the word of God?

There may have been a mode of revelation, using the process of channeling, that took place before the prophets began to emerge in Jewish history. The Ark of the Covenant, which the Israelites took with them as they traveled, may have served as a portable oracle shrine specifically for Yahweh. The Ark was a rectangular chest which was a cabinet for the Ten Commandments and, later, the Torah. It was considered the resting place of God, and it also was used as a pulpit.

On top of the chest was a cover of gold with a winged figure fastened at each end to protect it. Said the Lord to Moses, "There I shall come to meet you; there from above the throne of mercy [cover], from between the two cherubs that are on the Ark of the Testimony, I shall give you all my commands for the sons of Israel" (Exodus 25:23). This covering, or seat, was God's answering place. John Wyclyffe originally gave the name of this seat as "oracle" in his translation of the Bible.

Instructions for the sanctuary included special robes and a breastplate for the priest, incense, and a spice mixture for anointing the priests and equipment. The sanctuary was a tent; the Ark, altar, tables, and other equipment were made to be portable, to go with the people as they moved. The breastplate had on it something referred to as Urim and Thummim, also called an oracle. It is speculated that these were stones for divination, but knowledge of them is lost. Interestingly, Joseph Smith, prophet of the Mormon Church, said that he translated the Book of Mormon by using gazing stones called Urim and Thummim.

The Ark was thus a holy shrine which carried the presence of God. The divine instructions lay out ritual preparations, very similar to those that occurred later at Delphi. Perhaps their use could put the priest into a prophetic state in which he received the word of God. Thus, the Israelites could receive oracular communication from their own God wherever their travels took them. The priest could use the Ark as a pulpit, just as the Pythia spoke from the sacred tripod of Apollo. There was a social function to this portable shrine. It was a religious invention that replaced the elaborate temples of the Babylonians and Egyptians and the sacred oracle sites of the local gods.

In the Bible, there is no report of a priest going through the preparation ritual and then speaking the words of God. The writings do say that the voice of God spoke from the Holy of Holies where the Ark was kept. If the Ark was an oracle, then this voice could have been the priest, embodying the deity or reporting the words of an inner voice. Now, the traditions around the Ark are lost, and whatever they were, its use now is as a cabinet for the scrolls.

TIBETAN ORACLES

Oracles were used in Tibet before Buddhist times, but were incorporated into the religious and political structure when the country was united into a central government. The earliest, according to Lama Govinda (1966) in *The Way of the White Clouds*, was in the monastery of Samye. The high priest would become possessed by the ancient guardian spirits of Tibet whenever the ceremony in their honor was performed. In this trance, they would speak through him and answer questions. In the time of the fifth Dalai Lama (1617–1682), the Nanchung oracle at the monastery of Drepung was recognized as the official state oracle of Tibet. It was consulted on locating reincarnations of high lamas and on important political decisions. Questions of less import could be asked after the business of state was completed. Many of the important monasteries in Tibet had their own oracles. Each of the oracle priests had to be confirmed by the state oracle after going through rigorous training and testing. The Tibetan government in exile in India still uses the state oracle. In 1987, Asian scholar David Komito told me that the position was held by a frail, elderly monk. When the monk enters the oracular process, he goes through an astonishing transformation into a frenzied, vigorous being with the appearance and behaviors of the protector deities.

Govinda (1966) gives a vivid description of an oracle session at the monastery of Dungkar Gompa in Tibet. The priest was clad in brocade robes and wore a jeweled crown. Monks chanted gutturral invocations as cymbals, bells, and drums played. Incense from censers filled the temple. The oracle priest began to shake with convulsive movements, "as if the dark powers from the depth of the earth, the chthonic powers that governed humanity before the dawn of history, had seized his body and threatened to burst it" (p. 185). His face changed to become like a terrifying deity.

A senior monk held up questions, written on pieces of paper and tightly folded. The oracle priest, possessed by one of the six protectors, seized a sword and swung it about with flashing speed. Five or six of the monk attendants battled with him and, by weight of numbers, forced him back to the throne. Finally, he became calmer. He spoke and his words were recorded. Then he was possessed by another of the guardians, and the process repeated. The ceremony continued for hours, leaving the priest exhausted. Later the oracle priest told Govinda that he remembered nothing of the experience, though physically the aftereffects lasted for days.

The similarities of the Tibetan and Delphic oracles are obvious. There was a special temple ritual, a frenzied possession by the deity, and responses to questions. Each incorporated more ancient traditions. Each was consulted on matters of state and important religious decisions. The process is one of possession in which the individual is taken over by the deity.

THE ROLE OF THE ORACLES

The decisions of Delphi and Nanchung demonstrate the important role that oracles can play. There was no important question in the Near East that was not submitted to Delphi when the oracle was at its height. It was understood to be the embodiment of Apollo and to indicate the will of the god for city-states, colonies, commerce, and religious matters. The responses of Apollo provided guidance and authority in matters where reason or knowledge were inadequate and, in many cases, the decision might otherwise have been made by force. The high regard in which the oracle was held indicates it did this with success. Likewise, the Tibetan oracles provide information and authority for important societal matters, an example being the finding of children who are identified as reincarnated lamas. Today, in addition to those of the Tibetan society, there are similar oracles in many cultures such as Brazil, parts of Africa, and Asia. It is noteworthy that these and possession oracles in all societies are also available for personal questions on health, family, business, and other matters. Anthropologists sometimes distinguish between macro-decisions at the level of society or government and micro-decisions with regard to individual lives. The oracles lent their knowledge and authority to needs at both levels.

Classical scholar E. R. Dodds (1963), in *The Greeks and the Irrational,* suggests that the Pythia was a medium with psychic abilities which provided prophetic insight. Oesterreich (1974), in his classic work on possession, also takes this position. However, to my knowledge, no classical scholar has gone farther and suggested that the oracle gods really existed. In any event, the underlying process in oracles appears to be the same as in channeling. In both cases, the personality of the individual is replaced by the presence of another being. There can also be differences. The deities of the oracles often express themselves very energetically. The priestesses of Apollo were referred to as girls with frenzied mouths. We get our word "enthusiasm" from the concept of the embodiment of the god: "en-theos." The Tibetan possessions are similarly forceful. The oracle speakers seem to bring awesome forces from beyond the human realm. Those who are possessed by them must utterly surrender to their power. Present-day Western channelings of teachers and ascended masters are tranquil by comparison.

CHAPTER 6

PROPHECIES OF CATASTROPHE
AND OF TRANSFORMATION

Prophecy originally meant speaking for a god. The priests who reported the messages of the Delphic oracle were called *prophetes*. More generally, prophecy means speaking the words of God or inspired speaking in which God or the spirit speaks through the person. The term is often used now to mean a foretelling of the future. The prophets Isaiah and Jeremiah spoke the words of Yahweh to the Israelites, and Muhammad was the prophet of Allah for the Arabic peoples. The words or inspiration come from a source outside the mind of the prophet, the same process as in channeling. The Old Testament often calls the sayings of prophets "oracles," and says, "these are the words of Yahweh," or "the mouth of the Lord has spoken." The earlier Biblical prophets, such as Elisha and Samuel, spoke to kings and individuals, but the later ones like Amos, Isaiah, and Jeremiah addressed the Jews as a people. They reasserted the importance of the relationship between the Jews and God, called for social justice, and interpreted the meaning of the suffering that was being experienced by the people. They warned of the vengeance of God and foretold destruction if the people did not return to righteousness and justice. They held out hope of the coming of the Messiah and the establishment of New Jerusalem, the kingdom of God. Their prophecy provided values and meanings that transformed Judaism and continued into Christianity and Western civilization (H. Smith, 1958). In our time, similar prophetic messages of warning and hope are coming through channels. The following example channeled by Virginia Essene is from "The Christ" (1986):

> You must overcome the present level of negativity because your current environment of ugly thinking is not only destroying your own planet and threatening your physical future, but has now been carried into the streams of space far beyond that allowed by the Creator's laws which guarantee safety to other life.
>
> YOU MAY NOT TAKE THE EVIL THOUGHTS OF WAR AND VIOLENCE AND THE WEAPONS OF DESTRUCTION INTO SPACE! Hear this statement and heed it well. You are at a crossroad, a time of no return if you do [Caps in original] (p. 5).

If you allow a few maniacs to damage this exquisite planet—which was prepared for you to assist in your spiritual self-realization and in your devotion and love and appreciation of all living things—then you are foolish indeed (p. 7).

Contrasting to this warning of the danger of destruction, the message calls for action to change the world through individual and group efforts.

Therefore, each of you is called to join us in the work that must be done. You are reminded to put the usual habits and limitations of life aside and place your devotion, dedication, and energy toward accomplishing a *peaceful* planet. This is your gift against viciousness and violence. You are the corps of love and this is your opportunity for victory (p. 14).

Let each person on earth acknowledge that *behavior is the test of knowing.* How are you behaving? What have you learned, citizen of earth, that you would share with your own human family on earth? And what is it you would teach the rest of this galaxy's lifeforms about LOVE? Certainly those who teach love and peace will learn more about their subject but they must have some basic proficiency first (pp. 36–37).

Peace is possible by your example. Then let us march together in perfect union to achieve the purpose for which you came. In God's eternal name let this mighty achievement reign on earth by your love and service (p. 20).

The communicator of this message identifies himself as the Christ and says of himself, "There is now a greater Jesus for I have grown and expanded as you children of light are also doing" (p. 62). He explains that he and other beings are helping to carry out the divine plan for Earth, which is to manifest love and wisdom. At this particular time, they are providing assistance to help humans overcome the threat of man-produced destruction: "GOD HAS LITTLE TO DO WITH THE CONDITIONS ON YOUR PLANET. YOU HAVE BROUGHT THEM TO YOU BY YOUR OWN THOUGHTS, AC-TIONS, AND DESIRES" (p. 179).

The Christ says that he and his helpers cannot make the changes them-selves, but they can inspire and support humans in doing so. He says they are psychically showering love onto the Earth, communicating with people in meditation, and guiding with specific advice. For example, he discusses approaches to teaching children, what scientists should do, and even the value of television: "I must insist to all parents that TV is not an adequate babysitter, as you call it. Most programs are not fit company for adults, let alone children" (p. 169).

At first I was offended by the fire-and-brimstone style of the author, but some of the content would be difficult to disagree with.

CATASTROPHIC EXPECTATIONS: THE FIRE NEXT TIME

One of the themes that occurs in channeled messages is the warning of major changes, apparently to come in the near future. These are often catastrophic events such as nuclear destruction, wars, earthquakes, earth changes, famine, floods, and the disintegration of society (Mentor, 1985; H. L. Cayce, 1964; *Cosmic Awareness Speaks,* n.d.; Christ, 1986; C. Knight, 1981; Elkins and Rueckert, 1977; Elkins, Rueckert and McCarty, 1984; Steiger 1973; *The Law of One,* 1982a, 1982b, 1983).

Some of these channeled messages are oracle-like predictions that say the events are inevitable. Mentor, channeled by Meredith Lady Young, simply says that the thirteen years following 1987 will be filled with increased fear and bloodshed, wars and natural disasters (Mentor 1985). Edgar Cayce predicted major geological changes and continental shifts beginning in the period from 1958 to 1998. Like the comments from Christ, some prophecies see the catastrophes as caused by human failings and say that this is a purification. Rabindra Matori, channeled by Carol Bell Knight, says that it is the breakdown of the old order of greed, avarice, ignorance, stupidity, and exploitation, in which "it seems necessary for destruction to take place, leaving chaos in its wake, before the new world order can emerge" (Knight, 1981, p. 107). Gildas, channeled by Mary Swainson, tells her group, "Do not be afraid when we speak of 'the chaos' or 'the maelstrom.' Look beyond your fear and you will see that out of all this can only come forth purity, completeness, Godlikeness" (White and Swainson, 1971, p. 94).

The messages coming through Virginia Essene and others say that humans themselves can affect the course of events. Obviously, if these problems are caused by human behavior, then human changes can alter them. We should, they say, change our thoughts, feelings, and behavior in the direction of love, peace, compassion, and caring. These changes, both individual and group, will move the world away from man-created disasters and toward global peace and higher levels of spiritual development. The Christ (Essene) urges persons to meditate individually each day and once a week in a group to receive guidance and share inspiration. Matori (Knight) urges that hundreds of thousands of persons be prepared to serve and care for people needing help and to remedy conditions of improper housing and starvation.

EXTRATERRESTRIALS

Some messages through the channeling process purport to come from extraterrestrials. These are received telepathically through mental voices, and the entities identify themselves as space brothers, UFO occupants, or representatives of other galactic civilizations (Steiger, 1988; Vallee, 1975, 1979; Keel, 1970; Jung, 1959b). The individuals consider themselves contactees rather than channels and, often, cult-like followings develop around them. Often, the channeling follows an apparent physical experience with a UFO or UFO occupants. The messages speak of concern for the earth's peoples, the need for peace and spiritual values, and their willingness to motivate and encourage us. The themes of warning and prophecy occur frequently in these UFO entities' messages. Hatonn, a space being who has been claimed by several different contactee channelers, says that the earth's surface will be changed by a massive destruction (Elkins and Rueckert, 1977). This is a part of the preparation for earth people joining the galactic confederation. An entity identified as Ra, describing itself as a social memory complex channeled through Carla Rueckart, says that there will be a "harvest" associated with the destruction of persons moving from the level of third density to fourth density. The harvest means that some souls will go on to new lessons of love, while others will remain to repeat lessons they have not been learned. In several channeled communications, the third density is equated with physical reality while the fourth density is non-physical consciousness, or a psychic level of being. Third density beings may suffer death or physical harm in the foretold events.

There are statements by the space brothers that humans have influence in these matters, even the physical events. Prophecies are fulfilled, says one, by the realization of a pattern, but patterns can be changed. Dangers can be avoided if mankind changes its behavior (Elkins and Rueckert, 1977). The themes of a Confederation of Planets, a Solar System Council on Saturn, and other cosmic connections are prominent in channeled UFO material and in stories of contactees. The recipients are usually quite persuaded that they are being contacted by extraterrestrials and often receive technical information and theories. To my knowledge, none of these have proven workable or useful, but there is often a strong belief by the contactee that the material is very important. Other messages from UFO entities include calls for higher values, world peace, compassion, and love. Some messages, such as the widely read *The Starseed Transmissions* by Ken Carey (1982), are said to come from extraterrestrial beings who are also advanced spiritual teachers and guardians of the earth.

PROPHECIES THAT FAILED

It is indicated that in the year 1970 there shall be earth changes, that the actual axis of the earth is that which shall shift in a seismical stage where earth and moon and sun are at a particular alignment causing those changes that this Awareness has described, especially affecting the San Andreas fault from the area of Long Beach through California . . . Washington . . . Oregon. . . . It is suggested that by the year 1980 that accumulations of radioactive substance will have reached that point of contamination where life, animal life, and plant life will be seriously affected. . . . It is also indicated for the year 1990 this Awareness has indicated the nature of great cataclysm, that wherein land masses rise out of the South Atlantic, where there shall be eruptions from the center of this planet, indicating that change in reference to the great birds that shall fly, raining death on inhabitants and all that cries havoc (*Cosmic Awareness Speaks*, no date, p. 5).

A source called Cosmic Awareness made those predictions through Ralph Dube before his death in 1967. They are examples of predictions that have failed to be fulfilled. The axis of the earth did not shift in 1970, nor were there extensive earthquakes. The situation in 1980 did not match the prediction of radioactive pollution. Was there any reason to believe that the prediction of earth changes in 1990 might come true? Not on the basis of the previous track record. Earthquakes in general appear to have increased, but the magnitude portrayed in the prophecy is one of total cataclysm.

The axis of the earth seems to be a favorite topic of channels (and also of psychic predictions in general, I might note). John, channeled by Kevin Ryerson, was asked by a questioner if in the past there were shifts in the axis and if there is an upcoming shift in the axis. Said John, "We indeed as though notice as though there is the gradual shifting of the earth's axis. It has shifted as though by as much as one quarter over the last century. But it is as gradual." And he followed this up with the idea that we can change this by changing our thoughts. "And indeed as though if ye change as though thy inner thought, indeed as though ye may change the course of events itself" (Ryerson and Purcell, 1987).

The complicated language that John used is often found in channeled speaking and may be a kind of linguistic repetition used to maintain a trance state (Bronson, 1988). Regarding the earth, there is no evidence that the axis of the earth is or has been shifting over the last century. There is a normal precession (advancement) of the axis that is continual, such that the north pole of the earth slowly traces a circle in the sky. But this is slow, taking thousands of years to cycle, and the rate has not changed in recent times.

Cayce's Predictions

Another example of unfulfilled prophecy occurs in Edgar Cayce's predictions of geological events. In 1968 or 1969, said one reading, the land of ancient Atlantis would begin to surface near the Bahamas. There is no indication of this happening, despite expeditions to search for clues. (Some "walls" and "roads" were observed underwater, but these appear to be natural formations.)

Several of the Cayce readings in the 1930s designated a period from 1958 to 1998 when extensive land changes are predicted: the Western part of the U.S. will be broken up, the greater portion of Japan will go into the sea, the upper portion of Europe will change in the twinkling of an eye, there will be upheavals in the Arctic and Antarctic, volcanoes erupting, shifting of the poles, and inundations in California, Nevada, and Utah (H. L. Cayce, 1964, pp. 80–81). The readings directed Cayce to move to Virginia Beach, Virginia, because that location would be safe when much of the East Coast became submerged.

These changes and others predicted in the readings have not happened. Some of Cayce's followers have gone to great lengths to prove these events really happened on a smaller scale or that they were thought-form impressions (Stearn, 1967; H. L. Cayce, 1964; *Earth Changes: Past, Present and Future*, 1963). If one takes the predictions at face value, as is done with the other readings, then these forecasts are incorrect. Martin Ebon (1968) and Robert Sommerlott (1971), both open and sympathetic researchers, compare the predictions with objective evidence, including some provided by Cayce-oriented geologists, and find them wanting. "In the field of precognition," says Sommerlott drily, "Cayce's record is a catastrophe" (p. 245).

Cayce's family and organization moved to Virginia Beach on the strength of the readings and, regardless of the prediction, the move appears to have been a healthy one. But when Ramtha, channeled by J. Z. Knight, predicted that there would be earthquakes and natural disasters in California, several hundred of his followers moved to Oregon and Washington in the mid-1980s, some selling their property and leaving their homes. It was disruptive and divisive for many families. In the late 1980s, more than several thousand people moved to rural Montana, following the channeled guidance of Elizabeth Clare Prophet, who forecast that nuclear war was likely to begin in January 1990 and, when that did not occur, on April 23, 1990. There can be serious social consequences to uncritical belief in these messages.

The End of the World

A notable instance of the failure of channeled prophecy occurred in the middle 1950s in Michigan (Wallace, Wallachinsky, Wallace, and Wallace, 1980). Mrs. Dorothy Martin was receiving automatic writing from a group calling itself the Guardians who represented themselves as being part of a galactic civilization. They said their purpose was to teach humans the principles, ideas, and guides to right conduct to prepare the people of Earth for changes that lie ahead. A group of followers grew around the messages and teachings. The messages began to predict a cataclysmic disaster: "The Earthling will awaken to the great casting . . . of the lake seething and the great destruction of the tall buildings of the local city—the cast that the lake bed is sinking. . . ." (Festinger, Riecken, and Schachter, 1956, p. 55). The devastation was to include France and England sinking, Russia becoming a great sea, the Atlantic seaboard submerging, the U.S. becoming flooded, and new mountains rising in the Central States. One of the communicators, Sananda (identified as Jesus), told the group that they would be saved by a flying saucer spaceship which would pick them up the night of December

20, 1954. The leaders of the group, taking their social responsibility seriously, communicated these warnings to the media. Newspapers reported the story in a straightforward way, but there was also ridicule and humor at the expense of the believers. The group took the prophecy seriously and some quit their jobs and gave up possessions. The spacecraft did not arrive at the indicated time, and the automatic writing messages set another time several hours later. Again there was no arrival. This occurred several times over four days. The group was shocked and dismayed to realize that they were not going to be picked up and that the natural disasters were not occurring. A message then came saying "And mighty is the word of God—and by his word have ye been saved." The message implied that the group had loosed such a force of good and light that the catastrophes had been averted (Festinger, p. 169).

Social psychologist Leon Festinger and several colleagues studied the group almost from the beginning, even placing observers in the group masquerading as believers (which elicited criticism from colleagues later). It is clear that the group seriously and sincerely believed the messages that were coming to them. The book *When Prophecy Fails* (Festinger, 1956) points out that when the prediction was repeatedly disconfirmed, the group members belief system was shaken and they had to cope with the discrepancy between the messages and the events. Most surprisingly, many of the members chose to continue to believe in the validity of the messages, in some ways more strongly, as though the disconfirmation was a test that strengthened their faith.

Social Effects

This same sequence can happen in many movements where there are charismatic leaders or strongly held beliefs, including channeled teachings. Essentially, when a belief system is disconfirmed by circumstances or evidence, instead of being changed to fit the reality, the beliefs will sometimes be strengthened and even urged on others under the following circumstances: (1) The belief is held with deep emotional and/or intellectual conviction. (2) The believer has taken some important action or made a significant commitment based upon the belief. (3) The believer has the social support of others who believe. In these circumstances, even if events disconfirm part or all of the system, the person will frequently emerge unshaken, even more convinced of the truth of his or her beliefs. It is easier to rationalize, ignore, reinterpret, deny, accept contradictions, and do anything else rather than to accept being wrong or allow that the commitment was worthless. The individual may actually increase in his or her attempts to persuade others to believe. Scorn or persecution also makes it more difficult for the person to change.

This process of believing more strongly in order to reduce cognitive dissonance can be seen in a variety of movements. It applies to messianic or end-of-the-world groups—Millerites, the early Christians, Montanus, Shab-batai Zevi, and others—where events did not follow the expectations. It also applies to channeled messages. The disconfirmations of the statements of Cayce, Ramtha, Mrs. Martin, and others, do not create doubt or even discrimination in many of their followers. There ought to be no difficulty in accepting that a channeled entity might be 70 percent accurate on a health diagnosis, but zero percent accurate on geology. Unfortunately, there is an emotional need to make it all the same.

Disconfirmations

To my knowledge, in every case where prophecies of major disaster can be checked against real events, the channels do not stand up well. The events that are prophesied consistently do not occur. The dates come and go, and life goes on without the cataclysm. There are rarely minor events, such as small earthquakes or floods that conceivably might have been magnified. According to the entities, the events predicted are not symbolic or metaphorical. The sources treat them as real (Mrs. Martin's writing said "THIS IS DATED NOT IN SYMBOLOGY . . . REALITY YET! (Festinger, 1956, p. 56), and Cayce spoke about floods just as he spoke about someone's liver. There actually may have been a general increase in earthquakes, volcanic activity, and natural disasters in the past few decades, but specific events have not been predicted by channeled messages.

IS THERE AN UNCONSCIOUS DYNAMIC?

At present we are in a time of resurgence of these prophecies of warning. They come from psychics, survivors of near-death experiences, and others, as well as channels. It is curious as to what purpose these catastrophic predictions serve. They are stated in survival mode, yet they are not valid in specifics. They surely draw on psychological energy in their dramatic na-ture, but for what? In the cases that I have studied, I have been struck by the fact that the channeled predictions generally ignore major problems facing the human race: overpopulation, AIDS, pollution, increased drug usage, the thinning of the atmospheric ozone layer, and ecological destruction. Only occasionally is nuclear destruction treated as a danger. These are considered in the scientific and public community to be serious threats to the survival of large numbers of humans, but have not been in the scenarios of channeled predictions. Events of nature are much more frequent.

One possible motivation for the catastrophic predictions is the prevalence of anxiety about the future in the general population. The problems men-tioned above plus many others contribute to worry, anxiety, feelings of helplessness, and fear. Yet much of the time these have to be held at bay, simply because there seems to be little the individual can do about them. In the region of the psyche where channeling operates, there may be greater access to these preconscious feelings from the channel and from others. The channeled messages may construct specific events that release and focus the emotions. When there are inner issues or feelings, the individual tends to locate outer events that will match those feelings. If channels articulate prophecies of fearful events, this crystalizes the fear, making it less unknown, and also gives it an avenue of release through expression.

AN ARCHETYPE OF SOCIAL PROPHECY

The times are indeed troubled ones, and I see an archetypal pattern of prophecy arising in response. There are four elements that make up this form in its present manifestation.

1. There is recognition of a time of stress, despair, and fear, with social trouble and disintegration of values.

2. Prophetic warnings tell of danger, catastrophe, and destruction, caused by human failings and attitudes.

3. There is a call to transform actions, feelings or beliefs, to repent, to turn or return to higher values, express love and service, enter into harmony with nature, and so on.

4. The promise of a transformed world is given, a new age of love, growth, advancement, joining the galactic federation, or establishment of a spiritual era.

These four elements provide a structure for recognition of the problem, emotional mobilization, and motivation for change through a transformation This is an archetypal pattern of social prophecy, that is, a form that repeats itself in human history and has its own energy and structure. God, speaking through the Hebrew prophets, castigated the people for their failings, but promised a good life if they returned to their love and obedience. An example of this archetypal pattern is from Isaiah:

Listen you heavens: earth attend
for Yahweh is speaking.
. . .
A sinful nation, a people weighed down with guilt,
a breed of wrongdoers, perverted sons.
. . .
Your land is desolate, your towns burned down,
your fields—strangers lay them waste before your eyes:
All is desolation, as after the fall of Sodom.
. . .

A statue of the prophet Isaiah who spoke the words of God to the people.

Take your wrongdoing out of my sight.
Cease to do evil.
Learn to do good,
search for justice,
help the oppressed,
be just to the orphan,
plead for the widow.

Come now, let us talk this over,
says Yahweh.
Though your sins are like scarlet,
they shall be as white as snow;
though they are red as crimson,
they shall be like wool.

If you are willing to obey,
you shall eat of the good things of the earth.
But if you persist in rebellion,
the sword shall eat you instead.
The mouth of Yahweh has spoken.

(Isaiah I, 16, et passim, Jerusalem Bible)

This form is seen consistently in Isaiah, Jeremiah, Amos, Micah, Malachi, and the other prophets who spoke to those who had fallen away from trust and obedience. The prophecy is a combination of the stick and the carrot. In the time of the Biblical prophets, vengeance was threatened by the Lord, who also promised to bring the new messianic age. In our time, the new age is to come as a result of our own spiritual advancement, usually with the encouragement of beneficent entities. One of the extraterrestrial groups, with the name Calador Ramonsara, channeled through Helen Washburn Yamada, makes this prophetic archetype explicit:

> We from the galaxies beyond your solar system are impressing upon the minds of men and women . . . through many media the same message as the prophets of your Old Testament: "Repent!" We inspire science-fiction writers who are reaching one segment of the population which is on a different level than those who are on a more spiritual approach, [such] as those we reach through channels such as this one. We get through to many young people through their music; we reach you all in one way or another (Yamada, 1987, p. 49).

If this pattern can be seen as an archetype, then its current strength and prevalence should impel us to consider its relevance. Whether we believe in the existence of channeled entities or not, the emergence of this strong of a pattern at the present time indicates a powerful emotional concern for the state of our times. We do not need the angels to tell us we have problems, someone commented. One would think not, but experience suggests that we need many reminders of what is important. Roger Walsh puts it well in *Staying Alive:*

'Humankind cannot bear very much reality,' said T. S. Eliot, and repression and denial are the crutches we use to help us avoid it. . . . We wish to deny not only the state of the world but also our role in producing it (Walsh, 1984, p. 37).

These messages may be one modern equivalent of earlier forms of prophecy. Whether the channels speak with the voices of men or angels, these warnings parallel scientific concerns for world problems. It may be that some who will listen to no one else will hear the channels; it behooves us in any event to recognize the urgency of the message when it comes with such strength from beyond our conscious minds.

NEW AGE TRANSFORMATION

If the stick of prophecy is catastrophe, the carrot is the promise of a new age. For the Old Testament peoples, this was earthly bounty, protection from enemies, a coming messianic age, and a new covenant. For the early Christian church, it was the kingdom of God, established on earth as it is in heaven. Contemporary channels speak of a transformation in consciousness, or a change in individual spiritual level, which leads to social change. It is seen as within the power of the individual to make this change, though the exact steps are not often spelled out.

This need for change seems to grow out of the values and beliefs that emerged in American culture in the 1960s. This was a period in which remarkable psychological and spiritual events took place. Within that decade and since, the following social events and movements occurred:

Civil rights and women's rights movements; space exploration; increased interest in Zen, Buddhism, Yoga, Sufism, Taoism, and other non-Western religions; increased interest in mystical aspects of Western religions and meditation practices; rise in cult formation and membership; exploration of psychedelic drug effects; new psychotherapies such as Gestalt, TA, group work; interest in health and physical fitness; body therapies increase: acupressure, massage, Feldenkrais, Rolfing; Human Potential movement emerges; Association for Humanistic Psychology is founded; Association for Transpersonal Psychology is founded; spiritual experiences occur on space flights; interest increases in psychic phenomena; public opinion polls show increased belief in ESP, UFOs, reincarnation; rock music emerges.

These items clearly signal changes in cultural belief systems and assert the possibility of individual and social transformation toward an expanded consciousness. The various movements hold the expectation that people can change personalities for the better, toward greater authenticity, depth of communication, less defensiveness, and release of what might have been called neurotic limitations (but in current jargon would be called negative programs or negativities). Beyond this, there is acceptance of the spiritual or divine nature of the individual and the universe. Significantly, it is believed that one can make experiential progress toward the spiritual level of being, going beyond the personality level to the transpersonal self. Spiritual states are accepted as genuine and can be experienced directly, with practices and attitudes that facilitate that spiritual growth.

These are not new ideas, but they have taken on amazing vitality in the last few decades because of a loss of energy in the traditional religions, an attempt to make science impersonal and objective, and the rejection of deeper realities of human experience by mainstream beliefs. Many problems of our society—the nuclear threat, pollution, and the others already mentioned—are seen as coming from uncontrolled greed, ignorance, masculine values, desires, power needs, inertia, aggression, fear, and so on. No alternatives are seen in our present system to contain or change them. Old images of the self, with their emphasis on individualism, separateness, exploitation, will power and behavioral conditioning, are no longer serving us.

From these ideals, many have been inspired to formulate ideas of a better society. Channels reflect these ideals in their vision of a transformation that is coming. Some speak of it as following the destruction of the old order, while others see it as simply emerging out of our present chaos. Often it is with the help of beings on the other side who say they are sending energies of love, healing, and light to the earth. The quote from Calador Ramonsara tells how they are influencing society. Another statement of very specific, if far fetched, assistance comes fom Varcus, through the same person who channels Ramonsara: "Physically, we are keeping Earth Planet in balance with great spacecrafts with magnetic generators. We are cleaning your pollution with electro bombs in the atmosphere and in your oceans" (Yamada, 1987, p. 50).

Generally, however, humans are expected to do the work themselves, perhaps with the inspiration and guidance of the channeled forces. Says Christ, through Virginia Essene, "Unless a majority of you commit to this goal of peace and place every ounce of energy toward its accomplishment, the heavenly realms cannot . . . by the Creator's instructions to us . . . do it for you" (Christ, 1986, p. 18). Some channeled sources are strongly Christian, others more ecumenical or universal, but people are enjoined to develop spiritually, strive toward union with God, and express love and service for others as a way of moving toward the goal, whether individual transformation or social utopia.

A few channeled messages have addressed *social* action. The writings of The Tibetan, received by Alice A. Bailey, call for groups to be formed which are oriented toward meditation and service. People from this work have made efforts to promote world unity, for example advocating the support of the United Nations and the creation of world passports (A. Bailey, 1944; F. Bailey, 1955; Sinclair, 1984). Rabindra Matori, channeled by Carol Bell Knight, says that preparing for the new world order involves feeding, teaching, and finally freeing those who are homeless or starving. The U.S. is urged to propose a plan for this through the UN. Matori, along with Christ (Essene) and others, suggest that people meditate together or meet together as a way of strengthening their social effectiveness.

Most channeled messages give positive, but general, descriptions of the new age to come. They speak in idealistic ways of love, caring, and spiritual advancement. There is often talk of planes and vibrations and nonphysical realities. Gildas: "Because of the greatly increased vibrations your bodies will change; their material needs will be considerably less. . . . Men will walk with 'angels' and 'angels' with men . . . disease, weariness, all the things that worry you now will no longer be . . . the centres of love in man will be activated at a very high level and there will be peace and understanding all over the earth" (White and Swainson, 1971, pp. 97–98). Others say there will be channeling and psi abilities enabling communication with other people and with beings in other dimensions.

These are utopian visions, and they attempt to describe an ideal society. Plato's *Republic,* More's *Utopia,* and Huxley's *Island* are examples of utopian vision in fiction. Most utopian ideas focus on political (Plato) or societal (More) changes. *Island,* Huxley's last major novel, was concerned with higher states of consciousness in a social system, but went far beyond channeled ideas in its concreteness. Channeled visions of a new era almost never mention political issues, but instead define the transformations as values (justice, truth), personal qualities (love, compassion, trust in God) and psychic sensitivity. Sometimes there is transcendence of the physical plane—on to more lessons, as it were—or a joining of the Confederation of Planets. The changes in inner qualities are often simply assumed to lead toward global peace and a better world. These visions come from feelings and intuitions, not political or structural considerations, and they are the same urgings that caused thousands of young people in the 1960s and 1970s to form communes and intentional communities, believing that their inner states of love, honesty, openness, and certainty would create an alternative to the economic and political structures that governed mainstream life (Popenoe and Popenoe, 1984). The Findhorn community in Scotland is the best known of such groups and received guidance in its development through channeling (Hawken, 1975).

IN PERSPECTIVE

The entities who are making these prophecies are in the minority, perhaps a few dozen among the thousands of channelings now occurring. Still they receive much publicity, and followers often have strong emotional reactions to the prophetic messages. Undoubtedly this is because the channeled messages are correctly perceiving the dangers and dissatisfactions of the times, as well as reflecting generalized fears and anxiety. They fit into a social archetype of prophecy—warning of catastrophes and destruction and advising that personal transformation will enable us to survive or avoid the cataclysm.

Our modern society does not have a place for the functional role of prophet. Ministers, priests, and rabbis do not do this and neither does the institutional church. Psychics often make predictions, but valid ones, if any, are swamped in a deluge of media sensationalism. Scientists sometimes serve as prophets, but run into a conflict between the objective scientific attitude and the need for the fire of passion which is the engine of change. Nor do scientists address the values of interest to the channelers. Channeled entities are particularly suitable for prophesy because they are free agents, not of the system, though in it. They can present themselves as having an empathic, but outside, perspective on humans and the earth, with the voice of authority. This outside source of authority or perspective is essential for a prophet. The messages themselves are stronger in inspiration than in content. They are general, often disconfirmed when specific, and reflect idealism rather than specific programs. They are concerned, but not knowledgeable. The significance that I see to these messages is that they are a reflection from unconscious levels of our individual and collective minds telling us that our situation is serious. They are not to be dismissed, inasmuch as they correspond with data from other sources of knowledge and evoke our own concern about the problems that we have created and must confront.

CHAPTER 7

JANE ROBERTS AND SETH

In contemporary times, several channels have transmitted psychological and spiritual teachings that deserve detailed attention. We will look at three of them: the ideas on consciousness and reality from Seth, the occult system for service to humanity channeled through Alice A. Bailey, and *A Course in Miracles*.

JANE ROBERTS, ROBERT BUTTS, AND SETH

Jane Roberts (1929–1984) was a writer of poetry, short stories, and novels. She was married to Robert Butts, a painter. In 1963, she decided to write a book on ESP and so began experimenting with a Ouija Board. Within five sessions they were receiving messages from "Seth." Four sessions later, Jane started, much to her alarm, speaking the words aloud as they came into her head. As she became more experienced, she would go into a full trance, and Seth would speak through her body.

Seth defined himself as an "energy essence personality," as a future Jane, and also as a being who had various other incarnations and other realities. He never said that he was a separate outside entity. He referred to Jane as Rubert and to Robert as Joseph. Robert took notes as Jane channeled Seth. At first, Jane incorporated Seth's discourses in books she wrote, but soon Seth began to dictate books on his own. The text was given in virtually finished form. To my reading, it is not tightly organized and suffers from the effects of the oral style in which it came. The ideas are nevertheless distinct and clearly originate from an intelligence that is knowledgeable and communicates with intention. I spot-checked passages in two books and found that the rate of dictation was twenty-four to twenty-five words per minute, reflecting his deliberate speaking style (in contrast to the rapid mental dictation of Patience Worth and others). Like many channeled writers, he would stop one evening and begin exactly where he had left off the next evening, often with private sessions and class meetings in between.

Jane, herself, wrote poetry, fiction, and several books on her theory that the self was composed of many aspects, some in the physical world and this timeframe, others elsewhere (Roberts, 1973, 1975). Her writing is excellent

Jane Roberts, who channeled Seth, best known of the contemporary channeled teachers.

and more poetic and imagistic than Seth's. If he drew on her skills, he fared well.

Jane had a traumatic childhood and various health difficulties. Her father left the family when she was two, and she was emotionally abused by a seriously disturbed mother. Her mother had rheumatoid arthritis and was bedridden much of her life. Jane grew up under stressful conditions and, in her midthirties, began having the symptoms of rheumatoid arthritis. She later had to take synthetic thyroid for metabolic deficiencies and had many painful hospital stays. Her eyesight required strong glasses.

Jane explored many possible explanations for the nature of Seth. She did not believe he was a secondary personality or part of the subconscious, nor did she want to refer to him as a spirit. She speculated that he might be a personification of the superconscious part of her self, a kind of psychological structure that enabled her to tune into revelational knowledge. She also allowed that he might have an independent existence as another entity (Roberts, 1970). Her honesty in facing this puzzle indicates both integrity and intelligence.

Besides the Seth-oriented books, Jane channeled a book purporting to come from the consciousness of Paul Cézanne and another one from William James (Roberts, 1978). These puzzled and embarrassed her even more than Seth. William James, by the way, occasionally has written books through other mediums, such as S. Smith (1974), but none of them, including Roberts' book, are much like James' writing or thinking.

Jane died in 1984 from the effects of arthritis and a bone disease. The books continue to be influential, and there are small groups and individuals who continue to study their teachings.

The Seth Books

The messages channeled by Jane from Seth for over twenty years form a coherent body of literature on consciousness, reality, and human development. *The Seth Material,* published in 1970, introduced the concepts and philosophy along with the circumstances of the production of the material (Roberts, 1970). Two major books followed, *Seth Speaks* (Roberts, 1972), and *The Nature of Personal Reality* (Roberts, 1974). The latter was considered by Seth and Jane to be a textbook, with exercises for learning Seth's ideas for personal change. Other books followed, some by Seth, others by Miss Roberts, and two by Sue Watkins, reporting a first-hand account of the classes taught jointly by Seth and Roberts. Several million copies of these books are in print, making Seth the best known of the contemporary channeled beings.

SETH SPEAKS

You Are Part of a Larger Consciousness

A basic premise stated by Seth is that a person is a part of a larger entity that is outside physical space-time; thus, our individual self is an aspect of a greater self (which he called an entity or soul). Just as the unconscious is outside our awareness, so too we are not usually aware of the rest of this larger entity. Explained Roberts, "I think that the selves we know in normal life are only the three-dimensional actualizations of other source-selves from which we receive our energy and life" (1974, viii). The larger self exists in other dimensions or realities. We engage in the physical reality for mental training, feedback, and certain kinds of learning. Our own conscious aspect can reach to the larger soul-self for knowledge, experience, and energy.

Seth holds that reincarnation occurs (you will reincarnate whether you believe in it or not, he says), and the larger self is engaged in living several physical lives in different time periods, which are experienced simultaneously, since the soul is outside of sequential time. He means this literally, but it can also be seen as a metaphor for our many roles.

"You are not creatures of repression," says Seth, "You are creatures of expansion." The self is not limited. Where we have set up limits, we should explore and expand our capabilities. It is assumed that the expansion of

Seth, who referred to himself as an "energy personality essence," painted by Robert F. Butts in 1968.

consciousness is toward health and growth, and Seth's messages are com- pletely congruent with the interest in personal growth, transformation, and human potential that was emerging in the culture during the 1960s and 1970s. These ideas were motivating for Jane and Robert, and Seth found a ready audience of readers and seekers.

The Other Senses Discussed by Seth

Seth urged the development of inner senses. He named some, such as inner vibrational touch; psychological time; perception of past, present, and future; conceptual sense; and expansion or contraction of the tissue capsule. He gave specific guidance and exercises designed to evoke these senses. These were used by Roberts and her husband personally and in the classes she taught (Roberts 1970, 1974; Watkins, 1980, 1981).

Seth's emphasis that our conscious mind is a limited aspect of our self is a valid one in terms of the new psychologies of consciousness. It is evident that our ordinary consciousness is a conditioned and limited state. There are many alternative states of consciousness and variations within states. Many of these states facilitate special perceptions and abilities similar to those mentioned by Seth, such as hyperacuity of the senses, altered time perception, ESP abilities (perception of past, present, and future), emotional processing, imagery, mathematical skills, artistic ability, religious experiences, and others. These states often evoke changed perceptions of reality which are consistent across individuals. These issues have been explored by Charles Tart (1975), Lawrence LeShan (1976), John Lilly (1972), and Robert Masters and Jean Houston (1972).

The interest in consciousness states was very high during the time that Seth was presenting his material. He was drawing on knowledge that was in the culture and presenting it from his perspective.

The belief that our mind is part of a larger consciousness is consistent with psychologies such as those of Jung and Assagioli. The analytical psychology of Carl Jung (1959a, 1968) conceives of a greater self, beyond the ego-self, and on an archetypal level. The goal of therapy is to open the personal self to the nature of that greater self. Similarly, the Psychosynthesis therapy of Roberto Assagioli (1965) seeks to synthesize the personal self and the higher spiritual self. Seth's idea that we are manifestations of that larger entity into a physical plane is unique, but is as plausible as the other theories.

Beliefs and Our Reality

Seth emphasized that we create our own reality by projecting our beliefs and expectations into the world, individually and en masse. In a class exercise, he instructed people to write down beliefs they held about themselves and to study the implications. These core beliefs create our experience. Performing this exercise, Watkins reported that she found a core belief that women's bodies are faulty compared to men's, and she connected it to specific gynecological health problems that she had (Watkins, 1980). Beliefs about responsibility, poverty, wealth, illness, and so on, all create experience to confirm them. Their meanings affect our perception as well. Explained Seth: when meaning changes, perception changes.

These are sound psychological principles. Rational Emotive Therapy developed by psychologist Albert Ellis, general semantics, and other systems, all recognize the controlling influence of hidden beliefs and assumptions. Studies of perception show that, as Seth says, our physical senses create our world, and our states of mind influence what we think are factual perceptions. Seth has presented these concepts in a dramatic and motivating way, more powerfully than one finds in psychological or clinical literature. He has made them accessible, though whether individuals use them depends on their own perseverance and self-discipline.

He spoke against accepting the belief that we are determined by our past experiences. "THE PRESENT IS THE POINT OF POWER," he dictated in capital letters. "Your present beliefs . . . are like directions given to the entire personality, simultaneously organizing and reorganizing past experience according to your concepts of reality. The future—the probable future—is being altered in the same way, of course" (Roberts, 1974, p. 344). This is a powerful concept, echoed by therapists and spiritual leaders alike, who say to "live in the present." It goes further in saying that our present state can be used to selectively organize our experience of ourselves. This concept is related to procedures used in hypnosis and guided visualization, in which traumatic memories are recalled and processed, and positive experiences are utilized to change present attitudes and feelings. Seth's emphasis on the leverage of the present moment is realistic and provides a powerful therapeutic tool for personal change.

The assertion that we create our own reality, individually and collectively, is an attractive concept to many people. The validity of this can be placed on a continuum. At one end, it is almost certain that this is true for cultural conditionings; we experience the world as our culture portrays it. It is also true for personal attitudes, feelings, and thoughts. We also project on the outer world our values, judgments, and categories. At the level of physical events, this concept appears to be partially true. Some external events are a matter of choice. Some external events, or our participation in them, are created by us, consciously or unconsciously. Still other events appear to be random, but are synchronistic reflections of our inner beliefs, emotional issues, and processes. Other occurrences, such as earthquakes and the weather, appear to be beyond our creative abilities. In general, people tend to believe they have far less control in creating their reality than is actually the case; usually, it is the motivation and will that are limiting, not the creative opportunities. John Lilly has observed that the limits of our mind are beliefs to be explored, not facts to be assumed. Seth's position is, at the least, a challenge to examine beliefs and make choices—to expand rather than be contracted.

Seth and Jane as Co-Teachers

A brief comment is appropriate on Seth as a teacher. For several years, Jane Roberts conducted a weekly class concerning personal development. Seth would come out during most of the class sessions and, in a real sense, they were co-leaders. The accounts of the class sessions reveal an outstanding team in operation. They used both familiar and innovative techniques to get people to examine their lives and beliefs, with great awareness of individual and group dynamics. Examples of ESP, mutual dreams, and synchronistic events were incorporated into the teaching. One evening, three class members acted out a reincarnational drama, in which they each recalled being in a past life situation together. Personal issues were evoked as they each recalled and amplified mutual memories from the earlier period and confronted each other. Was it historically real? They never knew, but the memories seemed to be independent. Another session, both funny and instructive, was when Jane instructed all to dress as the opposite sex. The willingness or reluctance to do so again revealed their belief and attitudes. Through it all, Seth would intersperse lectures, comments on personal issues, and even confront individuals. The dynamics were clear. Seth was free to speak directly and authoritatively, going beyond Jane who had to manage organization and class process. It was Jane's class, but Seth was the prod. Jane was not passive, however; in one of the discussions concerning beliefs about sex, Jane calmly unzipped her dress, revealing that she was wearing no underclothes, and challenged the others to do the same! Some did, some did not (Watkins, 1980, 1981).

Other Topics

Other topics discussed by Seth were the nature of God (whom he defined as All That Is), probable realities, special teachers in human history, Christ, Christianity, dreams, and symbols as well as numerous other topics. Some of these are more difficult to evaluate than the themes previously described. His discussions are more psychological and metaphysical, with a strong emphasis on consciousness. There is little discussion of spiritual development, good/evil, love and compassion, God's role, mystical experience, or spiritual unity. There is forceful intellectual content to his discourse, and it is presented in a passionate, authoritative, almost evangelical style. It provides many powerful concepts with specific tools for personal self-knowledge, and it is among the best of the channeled transpersonal teachings.

IN PERSPECTIVE

After the death of Jane Roberts, several individuals have claimed to be channeling Seth, but there are few similarities to the original entity, and there is no reason to believe that Seth has returned. Jane Roberts' papers and recordings have been archived at Yale University. The Austin Seth Center (see the appendix) publishes *Reality Change,* a journal of Seth's ideas and their applications. There are occasional Seth conferences with workshops, papers, and presentations on the Seth material.

The books dictated by Seth continue to be popular and influential. His ideas articulate assumptions now held by many people interested in personal change and New Age thinking. Jane's work marks the dividing point between classical mediums, who called up spirits of the dead, and contemporary channeling, with its teachers, sages, and guides. Though there were other discarnate teachers before Seth, none communicated to the public so effectively. His presence created acceptance for the role of the channeled teacher that many others now play.

CHAPTER 8

ALICE A. BAILEY AND THE TIBETAN

The teachings of Seth are focused on individual self-development and expansion of consciousness. In contrast, the Tibetan master, Djwhal Khul, writing through Alice Ann Bailey, says his teachings are at the soul level, "the means whereby man can function as an incarnated soul. They do not deal primarily with the rules governing man's development" (A. Bailey, 1951, p. 93). The purpose is to enable the disciple to align the self with his soul and cooperate with the group (called the Hierarchy) of awakened beings on the planet to bring about world brotherhood, international cooperation, spiritual advancement, and an expansion of religion and science. Djwhal Khul (pronounced Jual Kool) explains soul development, tells of seven levels of initiation, and explains the metaphysics and rules of operation for these higher levels. The ultimate purpose is for the earth to join a cosmic brotherhood that is a part of the universe, though this is perhaps millions of years into the future.

There is a tradition in the writings about Bailey and Theosophy, which will be observed within this text, to use initials such as A.A.B. (Alice Ann Bailey), D.K. (Djwhal Kuhl), Master M (Moyra), Master R (Rakoczi), K. H. (Koot Humi).

BLAVATSKY AND CHANNELED THEOSOPHY

The concepts and metaphysics of Theosophy were first explicated in *The Secret Doctrine*, by Madame Helena Petrovna Blavatsky (H.P.B.) (1966). This massive work, first published in 1888, attempts to synthesize practically all religions and spiritual teachings in a psychological model of the cosmos, drawing on Western and Eastern traditions, and adding its own concepts. The book was said to have been telepathically channeled by H.P.B., principally from the Master Koot Humi whom Blavatsky says she also met in person during her travels in India. Concepts of an organization of adepts, initiates, and masters, the energies of creation, forces of evolution, the workings of universal consciousness, are all found in *The Secret Doctrine*. Each level of attainment takes in wider experience of the cosmic mind, moving from ordinary person to initiate, to master, and on up the planes of planetary and cosmic reality, with corresponding power and responsibility.

Around these doctrines, Madame Blavatsky and several colleagues founded the Theosophical Society. It became an influential metaphysical force in the early part of the 20th century. Irish poets W. B. Yeats and George Russell were members of a Society lodge. Austrian mystic Rudolf Steiner joined the Society, then later broke away to establish his own mystical system, which is named Anthroposophy. Theosophy has also influenced several religious movements in America, including I Am, channeled through Guy Ballard, and a group headed by Elizabeth Clare Prophet. A good summary of the origins, ideas, and influences of Theosophy is found in Robert Ellwood, Jr.'s *Religious and Spiritual Groups in Modern America*, where he characterizes Blavatsky's *The Secret Doctrine* as a psychological model of consciousness (Ellwood, 1973).

ALICE ANN BAILEY AND THEOSOPHY

When Alice A. Bailey was fifteen and staying at the home of an aunt in Scotland, she was astonished when a turbaned visitor, in otherwise European dress, walked into the room where she sat alone and told her that she had a role in future spiritual work, should she be willing (she reports this as a real experience, not a vision). Years later, she recognized his picture in a Theosophical lodge. He was Djwahl Khul, a Master of an Adept Occult Brotherhood. This did not sit well with the Theosophists, who were somewhat proprietary about the masters, and A.A.B. later left the Society.

After further contact and initial hesitation, A.A.B. agreed to work with D.K., who said that he was a Tibetan lama still in his physical body. Through A.A.B., he telepathically dictated about twenty books of metaphysical teachings, letters, and treatises. The first was *Initiation, Human and Solar* in 1922. Others included *The Light of the Soul,* (translations of the Yoga Sutras of Patanjali), *A Treatise on White Magic* (spiritual development of the disciple), and a massive five-volume work on the theory and application of the seven energy rays underlying the qualities of the universe. A.A.B. also wrote six books of her own. A listing of all these is found in *The Work of the Master Djwhal Khul with Alice A. Bailey* (1967).

A.A.B.'s Biography

Alice La Trobe-Bateman was born in England in 1890 and reared in the strict fundamental Christian households of her parents and grandparents. Her childhood was highly regimented and scheduled and, in her adult years, she was organized and intensely active. After she left the family, she worked as a voluntary evangelical worker in homes for British soldiers in Ireland and India. After the breakup of her first marriage, she struggled to keep her family of three children together in America. She was taught Theosophy by two students of H.P.B. She and her husband worked with

Alice A. Bailey, writer of metaphysical books dictated by the Tibetan, Djwhal Kuhl.

the Society until political issues caused them to separate from it. The marriage to Foster Bailey gave her a companion who supported her writing and helped organize the classes and organizations that resulted from it. She was a more reserved person than was the flamboyant Blavatsky, and an aura of seriousness, even secrecy, surrounds her work.

A.A.B. gave classes on the Tibetan's writings, *The Secret Doctrine,* and methods of discipleship. Out of these classes grew the Arcane School in New York, which is still active. It provides guidance, through correspondence, for students in meditation, study, and service, based on the A.A.B. works. Another organization, the Meditation Group for the New Age, in Ojai, California, mails monthly meditations organized around the Tibetan's writing, to about 10,000 people. There are other similar schools and organizations, all playing a part in building a new group of world servers intended to have a positive effect on world brotherhood.

A.A.B. died in 1949. Her husband and the organizations continued to disseminate the teachings (F. Bailey, 1954). There has been no successor to Bailey's role as a channel, though a further message from the masters was supposed to occur in 1975. The books by A.A.B. and D.K. are kept in print by the Lucis Publishing Company, New York, set up by the Baileys for that purpose.

A.A.B. wrote *The Unfinished Autobiography* (A. Bailey 1951) about her life and experiences. A sympathetic and informative book by Sir John Sinclair (1984), *The Alice Bailey Inheritance,* discusses her life and teachings and their connections in the world. An outside scholarly summary of her life and teaching is found in J. Stillson Judah's book, *The History and Philosophy of the Metaphysical Movements in America* (Judah, 1967).

THE HIERARCHY AND THE PLAN

Bailey's writing is matter-of-fact about the existence of a Hierarchy. This is a group of beings who are said to take responsibility for assisting humanity. They are human and spirit beings who are at various levels of spiritual development, including disciples, initiates, masters and, above them, the Chohans and the Kumaras who are the highest conscious beings in our planetary sphere. These beings are not dissimilar to angels and archangels in Western religions. There is a resemblance to the structure of a government or business corporation. At the pinnacle is the spirit of the solar system, which separates into three major figures, called logoi. From these emanate seven rays of energy. The rays will be described in more detail in Chapter 9. At our planet level, there is a being called Sanat Kumara who heads world evolution. He is accompanied by three other beings, also called Kumaras. Next are the leaders of each line of masters and disciples. The masters who contacted Bailey, Blavatsky, and the others are under these three leaders, who are identified as "department heads." Figures 8.1 and 8.2 show this complex organization.

The Hierarchy is said to have quarterly meetings during each century. The most recent would have been in 1975, the next presumably in the year 2000.

The Hierarchy has a plan which is actively concerned with the condition of Earth, seeking to create a peaceful and harmonious growth into brotherhood. The plan is seen as a continuation of evolution. As life develops from simple forms to plants, animals, and humans, so too does the human ego or soul continue that evolution into the paraphysical realities (referred to as astral, etheric, and causal levels). The human soul will make contact with the divine aspect and begin to transmit love and power from those realms to the Earth. D.K. says this will bring the Kingdom of God or the life more abundant referred to by the Christian Bible.

Practical Action

On a physical here-and-now level, the plan has specific concerns. In political areas, the attempt is to foster international cooperation and eco-

SOLAR AND PLANETARY HIERARCHIES

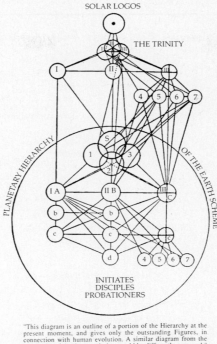

"This diagram is an outline of a portion of the Hierarchy at the present moment, and gives only the outstanding Figures, in connection with human evolution. A similar diagram from the standpoint of the deva evolution would be differently arranged."

(The connecting lines indicate force currents.)

Figure 8.1. Diagram of the Hierarchy described by the Tibetan.

nomic synthesis and to demonstrate the need to relinquish isolation, national egoism, and class hatreds. This is, observes D.K. quite correctly, one of the most difficult tasks the Hierarchy has ever set for itself. In religion, the aim is to foster the growth of spiritual consciousness and to further a more universal world religion, which will begin by the end of the century. This must be based on understanding, says D.K., or else people will be exploited by religious demagogues, fervent prophets, and reactionaries. In science, education, and psychology, the goal is to develop awareness of both tangible and intangible realms, expanding human knowledge, capabilities, and consciousness.

The members of the Hierarchy are said to be working behind the scenes, putting out thoughts, ideals, activities, and projects, attempting to influence the minds of governmental, business, and political workers toward this goal of brotherhood. The plan is idealistic, but more pragmatic than most such visions, whether they are channeled or expounded from political platforms.

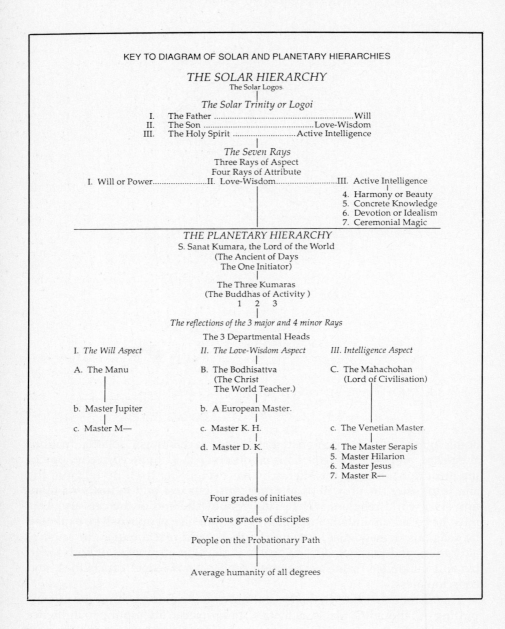

KEY TO DIAGRAM OF SOLAR AND PLANETARY HIERARCHIES

THE SOLAR HIERARCHY
The Solar Logos
|
The Solar Trinity or Logoi
I.   The Father ....Will
II.   The Son ....Love-Wisdom
III.   The Holy Spirit ....Active Intelligence
|
The Seven Rays
Three Rays of Aspect
Four Rays of Attribute
I. Will or Power.....................II. Love-Wisdom..........................III. Active Intelligence
|
4. Harmony or Beauty
5. Concrete Knowledge
6. Devotion or Idealism
7. Ceremonial Magic

THE PLANETARY HIERARCHY
S. Sanat Kumara, the Lord of the World
(The Ancient of Days
The One Initiator)
|
The Three Kumaras
(The Buddhas of Activity)
1   2   3
|
The reflections of the 3 major and 4 minor Rays
The 3 Departmental Heads

I. *The Will Aspect*   II. *The Love-Wisdom Aspect*   III. *Intelligence Aspect*
|
A. The Manu   B. The Bodhisattva   C. The Mahachohan
                                 (The Christ   (Lord of Civilisation)
                                 The World Teacher.)
| | |
b. Master Jupiter   b. A European Master.
| |
c. Master M—   c. Master K. H.   c. The Venetian Master.
                             | |
                             d. Master D. K.   4. The Master Serapis
                                                               5. Master Hilarion
                                                               6. Master Jesus
                                                               7. Master R—

Four grades of initiates
|
Various grades of disciples
|
People on the Probationary Path

Average humanity of all degrees

Figure 8.2. Key to the diagram.

It includes actual goals and objectives. D.K. refers to the Red Cross, for example, as a case of international cooperation. President Franklin Roosevelt's statement of the Four Freedoms is said to have been inspired by the Hierarchy. The point is made that many leaders are responsive to the ideas of general good, universal trade, and human equality, but their actions are often distorted by ambition, selfishness, and power, because there is no understanding of the inner source of the concepts. Students of these teachings are urged to further these goals in the world and, in recent years, they have supported world passports, the United Nations, and a group called Planetary Citizens.

The Reality of the Hierarchy

The concept of the Hierarchy itself is appealing to persons of a certain temperament. Believing in a hidden Hierarchy can reassure individuals that there is a conspiracy for good. From A.A.B.'s point of view, this should encourage us to do our part and to link up with those beings for service to the world. For some, it surely does just that; for others, the reassurance must relieve them of responsibility for effort on their part. Some are thrilled and inflated by their knowledge of the Hierarchy and take this to mean that they are part of the "in-group."

Does the Hierarchy actually exist? Is there actually a Master M, Djwhal Khul, and Sanat Kumara, head of our planetary domain? If so, they seem to have communicated only through the two women and their colleagues. H.P.B., A.A.B., and a few others in their groups said that they had met specific masters physically, in their apparitional form, or through psychic perception. They also claimed to have received psychically materialized letters from the masters, though there were charges of fraud against H.P.B. with regard to this matter. Later channelers, not from the Bailey groups, have claimed communications from some of the masters, including Morya, Saint Germain, and Hilarion, but these are pale shadows of the robust and intellectual beings that communicated through Blavatsky and Bailey. D.K., by the way, said that only about 15 percent of channeled material in general actually came from spiritual beings, and about 85 percent came from the subconscious of the channel.

The idea of a hidden group of sages or saints is found in several traditions. In yoga, there are stories of twelve sages who continually live in the world, preserving its spiritual nature. In Judaism there is a legend of Thirty-Six Saints, the *Lamed-vav Tzaddikim*. The world continues to exist by God's grace only because of the presence of these thirty-six and their unselfish work. No one knows who they are—a bus driver, shoemaker, pauper, banker—and in Sufism there is a similar tale about eight saints. One might see these tales as wish-fulfillment or a projection of our own repressed spiritual power. Perhaps there may be a realm in which there is truth behind the outer parables.

Disciples

We are training men and women everywhere so that they can be sensitive to the Plan, sensitive to their group vibration, and thus able to cooperate intelligently with the unfolding purpose" (A. Bailey, 1936, xviii).

Rules for disciples are set out in *A Treatise on White Magic* (A. Bailey, 1934) and throughout other books in the series, such as *Discipleship in the New Age, I, II* (A. Bailey, 1944, 1955). There is a systematic approach to the training of the disciple which concerns not the personality level but the development of spiritual levels through meditations, visualizations, outer service, and inner work with the chakras.

The essential requirement, repeated time and again in the early writings, is to make a connection between the ordinary mind—the lower self—and the soul (A. Bailey, 1934). The soul or egoic level is a higher self. Through meditation, the ordinary self aligns with the soul level, and energy downflows from the soul. The personality begins to reorient toward the soul as the director and center of identity. This brings one into contact with the master and the group of his disciples who are working with the plan.

Initiations occur as the person moves into higher levels of development. Descriptions of these are scattered throughout the writings, but especially in *Initiation, Human and Solar* (A. Bailey, 1922). For the first initiation, D.K. says, the control of the ego over the physical nature must have reached a high degree of attainment. The channel between the higher and lower selves must be widened and the obedience of physical desire practically automatic. The initiations take place in inner space and involve ceremonies with other spiritual beings.

Teaching

With these and successive developments, the masters begin to teach disciples. All the work, says Bailey, is done on the inner planes of consciousness. One passage says that teaching goes on between 10 P.M. and 5 A.M.. We can assume this is in the dream state or an out-of-body state. As many people who have practiced mental techniques can testify, one can have experiences of attending classes during the dream state. These are quite distinct from dreams of being in school. For most people, there is the sense of learning important information, truths, and principles, but usually this information is not retained with clarity. One artist told me that he received the answer to a color-mix problem by going to what he called "that great school in the sky," where some laconic librarian looked it up in a book for him.

Students are also advised to meditate on nights of the full moon and the new moon, as these are particularly propitious times for contact with the higher levels. One organization stemming from the Bailey teachings, the Meditation Group for the New Age, distributes guided meditations for full-moon meditation practice. Meditation and dreamwork experiences do suggest that there is more activity on the psychic and spiritual levels around the times of the full moon; many religious traditions, Tibetan Buddhism, for example, also schedule practices according to the lunar cycle.

"The main result I look for," writes D.K., "is one of *group* cooperation and understanding, and not of individual benefit. . . . We are building and planning for the future and for humanity, and not for the personal unfoldment of any particular aspirant" (A. Bailey, 1936, xvii). The individual becomes an outpost of the master's consciousness, in the service of the plan. In Freudian terms, perhaps it could be said that the plan becomes a transcendent superego. This is likely to evoke authority issues in many people, either to respond confidently to the authority and wisdom of the masters, or to indignantly reject their dictatorship.

In recent years, we have seen an increase in the need for group identity, trust, community, cooperative action, and consensual consciousness. This has been reflected in negative ways through abusive cults, but also in positive ways in ecology and consumer movements, international cooperation, associations, cooperatives, community building, and so on. The D.K. material presents a vision and calls for joining in group endeavor to accomplish it. Values of harmlessness and cooperation and a spirit of love are presented concretely as governing the performance of the work, which is to be done without publicity. These writings present a strong appeal for the concerned individual with these interests.

Education, Teaching, and Service

Educational activities through the Arcane School, the Meditation Group for a New Age (MGNA), and other organizations are described by John Sinclair (1984) in *The Alice Bailey Inheritance.* They support study, meditation practice, and transpersonal service with little publicity or fanfare. The goals of service and the transpersonal values of the work are admirable and visionary, whether they are furthered by the Hierarchy or simply one's own higher self. Without the continued messages from D.K., one wonders if the work will continue to attract students. The most important part of the attraction depends upon the genuineness of the experience of the inner work.

The actual work and activities of the Arcane school are not discussed publicly. The MGNA sends meditation guidance to over 10,000 individuals and holds periodic conferences in which students discuss ideas and activities.

The Writing

The scope of the A.A.B. writings is vast and majestic, with a vision of complex connections and levels, of inner planes and energies. The material is not easy reading because the language uses concepts and words that have no certain referents. Sometimes ideas are called by one name and sometimes another. The writing seems technical, but nevertheless vague in terms of consistency and precision. It is like reading a technical treatise in a field in which you are ignorant of the meanings of the basic elements: the sentences are grammatical but you are not sure what they mean. (I noted one sentence in *A Treatise on White Magic* that was fifty-five words long.) If one persists in the reading, eventually the meanings become clearer. A.A.B. said that she never changed a word that D.K. dictated or, had she done so, he would have stopped. Unfortunately, this laissez-faire attitude resulted in many of the volumes being disorganized and rambling with topics discussed in several different places; the volumes also contain inconsistencies, confusing typography, tangential digressions, and other normal faults of enthusiastic but inexperienced writers. Djwhal Khul was not a master of writing; this is obviously a different skill from mastery of the inner planes.

Transpersonal Themes

In metaphysical terms, the system described by A.A.B. is at the astral and subtle levels. These are the levels where there are auras, out-of-body states, psi functions, chakras, discarnate beings, personified deities, and other energy forms (Wilber, 1980). These realms are considered accessible to consciousness through meditation, visualization practices, altered states of consciousness, psychedelic substances, and shamanistic practices. Many spiritual traditions—Christianity, Islam, Buddhism, and Shamanism, for example—assume that, on these levels, there are higher beings or spirits that can relate to humans. However, these are not usually considered the highest spiritual levels of experience.

The path of most traditional mystics, in or out of religions, is to move higher in the levels of spiritual consciousness toward unity with the God-head or toward cessation of attachment in the Buddha nature. The Bailey writings emphasize putting oneself in service to humanity via the Plan, rather than continuing on the mystical path toward ultimate Being, which is seen as a much later stage involving many lifetimes. Also, they give little attention to personality level work. While D.K. is clear that the disciple must gain control over desires and thoughts, there is no discussion of how negative emotions, obstacles, or physical desires are to be eliminated. Of course, these instructions were given at a time when there were few psycho-logical tools for therapy; now the possibilities are somewhat wider. Trans-personal psychology suggests that spiritual work is likely to be handicapped by inner conflicts, negative emotional states, repressed issues, and similar problems (Vaughan, 1986). Those who study this system would be well advised to address emotional and psychological issues before or during their training.

Establishing communication between the lower self and the higher self—the ego or soul, in D.K.'s language—is a practice of spiritual growth that has broader value than just these teachings. This communication is a central process in the psychotherapy system called Psychosynthesis, developed by Roberto Assagioli (1965, 1973). Assagioli was a student of the D.K. material and is assumed to have incorporated some of the ideas in his psychology. He explains two stages of synthesis or integration. The first is to transform negative elements in the personality and synthesize them into an integrated, purposeful personality. The second level is to connect that personality with the higher self. To Assagioli, the higher self is the true self and is experienced in mystical or cosmic states. This higher self has independent existence and can exert an influence, a pull on the ordinary conscious self (which is also what D.K. says). The object of the spiritual synthesis is the realization of the spiritual self, the moving of self-identity to the transpersonal level. It is clear that these ideas are structurally similar to the D. K. teachings. Assagioli does not present the higher self as a link to advanced beings, but rather as the transpersonal potential in men and women, as an entrée into wider spiritual realities.

The Tibetan Connection

"Suffice it to say," wrote Djwhal Khul, "that I am a Tibetan disciple of a certain degree. . . . I live in a physical body like other men, on the borders of Tibet, and at times (from the exoteric standpoint) preside over a large group of Tibetan lamas, when my other duties permit" (A. Bailey, 1951, ix). This statement is printed in the front of all the books dictated by D.K. He was known as the Tibetan, he was said to be an abbot of a monastery, and he noted that he was known there by a different name than Djwhal Khul.

The religion of Tibet is Mahayana and Vajrayana Buddhism, with some shamanistic aspects from earlier religions. The doctrines and metaphysics presented by D.K. have very little similarity to Buddhist doctrines in Tibet or elsewhere. The concepts of the lower self and the higher self, the rays, and the hierarchy of masters are not found in Tibetan teachings. The idea of service to others, the chakras, and the planes of consciousness are indeed there, along with reincarnation, but these are beliefs common to the Hinduism and Buddhism throughout Asia. D.K., of course, did not say that he was presenting Buddhist doctrines; if he was a Buddhist abbot, his telepathic communications were quite different from his religion.

The Great Invocation

We will conclude this chapter with a mantram or prayer transmitted by Djwhal Khul and said to have come from the Christ in 1945, near the end of World War II. It is printed in all the Bailey/D.K. works. The Christ says it is a prayer for the world, voicing the great desires of humanity for the power of God to descend and for the halting of the course of evil.

From the point of Light within the Mind of God
Let Light stream forth into the minds of men.
Let Light descend on Earth.

From the point of Love within the Heart of God
Let Love stream forth into the hearts of men.
May Christ return to Earth.

From the centre where the Will of God is known
Let purpose guide the little wills of men—
The purpose which the Masters know and serve.

From the centre which we call the race of men
Let the Plan of Love and Light work out,
And may it seal the door where evil dwells.

Let Light and Love and Power restore the Plan on Earth.

CHAPTER 9

THE SEVEN RAYS AND THE ENNEAGRAM

The writings of Blavatsky and Bailey added several important concepts to the Western metaphysical tradition. These included body energy centers (the chakras), kundalini energy, the astral, etheric, and causal planes, and particularly the model of the seven rays. The chakras, kundalini, and the planes of consciousness are a part of Hindu and Buddhist metaphysics and were somewhat familiar at the time through translations of Oriental literature and visits to the East. The seven rays, so far as I know, do not appear in earlier Eastern religious writings or Western occultism. They are first referred to in H.P.B.'s writings and receive their fullest discussion in Bailey's works, beginning with *Initiation, Human and Solar*, (A. Bailey, 1922) and culminating with *A Treatise on the Seven Rays* (A. Bailey, 1936–1960), which comprises five volumes and 3359 pages of text, plus indexes. (One of the considerate and professional aspects of A.A.B.'s writing is that all volumes have indexes.)

The concept is a simple, yet vast one. There are seven fundamental rays or emanations that influence all reality. These are qualities of existence, life, and action. As the ancients held that all reality was of four elements, so this principle says that the Absolute divides into seven qualities:

> The seven rays are therefore embodiments of seven types of force which demonstrate to us the seven qualities of Deity. These seven qualities have consequently a sevenfold effect upon the matter and forms to be found in all parts of the universe, and have also a sevenfold interrelation between themselves (A. Bailey 1936, p. 19).

An obvious comparison is that of white light fanning out into a spectrum of different colors. The term "ray" implies vibration, radiation, and energy. D.K. also describes them as builders, lords and rulers, and deities. The members of the Hierarchy (see Chapter 8) personify and direct their influence. In the same way, Tibetan Buddhism personifies qualities of the enlightened mind into bodhisattva beings of compassion, power, and intelligence. Esoteric Christians say that Jesus embodied Christ Consciousness, and Hindus personify the activity of the universe as Brahma, Vishnu, and Shiva. The qualities of the seven rays are described as follows:

Ray I   Will or Power
Ray II   Love-Wisdom
Ray III   Intelligent Activity
Ray IV   Harmony and Beauty
Ray V   Concrete Knowledge
Ray VI   Devotion
Ray VII   Ceremony and Magic

The first ray is the Ray of Will or Power. Its qualities are the expression of will, intention, dynamic purpose, creation, and destruction.

The second ray is the Ray of Love-Wisdom. It is the principle of love, attraction, coherence, inclusiveness, responsiveness, and sensitivity of forms.

The third ray is the Ray of Intelligent Activity. This is the quality of intelligence in action, of adaptability and creativity. In a larger sense, it is the intelligent response of form building to express the divine purpose.

The first three rays are the major rays, the dominant aspects of deity. The teaching equates them to the Christian Trinity. The Father is Will and the Holy Spirit or Mother is Love-Wisdom; together they manifest the Son in matter and intelligent activity.

The fourth ray is the Ray of Harmony. This is the quality of beauty, organization through form, creative art, and the harmonious interplay of divine manifestations. D.K. comments that mathematical exactitude reflects this quality. The fourth ray is sometimes called Harmony Through Conflict and Harmony, Beauty, and Art.

The fifth ray is the Ray of Concrete Knowledge. Its qualities include knowledge, intelligence, and analysis. It produces science.

The sixth ray is the Ray of Devotion. It expresses a one-pointed idealism, an awareness of and orientation toward the idea behind the form, persistence, and adherence.

The seventh ray is the Ray of Ceremony and Magic. It is the quality of transformation through order. It is a coordinating energy, organizing, bringing different levels into unification and fusion.

At higher levels, the last four rays are a part of the third ray and are synthesized with it. At planetary, personality, and soul levels, all seven are operating and influencing the nature of forms. Various ray energies and ray lords take part in the initiations of the disciples until, at the highest levels, the aspirant is situated on one of the three primary rays.

Each of the rays has seven subrays that incorporate its basic quality in the form of the other ray qualities. For example, the entire solar system is said to be dominated by the second ray of Love-Wisdom, and the seven rays found in manifestation on this planet and in humans are colored with the underlying tone of the overall second ray. D.K. comments that there are no pure first ray individuals on the planet. Current first ray forms are actually the power subray of the Love-Wisdom ray. "A pure first ray ego in incarnation at this time would be a disaster. There is not sufficient intelligence and love in the world to balance the dynamic will of an ego on the ray of the destroyer" (A. Bailey, 1936, p. 27).

As the rays emanate into our solar system through physical and nonphysical planes, the members of the Hierarchy personify and direct their influence. The organization chart in Chapter 8 shows the relationship of the rays to the Hierarchy. D.K. is on the Love-Wisdom aspect. It is said that this is one reason he emphasizes group cooperation and the linking of common effort, since those are characteristics of the magnetic quality of the second ray. The master who wrote most of H.P.B.'s channeled material, Koot Humi, is also on the second ray. There have apparently been no channeled teachings from the first and third ray lines.

THE RAYS AND PERSONALITY

In life, people manifest their rays in personality, work, and social roles. In the volumes on the rays, D.K. presented several descriptions of how people reflected the rays in their personalities. For example:

The power type, full of will and governing capacity.

The love type, full of love and fusing power.

The active type, full of action, and manipulating energy.

The artistic type, full of the sense of beauty and creative aspiration.

The scientific type, full of the idea of cause and results. The mathematical type.

The devotee type, full of idealism.

The business type, full of organizing power. Given to ritualistic ceremony.

(A. Bailey, 1936, p. 329)

D.K. gave detailed descriptions of the actions and results of ray activity in humans. For persons on the first ray of will or power, he listed the special virtues of strength, courage, steadfastness, truthfulness arising from absolute fearlessness, power of ruling, capacity to grasp great questions in a large-minded way, and ability to handle men and measures. The vices he described were pride, ambition, willfulness, hardness, arrogance, desire to control others, obstinacy, and anger. The virtues that the person on this ray should cultivate are tenderness, humility, sympathy, tolerance, and patience (A. Bailey, 1936, p. 201).

This description captures very well a type often seen in the role of leader, warrior, statesman, fanatic, visionary, or reformer. Similar descriptions are given for each of the seven ray expressions. For some of the inner groups taught by Bailey, D.K. would write letters to students telling the ray that they were on, which would indicate what lines of endeavor would be easier, and which ones would involve conflicts.

Others have applied the rays to human personality and activities. Geoffrey Hodson (1968), in *The Seven Human Temperaments,* spells out the seven types, their societal roles, goals, achievement styles, strengths and weaknesses, and associated colors, religions, art, jewels and symbols. Jack Schwarz (1980), an accomplished nontraditional healer, has described the seven rays in human aura fields and says that a trained clairvoyant can see the ray energy as an input directed down through the crown chakra. He observes that some people have more than one ray entering their field. For example, when he "looked" at my ray energy, he told me that I had mostly yellow ray, with some rose. The colors he associated with the rays are the same as Hodson; with some of the qualities Schwarz gives to them, these are:

   I.   Electric blue, white, and vermillion red—power, will
  II.   Azure blue and golden yellow—love, wisdom
 III.   Emerald green—comprehension, mental power
  IV.   Tawny bronze orange—stability, harmony, balance
   V.   Lemon yellow—logic, accuracy
  VI.   Rose pink—one-pointedness, devotion
 VII.   Purple—grace, ritual, precision

The colors given for the rays in the A.A.B. writings are not consistent; for example, at one time ray four is green, another time it is yellow-orange. A publisher's footnote says this is because the distinction is not always made between rays and subrays, but this does not seem evident in the text.

THE ENNEAGRAM OF PERSONALITY

Another esoteric system of human typology has a remarkable resemblance to the ray qualities. The Arica Institute training, originated by Oscar Ichazo, includes an application of the enneagram structure to personality (Lilly and Hart, 1975). The enneagram is a Sufi symbol, a nine-pointed diagram. It was introduced to the West through the teaching of G. I. Gurdjieff. Each of the nine points is associated with specific qualities, and these qualities have been applied to personality types by Ichazo. Knowledge of these types is taught as information to help in personal and spiritual development. The most accessible discussions are in *The Enneagram,* by Helen Palmer (1988), and *Personality Types,* by Don Riso (1987). Ralph Metzner's book *Know Your Type* gives brief descriptions of this and other typologies (Metzner, 1979), and Robert Lincoln (1983) has suggested how the enneagram types can be described in terms of human development and depth psychology. The following table lists the enneagram points, with the character aspects described by Riso and Palmer and the negative fixations identified by Ichazo.

Riso	Palmer	Ichazo (Fixation)
1. Reformer	Perfectionist	Resentment
2. Helper	Giver	Flatterer
3. Status Seeker	Performer	Go [i.e., Type A behavior]
4. Artist	Tragic Romantic	Melancoly
5. Thinker	Observer	Stinge
6. Loyalist	Devil's Advocate	Coward
7. Generalist	Epicure	Planner [i.e., schemer]
8. Leader	Boss	Venge
9. Peacemaker	Mediator	Indolent

It is said that Ichazo received the personality enneagram from channeled sources, specifically the archangel Metatron. I was told that Ichazo was given the types one at a time, and he spent some time living as each type before going on to the next one. As can be seen, the first seven points have similar qualities to the seven rays. For example, point one on the enneagram is a person whose goal is focused on perfection; when negatively fixated, this personality moves into resentment and anger. Perfecting seems to be another phrasing of the goal of the first ray—manifesting the divine will. The fixations are virtually the same as the vices listed by D.K. Another example of correspondence is at enneagram point five, whose essence is the holding of knowledge and omniscience. The fifth ray is the ray of knowledge, science, and concrete intelligence.

Ichazo uses several names to identify the dominant qualities of each point. Palmer and Riso have used type names that they feel are most appropriate for contemporary social roles and relationships. The descriptions of the rays and the enneagram points are not completely identical, but they are similar enough to suggest that they express the same essences taken from slightly different points of view and vocabulary. I have worked personally with the enneagram and chakra systems, and my study of the ray system has illuminated each of the other approaches.

One question arises. The enneagram has nine types, rather than seven;

how does one account for the two additional ones? A possibility is that the rays begin to repeat in a spiral, so that point eight is another form of point one. Ichazo described point eight on the enneagram as motivated toward truth and justice. Riso describes this type as heroic, aggressive, destructive, and expressive of power. These appear to be the way the first ray, the Will of God, could manifest in the world. Thus, enneagram point eight appears similar to the first ray type, but less moderated by the Love-Wisdom ray influence. It may be a more pure first ray type, which D.K. discusses as the destroyer. The ninth point of the enneagram is characterized as uninvolved, balancing, oriented toward union, receptive. It may be a version of ray two. This could also be a person who is on the one hand either so balanced that no one ray predominates, or who has achieved a certain level of connection with the unity beyond the ray spectrum. Alternatively, these could express two further qualities added to the original seven of the rays.

THE CHAKRAS

Another metaphysical model that is similar to the rays is the system of chakras, which are described as energy centers in the human body, a kind of psychic anatomy (Radha, 1978). The chakra model is most fully developed in yoga, but it is also found in mystical aspects of Buddhism, Islam, and Christianity. There are seven major centers, and each has associated with it particular qualities of energy and a location in the body.

1.   Survival, purpose, basic energy of creation and life. Located in the body at the base of the spine.
2.   Sexuality, emotional relationships. Located in the body at the level of the genitals.
3.   Power, action. Located at the level of the navel, the solar plexus.
4.   Love, compassion. Located in the area of the heart.
5.   Communication, ideas, creativity, conceptual thinking. Located in the throat area.
6.   Single-pointed attention, unity, non-duality. Located in the forehead; third eye.
7.   Transcendence, enlightenment. Located at the top of the head, the crown.

While there is not an exact correspondence, the qualities of the chakras seem similar to the character of the rays. As with the enneagram, there are meditations, exercises, and ways of working with the energy of each chakra. A difference to be noted is that the enneagram system identifies a person as completely or predominantly one of the nine types. The chakra system is not a typology: every person is assumed to have all seven qualities of energy, at various levels. The parallels of these models, each in its own language and context, suggests that there is a basis in reality for the seven qualities, or else they make up an exceptionally ingenious practical formula.

HOW REAL ARE THE RAYS?

Some people may wonder if the rays and their assorted deities, powers, and activities actually exist. The ray model and the enneagram typology, like all models, must of necessity select and organize data. In one sense, the question is whether they make sense out of the experience of perceiving oneself and others. I have noticed that if a system works in identifying a person to himself or herself, then it probably will enable the person to apply it to others as well. If it does not fit, then it rarely makes sense when that person applies it to others. Public awareness of the enneagram model is increasing, and many are finding it a practical system of self-knowledge. Perhaps an enterprising student of these systems will explore psychological tests for identifying and measuring a person's characteristics according to the concepts of these systems. This will enable a more extensive testing and use of the ideas presented.

In their application to personality, these models are similar to the theories of Freud, Jung, and other psychologists. They deal with unmeasurable, inferential forces and hypothetical entities—id, libido, archetypes, the unconscious. One may sense experientially their plausibility, learn to intuit the dynamics of their operation, and measure their expression in behavior. The reality is there in a pragmatic sense. Sometimes there are criteria and objective measures that can be articulated, sometimes not. It seems to me that the ray model is a system of consciousness to be entered, rather than a description of electromagnetic vibrations. The enneagram of personality is also a mode of perception and experience. Entering the system enables certain perceptions, experiences, understandings, knowledge, and powers. Science, cooking, music, falling in love, and other human endeavors are no different. James Hillman (1983), in his book *Healing Fiction*, writes about this paradox. He says that psychological theories—id, ego, even the self—are in one sense fiction, but accepting them as true leads to knowledge and growth. In a way, these are beneficent self-fulfilling prophecies in the service of healing.

It appears that these theories have as much potential as other typologies and possibly more, because the categories have spiritual as well as psychological meaning. The ray and enneagram models propose the radical idea that a person does not become less individual as he or she grows psychologically and spiritually, but rather becomes more capable of expressing his or her particular individuality, going beyond the ego personality to what has been called essence or true purpose.

CHAPTER 10

A COURSE IN MIRACLES

HELEN SCHUCMAN, BILL THETFORD, JUDITH SKUTCH WHITSON

Helen Schucman was a reluctant, ambivalent scribe for *A Course in Miracles*. She heard a mental voice dictating the material, transcribed it in her own form of shorthand, and read it aloud to her colleague Bill Thetford who typed the manuscript. She was so upset by the process that she often could not see her own shorthand to read it. She asked the inner voice why she was chosen to do this writing. The answer came clearly that she was the best choice. "But why?" she asked. "Because you'll do it," came the certain reply, and Helen knew the answer was right.

Mrs. Schucman was born Helen Cohn in 1909 and grew up in New York City. Her father was a nonpracticing Jew; her mother had tried many religions and considered herself a Theosophist. Helen was very interested in God and religion as a child and was even baptized by an evangelist. When nothing changed, and she could not see God, she simply lost her faith. In later years, she considered herself an atheist, as much from anger at the absence of God as from disbelief. Turning to intellectual pursuits, she read widely in high school and majored in English at New York University. She had secret hopes of becoming a great writer. She married Louis Schucman in college and, after graduation, worked in his bookstore; this work was not for her, and she became ill and dissatisfied.

Ten years later, at her husband's urging, she entered New York University Graduate School of Psychology and received her doctorate in 1957. Shortly afterward, she joined the Psychology Department at Columbia University College of Physicians and Surgeons. Dr. William Thetford was department chair. He held a Ph.D. from the University of Chicago where he had been a teaching assistant for noted therapist Carl Rogers. Even though he had hired her and liked her, they often brought out the worst in each other. Further, the department was rife with competition and mutual suspicion. One day in 1965, after a stressful faculty meeting, he said to Helen, "There must be another way." He announced that he was going to try to change his negative attitudes and look at things differently. To his surprise, Helen said that he was right, and she would help him. Department meetings began to become slightly less tense.

Dr. Helen Schucman, scribe for A Course in Miracles, *and her colleague Dr. William Thetford.*

Helen had, from time to time, heard an inner voice along with having vivid and apparently symbolic visions. These seemed to accelerate after their pact to find a better way. One evening in October, 1965, a voice said to her, "This is a course in miracles. Please take notes." In a panic, she phoned Bill. "What am I going to do?" she asked. "Why don't you take the notes," said Bill calmly.

In 1972, a manuscript of 1500 pages was completed. Bill showed it to only two friends, not even telling one of them its origin. In 1975, Bill heard Judy Skutch, an energetic and enthusiastic supporter of psychic research, at a conference and arranged a lunch with her and researcher Douglas Dean at Columbia. Judy, for a reason unknown to her, said to Helen over dessert, "You hear an inner voice, don't you?" Helen blanched and Bill adjourned the lunch. He led them back to the office, locked the door, and told them the story of the voice and the Course.

Though highly successful with work and family, Judy had felt a lack of fulfillment in her life. She began to read the manuscript and continued for eight hours straight. She was completely taken by it. Within a year she, along with friends and associates, published the Course first in manuscript form and then typeset. The Foundation for Inner Peace continues to be the nonprofit publisher, with 700,000 copies now in print.

Helen continued to have mixed feelings about the Course and her role.

Dr. Schucman and Judith Skutch Whitson of the Foundation for Inner Peace.

On one hand, she was pleased that it was valued by so many people; on the other hand, she seemed to reject its application for herself. "I know it's true," she once said, "but I don't believe it."

Helen died in 1981, Bill in 1988. The account of Helen, Bill, Judy (now Judith Skutch Whitson), and others, and of the writing of *A Course in Miracles* is told in *Journey without Distance*, by Robert Skutch (1984), who knew all the participants personally. At Bill's request, Helen wrote an unpublished autobiography (1973). Biographical material is included in the introduction to the Course and in books about it (Wapnick, 1983, 1985). A video *The Story of* A Course in Miracles (1987) is available from the Foundation for Inner Peace.

A METAPHYSICAL, SPIRITUAL PSYCHOTHERAPY

A Course in Miracles is specifically a spiritual teaching. Its language is that of Christianity. God, Jesus, and the Holy Spirit are major figures in its doctrines and, indeed, the author sometimes refers to Jesus in first person— as himself. The human spiritual problem that it addresses is the ego's perceived separation from God, and the goal is to guide the person to reconnect with God through the inner teacher called the Holy Spirit. The

Course is unique in that it contains metaphysical spiritual teachings from a psychological point of view. It analyzes the effects of the supposed separation in terms of psychological processes. The separation is illusory, the Course teaches, because one is never really separate from God.

The word "miracle" is used differently in the Course than in ordinary parlance. Its usage within the course means a shift in perception from the ego world of fear, guilt, and anger to the world of the Holy Spirit, which is love, forgiveness, and inner healing. It means perceiving things differently through a changed state of mind. "There is nothing either good or bad," Hamlet says, "but thinking makes it so." These are miracles of inner states rather than external events. After all, it is a miracle to get some people to change their minds. Nevertheless, one's behavior and the external world is affected by these inner states. Still, there is confusion about the meaning. When Dr. Frances Vaughan was traveling in India, she was asked to speak at a local university because they heard she taught a course in miracles at the Institute of Transpersonal Psychology. She had to explain it was not what they imagined!

The Course is organized in three parts. The first is the Text, in which the conceptual framework is explained. The ego is described, as are the obstacles it raises to knowledge of the existence of spirit. The Course says that the ego we have made is not reality, spirit is. The second section is the Workbook for Students. There are 365 lessons, which might be attempted by a diligent student at the rate of one a day. A short Manual for Teachers makes up part three, organized around questions on teaching, teachers, and various topics. These were dictated sequentially, without headings or format. Schucman, Thetford, and Dr. Kenneth Wapnick, a psychologist who joined them after the manuscript was completed, divided it into paragraphs and sections and supplied headings, with assistance from Helen's inner voice. Two further essays were dictated to Helen. The first was *Psychotherapy: Purpose, Process and Practice* (1976). The topics of the title are discussed from the framework of the spiritual purposes of the Course. The second is *The Song of Prayer: Prayer, Forgiveness, Healing* (1978), an essay on levels and purposes of prayer.

The Text

There are many concepts and themes interwoven in the Text (*A Course in Miracles*, 1985a). I will select some of the key ideas to discuss. The first words taken down by Helen are famous among readers of the Course and in writings about it.

This is a course in miracles. It is a required course. Only the time you take it is voluntary. Free will does not mean that you can establish the curriculum. It means only that you can elect what you want to take at a given time. The course does not aim at teaching the meaning of love, for that is beyond what can be taught. It does aim, however, at removing the blocks to the awareness of love's presence, which is your natural inheritance. The opposite of love is fear, but what is all-encompassing can have no opposite.

The course can therefore be summed up very simply in this way: Nothing real can be threatened. Nothing unreal exists. Herein lies the peace of God. (p. ix)

The last paragraph is a spiritual koan, a paradox, like the famous Japanese Zen questions. The thought reflects the words of Krishna in the Hindu *Bhagavad Gita:* "The unreal has no existence, and the real never ceases to be; the reality of is and is not has thus been perceived by the seers of truth. Know that to be imperishible, by which all this is pervaded" (II, 16–17). There are many instances in which the Course puts into its language the concepts of different religions.

A Spiritual Curriculum

The Course is designed to be a spiritual curriculum. At one point it calls itself a mind training program. The tone is practical, and the analysis has a psychological quality. Even in the introduction, there are specific descriptions of the relations of love, fear, choice, and mental polarities. To take one example, the text states that the original nature of the mind is a state of love, which is now obscured by obstacles—fear, guilt, and so on. The logical implication is that if the obstacles are removed, love will be able to manifest naturally. This theme continues through the entire Course, in which exercises and explanations are given to clear the mind of conditionings.

Love in the Course does not mean sentimental romance, but the relation of God and creation, the manifestation of forgiveness, and the force that joins together (Wapnick, 1982). The premise that human nature is essentially one of love is not an orthodox Christian doctrine because it conflicts with the principle of original sin. The orthodox Christian position is termed Redemption theology, meaning that Christ had to redeem humankind's sins, which began with the fall from grace in the Garden of Eden. Christ is seen as a sacrifice to atone for original sin. More consistent with the Course is Creation Spirituality (Fox, 1983), a distinct minority viewpoint in Catholicism which holds that human beings are spiritual creations of God and thus good. The position of the Course is also similar to Vajrayana Buddhism, which teaches that the natural condition of the mind is enlightenment, but that it is obscured by negative emotional states. Remove the obstacles, and the enlightenment is there.

The Course does use the term atonement, saying that it is the reuniting of all creations with God and the canceling of errors. This is reality, the state of oneness with God. This task of atonement has been taken on by Jesus, and as people return to their natural state, they become part of it also. At this point in the text, the author speaks in first person and appears to be Jesus saying, "I am in charge of the process of Atonement" (1985a, 6). Jesus is presented (or presents himself) in the Course as a brother and a companion, not as a deity. He says he is the Son of God, but so are all people. It distressed Helen (who, you may recall, considered herself to be an atheistic Jew) to consider that the voice speaking to her was actually Jesus.

There is also a hint of the Buddhist view in the paradoxical lines that nothing real can be threatened and nothing unreal exists. In Mahayana Buddhism (for example, Zen and Tibetan) a statement is made that samsara, the state of illusion, and nirvana, the enlightened state, are the same; one's perception has changed. This is not something that can be accomplished through analysis, but rather must come from a change in experience and perception, which requires both understanding and practice.

The Course explains that people see themselves in a state of separation from God. The ego, as defined by the Course, is that part of the mind which perceives itself as split from its creator. It has chosen this split in order to create itself; however, the Course says that this is not really possible, it is an illusion. The ego feels guilt from the imagined separation which it chose. It experiences fear because it feels the need to be punished for the guilt. Then, it uses the psychological defense mechanism of projection to attribute the punishment and to attack the outside world. Wapnick (1982) summarizes:

> Fear is the expected punishment for our sins, which our guilt demands; the resulting terror over what we believe we deserve leads us to defend ourselves by attacking others, which merely reinforces our sense of vulnerability and fear, establishing a vicious circle of fear and defense (p. 57).

The solution offered by the Course is to turn to the voice within, called the Holy Spirit, which is our link to and communication with God. This puts us back into one-mindedness with God, changes our perceptions of the world, and allows forgiveness of others and ourselves. The text emphasizes that the contact with the Holy Spirit is within the choice of the person. If forgiveness can be allowed, one's own guilt is released. Forgiveness comes from the Holy Spirit, so when one forgives, one experiences the Holy Spirit. Since the perceived attack of others is based on projection, genuine forgiveness is forgiveness of oneself.

One can choose to will, invite, or open up to the presence of the Holy Spirit, and there will be a response to that invitation. The individual is urged to turn over self-direction to this guide or teacher. The result is a holy instant in which perception, fear, guilt, and self-judgment can change.

In Chapter 30, there are specific practices for making decisions. The person begins by reflecting on the kind of day that is wanted, then choosing not to make any decisions based on prejudgments and the ego self. He or she holds the outlook "Today I will make no decisions by myself" (p. 581). Essentially, the decisions are to be guided by the inner spirit. The text gives a carefully graded sequence of what to do if one forgets and loses that attitude, for example at one point simply saying, "I want another way to look at this" (p. 583).

There is a similarity to the model that Assagioli developed for spiritual growth in Psychosynthesis, in which the personality relinquishes its identification with the ego and orients toward the transpersonal self. In Psychosynthesis, as in the Course, this higher self is considered to be different from the ordinary ego. It is an intermediary between the ordinary self and the spiritual domain of the universe. "The Holy Spirit mediates higher to lower communication, keeping the direct channel from God to you open for revelation" (p. 6).

In transpersonal psychology, this process is often described in a nonspiritual framework as the use of intuition or inner guidance. Frances Vaughan (1979), in *Awakening Intuition,* gives ample evidence that there is a process of inner knowledge that can be drawn upon, a source of wisdom that is beyond the logical or emotional levels of the conscious ego. This may be personified as a guide in mental images, as a power animal in shamanism, or experienced through sensations, feelings, voices, or hunches. The instructions given by Vaughan for cultivation of intuition include meditative, therapeutic, and imagery techniques. These are quite compatible with the principles of *A Course in Miracles.* Another book, *Higher Creativity,* by Willis Harman and Howard Rheingold (1984), takes up the same topic, but with more emphasis on problem solving. Again, these accounts imply a source of knowledge that appears not to come from the conscious mind with its knowledge and thinking.

In the Course, this knowledge is identified as coming from higher spiritual levels. The contact with this level leads to a change in how the world is seen. In this, the Course is aligned with almost all spiritual traditions which seek changes in the self and in the perception of the world.

Throughout the text, the elements and principles of inner experience are used to explain these themes. For example, here are two sentences expressing a psychological principle, "And value no plan of the ego before the plan of God. . . . Every allegiance to a plan of salvation apart from Him diminishes the value of His Will for you in your own mind" (p. 288). This is a thought worthy of William James who pointed out that what you give attention to, you identify with.

The Course takes up self-judgment, self-image, atonement, forgiveness, healing, guilt, peace, and other familiar topics, but often from new spiritual or psychological viewpoints. For some individuals, the analysis is probably quite accurate, but it is difficult to say how universal it is; that is, does guilt result for everyone from a perceived separation from the divine, and is this projected as fear of attack? Does forgiveness enable the healing of this for everyone?

At first, Schucman and Thetford believed that the Course was given to them for their own personal work. They considered it the answer to Bill's yearning for another way. They had no thoughts that it might be published for others. As they were both psychologists, it is quite reasonable that the language and principles should be in the framework of psychology. Helen's autobiographical writings show much detailed self-analysis, and it appears that the Course drew on these introspections as knowledge of how the mind works or, at least, how Helen's mind worked. The Course seems directed toward releasing negative obstacles of fear, guilt, feelings of inadequacy, and self-judgment, and is directed toward evocation of nonjudgmental, transpersonal states of knowledge and perception. Perhaps those negative issues and positive visions were of special relevance to the two recipients and spoke to their inner and outer needs. To the extent that others share those concerns, the Course speaks to them as well.

Workbook for Students

When the text was completed, Helen assumed that the Course was finished. Soon, she began feeling that there was more to come, and the voice began with a workbook for students (*A Course in Miracles*, 1985b). The format of the Course uses an academic model—a textbook, a workbook, and a teacher's manual. This model was familiar to teachers such as Schucman and Thetford. As with other channeled material, it appears likely that the intelligence behind the voice drew upon the knowledge, skills, and experience of Helen (and probably Bill) for the language, information, and psychology of teaching. Thus, congruent with Helen's experience, it is presented like an academic course, with psychological orientation and graduated exercises. I would not be certain that the workbook was intended from the start. I get a sense that the larger format of the Course may have developed as the dictation of the text was emerging.

The workbook contains 365 lessons, consisting of exercises, meditations, affirmations, and reviews. The text has exercises in it such as visualizations, but they are occasional. The workbook is systematic and focused. The lessons are graduated to help the individual experience the material of the text. The instructions say to do no more than one lesson a day, and they comment that the lessons do not need to be believed or understood, simply done. This is very sensible, as it avoids the defenses of the rational mind or the need to understand the theory. The ideas of the text are to be grounded by experience, even if the experience is not verbalized. A universal theology is not possible, says the Course, but a universal experience is. The workbook is clear as to what the experience is: "the undoing of the way you see now . . .," and "the acquisition of true perception" (p. 1). It is a shift from seeing the world as fearful and the self as victimized to a world of choice, forgiveness, and peace. The psychology involved in these lessons is well worth studying for its insight into a transformational method. Though the lessons could be practiced at the rate of one a day, I have heard from many people that they are not successful at this pace. They report forgetting to carry out the instructions or saying the words of an affirmation and blanking out their meaning. The Course is designed for self-study. Many people spend as much time as they choose on each lesson. Some readers begin with the text, others with the workbook, others in some other way.

The Lessons in the Workbook

The very first lesson is likely to shock the student. It is an exercise with the theme "Nothing I see in this room means anything." The student is told to experience this idea by looking around and applying it to everything he or she sees.

> This table does not mean anything. . . .
> This chair does not mean anything. . . .
> That lamp does not mean anything. . . .
> That shadow does not mean anything (p. 3).

The student is told to do this no more than twice a day, only for a minute or two, and to not exclude anything that is seen.

The second lesson continues "I have given everything I see in this room [on this street, from this window, in this place] all the meaning it has for me" (p. 4). Again, this is applied to anything the student sees, taking subjects as they are noticed.

These first two exercises go to the roots of perception and meaning. It is quite true that the physical world has no meaning in its own nature. Sensations, objects, events simply exist at their nonverbal levels. There is no inherent meaning to them. In recognizing that something has no meaning, there is an elimination of name, function, social context, history, use, values, and other associations. There is an experience of the nonverbal level of pure phenomena, without interpretation.

The second lesson says that the meanings that are perceived are ones that are projected by us onto the world. The General Semantics movement in American popular philosophy has emphasized this; meanings are in people, not in words. The ease with which hypnosis can change attitudes, beliefs, and even sensory perception is well established. What most people do not realize is that we project meaning at even the basic level. A hypnotized person may see a hat as a rabbit, and some observers naively laugh, assuming the object is really a hat. But seeing it as a hat is just as much a construction of our perception as seeing it as a rabbit.

In psychotherapy, it is well known that our experience is affected, even created, by hidden assumptions. Rational-Emotive Therapy, developed by Albert Ellis, notes how beliefs (such as "I am shy," and "Men don't like me") affect perceptions of self and others and determine how people act. Projections, either at a neurotic level or the level of ordinary perception, literally construct the meanings in our world based on our past experience and ideas.

Perceiving reality without conditioned meanings, as in the first lesson, is often associated with mystical or peak experiences. In these, the person reports seeing the suchness or beingness of things, separate from name, function, or purpose. Abraham Maslow studied peak experiences, and one of the characteristics he found was that the perceiver did not project purposes on nature. "In a word, he can see it in its own Being (as an end in itself) rather than as something to be used or something to be afraid of or something to wish for or to be reacted to in some other personal, human, self-centered way" (Maslow, 1964, p. 61). Aldous Huxley, when he took the psychedelic substance mescaline, said that he experienced objects in this way, seeing Reality, not his overlays on it.

These mystical experiences have a positive-feeling tone to them, but there are also experiences of existential meaninglessness that are fearful. Lesson Thirteen says that this occurs because the ego fears it cannot fill the void, whereas actually God provides meaning for the world beneath the words of the ego. Here, as in the text, there is the presumption that the cause of anxiety is separation of the ego from the truth of God.

One spiritual teaching, the Tibetan Buddhist Dzogchen tradition, holds that the enlightened mind perceives the world at the level before associations—bird songs are pure sound, for example. In yoga, there is reference to the mind as conditioned, with mental reactions that have been built up through experiences.

In addition to the transcendent aspect of the experience, there is another dimension. The conditionings and meanings that we project are overlaid on the naked reality, like clothes. These projections fall into place. They are evoked by context, purpose, needs, and so on. They preclude any alternative perceptions and any other associations at variance with the predominant set. We have little choice in how we perceive our experience, and we do not usually realize that other views are possible. Carlos Castaneda, the anthropologist-writer, once spoke to a college class taught by transpersonal psychologist Robert Frager. Castaneda told the students that they were just like their parents. The students, including barefoot hippies, protested this charge. Castaneda said, "Well, you still see trees like your parents do, don't you?"

Most of the conditionings of meaning come from our society, our emotional needs, and our language, and these determine our experience. If these are derived from fear, feelings of inadequacy, anger, defensiveness, judgmentalness, and other negative elements, then the meaning projected on the world reflects those reactions. Through these lessons, the Course clearly intends to undo these influences on our experience, first to remove the pathological, negative, view of people and things, and second to allow an alternative spiritual viewpoint to be cultivated.

The early lessons are designed to destructure past associations and judgments. Lesson Three has the student saying "I do not understand anything I see in this room." The point is to make no judgments on whatever is seen and to separate one's self even from understanding, because understanding is a product of past conditioning. Lesson Four says "These thoughts do not mean anything," like the things of Lesson One. For people who value their thinking, this is a hard lesson indeed. The instructions drily say "you may find the suspension of judgment in connection with thoughts particularly difficult" (p. 7). It is like the contemplative exercise that led Indian yogi Ramakrishna to enlightenment, part of which is meditating on "I am not my thoughts." For persons who are more inclined to value their feelings, an equivalent lesson would be "These feelings do not mean anything." (Lesson Four suggests to me that Helen strongly identified with her thoughts, so naturally this is the way the lesson was phrased.)

Lesson Five attempts to dis-identify from emotional judgments, using the phrase "I am never upset for the reason I think" (p. 8). The student is to apply it to any upset, saying "I am not angry at Joan for the reason I think," or "I am not depressed at losing my money for the reason I think." It is to be applied to worry, depression, fear, anger, anxiety, and other negative emotions. One is not to try to find the "real" cause, but rather to disengage from the belief.

The next lessons take up the idea that past experiences and thoughts make up our projections on the world. Lesson Eleven states it specifically, "Your thoughts determine the world you see" (p. 18). This idea is not new, though it is rarely taken seriously; the Course presents it in the context of exercises that will ground it in practice.

The point developed by further lessons is that if the world is meaningless, it is neither good or bad. Why, then, should one be upset? The goal of inner peace is found in one way or another in all traditions, though the method of achievement may be different. In Christianity, this idea is presented as giving up the things of the world, giving no thought to the morrow; in Buddhism, it is equanimity coming from the cessation of desire.

As the lessons progress, an alternative perspective is constructed. The student is instructed to be aware of the stream of thoughts, noticing dispassionately, but not dwelling on them. Lesson Thirty-one is "I am not the victim of the world I see" (p. 48). This lesson is similar to vipassana mindfulness meditation, a technique for decreasing the influence of emotional reactions to thoughts.

The student practices "God is in everything I see because God is in my mind," (Lsn. 30, p. 47) and "My mind is part of God's" (Lsn. 35, p. 53). I see these, and many later lessons, as intended to evoke spiritual states or energies in the self. These states or energies are then projected onto the world, thus changing perception. It should be noted that the idea that one's mind is a part of God's mind is at variance with the fundamentalist Protestant and Catholic theological position that humans are separate and creations of God, not a part of God.

Further lessons develop specific experiences related to forgiving others, salvation, feeling the peace of God, spiritual understanding, new attitudes, divine reality, and alignment with the Holy Spirit.

The lessons all are titled with a sentence or statement. Some students use these as affirmations; that is, they repeat them as a way to hold the thought in their minds and to evoke its meaning in their lives. This is similar to the use of prayer in Judaism and Christianity and mantra in Eastern traditions. In the former, there is presumed to be a deity who responds; in the latter, the formulas themselves are understood to have spiritual energy. The use of affirmations has become popular in contemporary popular growth psychology, but there has been little actual evaluation of their power. In my observation, they may provide guidance to orient the forces of the self, but they can also be simply emotionally reassuring without being effective. The Course does not advocate these phrases as affirmations, but rather as ideas for contemplation and application, a technique deeply rooted in traditional spiritual practice.

In any event, the lessons set out an intensive course. They are well thought out to accomplish the purposes of undoing ordinary perception and systematically training a different view of the self and the world. They stimulate powerful intellectual and emotional reactions, and many people find that their mind engages its defenses to deny, avoid, or misinterpret the ideas and the applications. The text states, "This is a course in mind training," (1985a, p. 13) and the lessons bear this out.

Manual for Teachers

When the voice began dictating the workbook for students, Helen knew that there would also be a teacher's manual because, "that's obviously what professors have to teach. And I did feel that it was going to organize itself in that way. And it did" (Hammond, 1975). The manual (*A Course in Miracles,* 1985c) is the shortest of the three parts, 88 pages in print against the 622 pages of the text and 478 pages of the workbook. It is organized around questions: Who are God's teachers . . . who are their pupils . . . how is judgment relinquished . . . is reincarnation so . . . and so on. There is a second part to the manual which contains a discussion of terms used in the Course, including mind-spirit, the ego—the miracle, forgiveness, and Holy Spirit.

A teacher of God, says the manual, is anyone who chooses to be one. This is a choice in which the person sees his interests to be at one with other people, rather than separate from them. A teaching-learning situation reduces separation; therefore, the relationship is holy (would that more schools and teachers recognized this!). The manual says that these situations occur at three levels. The first are apparently casual encounters,

a 'chance' meeting of two apparent strangers in an elevator, a child who is not looking where he is going running into an adult 'by chance,' two students 'happening' to walk home together. These are not chance encounters. Each of them has the potential for becoming a teaching-learning situation. Perhaps the seeming strangers in the elevator will smile to one another; perhaps the adult will not scold the child for bumping into him; perhaps the students will become friends. Even at the level of the most casual encounter, it is possible for two people to lose sight of separate interests, if only for a moment (p. 6).

The second level is a sustained relationship for a period of time (a class, a work associate), where there is intensive teaching-learning. The third is a lifelong relationship, where "each person is given a chosen learning partner who presents him with unlimited opportunities for learning."

The foundation of teaching ability is said to be the learning of trust in the power of God in the world. Several stages of development are given for this. The first is a period of undoing of beliefs and circumstances. Next is sorting out, determining which things are helpful and which are hindrances. This is followed by relinquishment of the valueless. Then comes a period of settling down, a respite, with the theme, "Give up what you do not want and keep what you do." This is followed by an unsettled period in which the person must take each situation as it comes and ask simply what he or she really wants each time, with no judgment of his own. Finally, at some point, there is a level of achievement, with understanding of the learning, deep tranquility, and the ability to apply the understanding to all situations (the psychological term "transfer" is used for the last quality, using Helen's professional language to make the point).

The stages of spiritual development given by the Course have similarities to those outlined in some religions. For example, there is renunciation in Christianity, Hinduism, and Buddhism, where the follower relinquishes the things of the world. There is a period similar to the "settling down" in which the grace of God seems to be flowing. This is followed by what Saint John of the Cross characterized as a dark night of the soul, in which divine presence seems to have disappeared, and the person is bereft of guidance. This is paralleled by the Course's period of unsettling. Other qualities that are discussed for teachers include honesty, tolerance, gentleness, defenselessness, and patience, which are good characteristics to cultivate regardless of the kind of teaching one is doing.

The answers to the questions combine inspirational and practical advice. Saving time is suggested as a practice for managing daily life; avoiding magical thinking is urged. There is discussion of healing, justice, peace, Jesus, and Christ. In regard to Jesus, the manual makes a remarkable comment. "This course has come from Him because His words have reached you in a language you can love and understand. Are other teachers possible, to lead the way to those who speak in different tongues and appeal to different symbols? Certainly there are. Would God leave anyone without a very present help in time of trouble? . . . symbols must shift and change to suit the need. Jesus has come to answer yours. In Him you find God's Answer" (p. 56). It is usually difficult for founders and followers of a faith to acknowledge other spiritual paths, but the Course is explicit that the curriculum is multifaceted. It is also evident that the Course is oriented toward those who find spiritual meaning in its concepts: ideas of God, Jesus, Holy Spirit, atonement, fear, guilt and sin, forgiveness, and redemption. This is so even if many of these are redefined or used in ways that are unexpected.

Reincarnation and Psychic Powers

"Is Reincarnation So?" asks the title of one section. When Buddha was asked the same question, he commented that a consideration of the question did not further one's enlightenment. The Course essentially takes the same position: "It would not be helpful to take any definite stand" (p. 57). It points out that if reincarnation is responsible for current difficulties, the person still has to deal with the issues now. If he is trying to make his future lives better, he can still do it only in the present.

The existence of psychic powers is acknowledged: "Communication is not limited to the small range of channels the world recognizes. . . . The limits the world places on communication are the chief barriers to direct experience of the Holy Spirit, Whose Presence is always there and Whose Voice is available but for the hearing" (p. 59). That is, listening to the inner voice requires sensitivity and "tuning in" to a different level or source of consciousness.

In comments about psychic powers, there are traces of Saint Paul's observation in I Corinthians, 12, that these abilities are gifts of the Spirit. "The seemingly new abilities that may be gathered on the way can be very helpful. Given to the Holy Spirit, and used under His direction, they are valuable teaching aids. . . . Taking them as ends in themselves, no matter how this is done, will delay progress" (p. 59). This position is taken by most religious traditions. The Yoga Sutras of Patanjali say that when gaining powers becomes an end in itself, they become obstacles to liberation.

Sometimes the manual takes the opportunity to say a few more words about redemption or whatever, to elaborate on a topic from the Text; mostly, it is oriented toward spiritual advice for the teacher. It emphasizes that the teacher and learner are not separate. To teach is to learn, and one teaches that which one wishes to learn. Teaching is demonstration and reflects one's beliefs about oneself. The manual is not directed toward lesson plans, but more toward the attitudes and understandings of those who are in the roles of teachers and who are the learners as well.

CRITIQUES OF *A COURSE IN MIRACLES*

The Course is becoming well known enough to be discussed in public and professional forums. Psychiatrist Roger Walsh, writing in *Common Boundary,* showed parallels between the Course and traditional spiritual systems (Walsh, 1989). An article in response, by Jungian psychologist James Hillman, called the Course an omnipotent spiritual fantasy, arguing that it promotes the belief that the world is illusion, and that one can change reality by changing one's beliefs (Hillman and Dunn, 1989). Hillman also challenged the idea of forgiveness, saying that forgiving leads to forgetting and denial. Would we forgive Hitler? asks Hillman, posing a question that has troubled persons of many religions. He asserts that the emotions of justice, anger, sadness, and others motivate people to take action to improve the world, but that if these emotions and the world are seen as not real, then passivity and inaction result.

If I understand the Course correctly, Hillman is mistaken in his interpretation of what it means by forgiveness, reality, and other ideas. Forgiveness, for example, is primarily the forgiveness of oneself and a shift of perception causing a withdrawal of projections onto others. Action in the world is not rejected. The Course says that peace comes through offering peace, not war. Justice is said to be the divine correction for injustice. In asserting that anger, sadness, and other negative emotions are essential for social action in the world, Hillman articulates a position that deserves discussion, but is contradicted by many persons engaged in social action. Furthering passive omnipotence does not appear to me to be an intrinsic quality of the Course, but rather the way some interpret its concepts to justify their own tendencies.

Another critique in *Gnosis* by Richard Smoley (1987) says that the Course can produce an attitude of denial, with the individual rejecting criticisms and judgments, becoming spacey, and using the lessons as affirmations to stay at the conceptual level. I have noticed that some people use their ideas of the Course as a basis for denying reality, ignoring responsibility, and avoiding self-knowledge, but I would not blame this on the Course. Any spiritual or therapeutic system has aspects that can attract people with particular blind spots and imbalances.

The Course says little about the body and its role in psychological and spiritual work. Smoley and others feel that its treatment of the body as an illusion amounts to a rejection of it. Certainly contemporary psychotherapy is coming to acknowledge the importance of body-mind awareness and the physical aspect of emotional health.

The terminology has been criticized for being masculine: the Holy Spirit is masculine, teachers are referred to as male, and people are always brothers. Feminine references are used only once in the three volumes. In this time of sensitivity to the language of gender, the effect is to exclude the feminine qualities of the divine, or to co-opt them as a part of masculine identity. Some readers have remedied this personally by changing masculine language to feminine terms in the Course, and they report the meaning becomes more balanced and richer for them, without altering the conceptual principles.

Some people who are interested in mystical traditions have criticized the Course for being Christian in its terminology. It certainly is that, but behind this terminology is a less orthodox theology. The Course reinterprets the creation, the atonement, the resurrection, the fall of man (and woman), sees Jesus as a brother, and considers the human problem to be imagined separation of the ego from its Source (God), rather than original sin. These and other concepts are divergent from mainstream Christian doctrines, and some of them would be considered heretical in relation to official Church dogma. In fact, the Course has been condemned as anti-Christian by fundamentalist Christian advocates. On the other hand, many acknowledged Christians find the principles of the Course very compatible with their beliefs (Wapnick, 1978, 1983). Whether or not it was dictated by Jesus, the Course is at least neo-Christian in its imagery and teaching.

A Course in Miracles continues to gain readers and followers. The three volumes and material scribed by Mrs. Schucman are published by the Foundation for Inner Peace. There is no formal organization for students of the material, but there are many autonomous study groups organized by interested individuals to discuss and practice the teachings. Writings, study materials, teachers, and seminars have grown around the Course. The development of the Course as a contemporary spiritual movement is unusual in that there is no charismatic prophet or any organizer to create an official institutional structure. The founders believed it was simply their task to make the material available for others, to be used, as Helen said, for the purpose of obtaining inner peace.

CHAPTER 11

INNER VOICES AND INNER GUIDES

One of the ways in which information is received from outside the conscious mind is through an inner voice. Some people only hear a word or phrase or their name being called; for others, the voice is an inner adviser, and they can engage in dialog with it. They may even communicate its messages to others or write material from its dictation as we have seen in the case of Helen Schucman. Hearing an inner voice is far more common than might be expected, being experienced by perhaps more than 15 percent of the general population. Sometimes the voice is accompanied by seeing a figure in inner vision who is usually interpreted as an inner guide. Since hearing voices or seeing visions is often considered to be a sign of mental illness, it will repay us to look at cases where disturbance is not evident and the messages prove to be of value. The experience of an inner voice is quite different from the more flamboyant trance speaking or Ouija Board manipulation, but it is another manifestation of the process that occurs in channeling.

SUBPERSONALITIES AND INNER SELVES

We will begin with the methods used to develop inner guides in channeling and note similar psychological techniques that evoke inner imaginal figures. During the interest in channeling that occurred in the decade of the eighties, classes and seminars were offered to teach people how to channel. They often began by teaching the person to develop a relaxed meditative state. Then the mental imagery of a door was created, behind which was to be the spirit guide. After psychological and emotional readiness was achieved, the door was opened, and the channeled entity appeared. Individuals reported contacting guides and various entities using this technique (Roman and Packer, 1987).

This is similar to a technique used in Psychosynthesis, the psychotherapy developed by Roberto Assagioli (1965). Psychosynthesis holds that our personality contains various aspects, feelings, and roles—conceptualized as subpersonalities. These roles could be as mother or father, our job personality, an outdoor person, a teacher, the self-critic, a frightened child, a religious figure, and so on. These parts are often split, and one of the tasks of therapy is to integrate or synthesize them into a whole self.

The subpersonalities can be identified by repeatedly asking "Who Am I?," by introspection, or by inviting them to appear from behind an imagined door, marked "Subpersonalities" (Vargiu, 1974). They are often imagined vividly as persons (or animals or other figures) dressed in an appropriate way and speaking quite independently inside the mind to the person. The subpersonality may explain its contribution to the self, state its needs, engage in dialog, or give advice. Beyond these "horizontal" parts of the personality, the inner imagination technique also can communicate with what Psychosynthesis practitioners refer to as the higher self. This may be personified (as a wise old woman or an angel, for example) or may be an intuited presence which gives messages for guidance and insight.

There are other psychotherapies that call out parts of the self and that acknowledge a higher aspect. Hal Stone and Sidra Winkelman's voice dialogue has the client sitting or standing in various locations and speaking in different voices as he or she personifies different selves. Again, these tend to appear as critics, protectors, perfectionists, children, and other parts of the self. As the critical, inconsistent, and quarrelsome parts begin to reform and relate, there is communication with the part that is a higher self or spirit and concerned with being, meaning, and energy (Stone and Winkelman, 1989).

In *Memories, Dreams, Reflections,* C. G. Jung (1973) writes of such a higher self from personal experience. In his inner work, he began to experience a wise figure named Philemon who acted as a guide for insights and for Jung's self-exploration. Philemon was autonomous and participated in dialogs with Jung. Jung felt that he had not personified Philemon, but that such figures have a personal nature from the beginning. Later, another inner guide whom he called Ka appeared. Their origins, felt Jung, were outside the personal conscious and unconscious minds. The analytical psychology developed by Jung postulates that beyond the ego is a greater self and a collective unconscious where these figures may originate.

INNER CHARACTERS, SOME CONSTRUCTED, SOME NOT

We can now turn to inner figures that have been created in some sense by the individual in a context other than channeling. Businessman Napoleon Hill deliberately constructed his inner guides. Hill, author of the best-selling book *Think and Grow Rich,* tells of his inner council of advisors, selected by him and created in his mind (Hill, 1960). These were Emerson, Paine, Edison, Darwin, Lincoln, Burbank, Napoleon, Ford, and Carnegie. He selected them because he admired their qualities and wished to rebuild his own character. He studied their lives and carried on dialogs with them

before falling asleep at night. Before long, these imaginary characters became real, speaking to him and each other and having character traits.
Lincoln was always late to the meetings. Luther Burbank and Tom Paine
exchanged witty repartee. Hill became frightened of their realism and
actually stopped the meetings for several months, lest he forget that the
counselors were imaginary. Their guidance, he reported, helped him in
emergencies and with many problems.

Inner figures and voices also are found in the experiences of many literary
authors. While Hill systematically constructed his characters, with writers
the development of inner voices and figures is more spontaneous, responding to the writing intentions of the person. We have already noted Blake's
comment that *Jerusalem* was dictated to him. Others such as R. L. Stevenson
and Enid Blyton reported seeing scenes acted out in detail. Merlin Stone
says that she was directed by the Goddess to particular libraries and even
pages in books when she was writing *When God Was a Woman. Invisible
Guests,* by Mary Watkins (1986) reports that some authors have an even
more intimate relationship with their "creations." Alice Walker spoke with
the characters of *The Color Purple* for a year during the writing. She felt them
trying to contact her, to speak through her. Celie, Shug, and the others
would sit and talk with her. They would give her perspectives that differed
from hers and even got her to move from the city to the country. Watkins
calls these various figures "imaginal others." They are autonomous in that
they appear unexpectedly, and we cannot predict what they will say. They
carry on dialogs and conversations. These situations are not pathological,
says Watkins. She suggests that they call for building a relationship with the
other, rather than depotentiating and trying to co-opt their energy. This
relationship values dramatic thought rather than abstract unity. It is one of
respect in which the self does not attempt to abolish the autonomy of the
other.

CHANNELED COMMENTS ON INNER GUIDES

If we move to channeled writings, we find several channeled teachings
that assert the existence of an inner spiritual entity that can be contacted by
the person. The books by Alice A. Bailey assert that there is a soul for every
person, and the individual's task is to contact the soul through spiritual
work and invite its help. Energy, purpose, and communication flow down
from the soul to the personality in order to stimulate intelligent activity. The
Bailey writings say that this soul is in communion with other souls, so the
contact enables the person to work together with others to benefit humanity. As mentioned in Chapter 8, Assagioli is presumed to have developed his
Psychosynthesis model of the self from the Tibetan's writings. See the
discussion of this model in Chapter 16.

In the *Urantia Book* (1955), every person is said to have a part of the

Godhead within him or her. This Godhead is given rather odd names, being called the Mystery Monitor or Thought Adjuster. It is also defined as God in man. Its purpose is to receive messages from the universe's spiritual intelligences and translate them to the mind, so to make a new mind. It is to create the conditions for spiritual growth, which include making one's life reasonably rugged and difficult, so decisions will be stimulated. As in the Bailey writings, the person must desire this contact, as the adjusters respect the will of the individual. The text says that the adjuster may be heard by some as the still inner voice, the voice of the Divine.

A Course in Miracles (1985a, 1985b, 1985c), written in Christian language, refers to the Holy Spirit as the communication link between God and His separated sons. The Holy Spirit is a part of God that dwells in the Christ mind of the person. The Holy Spirit can provide guidance, teaching, and comfort to the person. It is described as the voice of God, literally being heard within. One is advised to call on it for any problem or perplexity, not just spiritual issues. The course says that the Holy Spirit will respond only at the invitation of the individual. "Ask and He will answer" (1985c, p. 67), which echoes the Biblical statement by Jesus, "Ask, and it shall be given you . . . knock, and it shall be opened unto you."

Other channeled literature refers to an inner guide or spiritual element in the mind, for example, Ken Carey's Return of the Bird Tribes, communicated from a native-American perspective, says that people have within them a higher self, called a hokseda.

RELIGIOUS CONCEPTS OF GUIDANCE

This concept parallels the orthodox Christian doctrine of the Holy Spirit. The Holy Spirit was believed to be an actual presence that entered the individual and gave abilities called gifts of the spirit. These included speaking in the tongues (languages) of angels, interpreting what was said, and prophesy (inspirational or revelatory speaking, that is, channeling). Morton Kelsey, Episcopal theologian, suggests that the Holy Spirit enters at the unconscious level of the personality, then communicates with the conscious mind (Kelsey, 1978). Jesus refers also to the spirit of truth, called the Paraclete, Advocate, or Comforter, who, he says, will come to dwell with and in the person (John 14:16). In several religious traditions, there is the belief that each individual has one or two guardian angels who provide guidance and assistance.

INNER VOICES

An inner voice can be heard by quite respectable, healthy individuals, but is rarely reported or discussed, even to family and friends. One of the circumstances in which such a voice is heard is in a crisis that admits of no solution from ordinary mental resources. Psychotherapist M. Scott Peck (1978), in *The Road Less Travelled*, tells of a time in adolescence when he was in despair and terrified about his reluctance to attend a particular school, an action which would go against his family's wishes and tradition. "At the moment of my greatest despair, from my unconscious there came a sequence of words, like a strange disembodied oracle from a voice that was not mine: 'The only real security in life lies in relishing life's insecurity' " (pp. 136–137). This gave him the courage to make the decision not to go.

A health crisis in the life of David A. Tate (1989) stimulated an inner voice for him. In *Health, Hope, and Healing*, he tells how he was in despair. Feeling he had in some way brought on a life-threatening disease, he desperately wanted to reverse the process. But how could he begin?

> A voice—not external but not quite internal either—began to speak to me. The voice was clear and calm and spoke with absolute authority. It told me that if I wanted to be cured, I would have to know that I was already well and then I would find the means of survival. I tried to explain to the voice that I hadn't received the chemotherapy yet, that I couldn't possibly be cured now. But it insisted: you must *know* you are cured *now* (p. 58).

Against rationality, Tate finally assented and, he said, it felt like a baptism. Though he was not always able to hold that belief in the years to come, it changed his journey to a healing one.

Those were brief experiences of voices, but many people hear a voice more than once. A frequent inner voice was experienced by Helen Schucman, scribe of *A Course in Miracles*. This voice dictated the material to her, but she heard it long before that and learned she could ask it for advice and information. Later, as the manuscript moved toward publication and dissemination, others associated with the work began to call upon their inner voices as a group (Skutch, 1984). When several of them asked on the same question, they found the answers were often in agreement, for example, as to whether a particular publisher should be used.

A case in which a continuing voice served as a personal teacher is that of Paul Tuttle, a Washington state businessman (Tuttle, 1985). Faced with problems in his business, he heard that everyone had a spiritual guide, so he began to request this in meditation. For three weeks nothing happened, then he heard a voice; it identified itself as Rajpur. In response to a question, it indicated that it was communicating with Tuttle through meanings without language, which he (Tuttle) then translated into English. In subsequent sessions, it gave Tuttle guidance on his life and also explained various metaphysical ideas. The guidance was sometimes difficult for businessman Tuttle to accept, for example:

> **PAUL:**   Are you saying that I need to sit here without raising a
>   finger in response to anything that is going on, and let
>   the axes fall as they appear to be going to?

RAJ: That is exactly what I am saying. . . .

PAUL: And you are saying that you cannot tell me why I should do such an extreme thing?

RAJ: That is correct.

PAUL: You understood when I said "axes falling" that I was referring to the possibility of being kicked out of our house because we can't pay the rent, being sued . . . and so on?

RAJ: I understood exactly, Paul.

PAUL: And your answer remains the same?

RAJ: It remains the same (pp. 210–211).

To Tuttle's surprise and relief, some unexpected money turned up. This was a trying time for Tuttle, with business problems, family moves, and emotional turbulence. Nevertheless, he relied on guidance from Raj. It was initially for himself and his wife Susan, but then, with Raj's permission, Tuttle put the material in a book, *You Are the Answer* (Tuttle, 1985), and began to present workshops in which Raj answered questions put by participants. Curiously, in the course of their conversations, Raj also made predictions (for example, about world events, the coming of the Messiah, visitors) which failed to occur.

Raj's teachings developed followers, some cultish, some not, like other channeled material. Tuttle's life became more stable. He remained low key about his work, continued to smoke (against Raj's wishes), and acknowledged the value of Raj's guidance during a difficult time. I asked him in 1987 what he learned from his experience. He told me that he had been at the end of his ability to deal with the situation. He could not think his way out of it. Raj's direction took him beyond what he could do. And, he added, even during the worst times, his family always had a roof over their heads, and he always had cigarettes to smoke.

Historical Voices and Guides

There are several examples of historical figures who have experienced an inner voice. Plato and Xenophon report that Socrates had an inner voice, called a *daimon*. It often acted as a warning voice to him. For example, it once told him not to go down a particular street in Athens, enabling him to avoid a herd of pigs which knocked down his friends who had ignored his warning. It also advised him not to defend himself at his trial.

Joan of Arc (1312–1331), who began hearing voices at age thirteen, was led by them to champion the cause of Charles VII in France. The Maid also saw the visionary figures of Saint Michael, Saint Margaret, and Saint Catherine. She called them her Counsel (this reminds me of Napoleon Hill's

Council). Her voices directed her to brilliant acts of military strategy and heroism, which succeeded in restoring the king to the throne, and proved a turning point in the Hundred Years' War. They also resulted in her being tried for witchcraft by the church. In the trial, she refused to deny the voices, which told her incorrectly that she would be freed. She was found guilty and killed. Later, the church recanted its decision and acknowledged her sainthood. While the trial decreed that her voices were from demons, the orthodox psychological view would be that they were hallucinations. George Bernard Shaw's treatment of this in his great play *Saint Joan* is instructive.

ROBERT: What did you mean when you said that Saint Catherine and Saint Margaret talked to you every day?

JOAN: They do.

ROBERT: What are they like?

JOAN: (Suddenly obstinate) I will tell you nothing about that; they have not given me leave.

ROBERT: But you actually see them; and they talk to you just as I am talking to you?

JOAN: No, it is quite different. I cannot tell you; you must not talk to me about my voices.

ROBERT: How do you mean, voices?

JOAN: I hear voices telling me what to do. They come from God.

ROBERT: They come from your imagination.

JOAN: Of course. That is how the messages of God come to us.

POULENGY: Checkmate (Shaw, 1958, pp. 810–811).

F. W. H. Myers, the great psychical researcher, in *Human Personality* concluded that there was no reason to assume that the voices came from anywhere other than Joan's own mind. But he also pointed out that she was not insane; rather, indeed, a model of sanity, being able to draw on all her being to cope with the needs of the real world (Myers, 1903). Shaw also contends that Joan was unusually sane, pointing to the quality of the military orders and advice from her Counsel. There were also several incidents suggestive of ESP, in which the voices told her of the location of a hidden sword and predicted battle events.

Psychological Studies of Inner Voices

Some psychologists have acknowledged the occurrence and role of these inner voices. They have verified that beneficent, positive voices can be heard by normal, healthy individuals. Alfred Alschuler (1987, 1990) reports that many inner voices provide healing, superior information, inspiration, and authorization. They resolve problems and offer feedback. His research turned up 150 individuals in history who heard an inner voice, including Martin Luther, Saint Teresa, French mystic Madame Guyon, and, ironically, Adolf Hitler, who was saved from death in the First World War by a voice that told him to move down a trench just before a shell exploded, killing every person in the group where he had been sitting. Alschuler cites surveys that indicate about 15 percent of the population have heard a voice as a part of a spiritual experience, so the general percentage is probably much larger. Alschuler was motivated to study these cases because he himself began to hear a voice about 1977. Like Helen Schucman, he feared this meant a breakdown, even though his life and professional work were productive and normal. He was relieved and reassured by his research which showed that there were sane, loving, and capable people who were better for hearing an inner voice. He was angered by learning about Hitler and says he had to acknowledge that the inner voice also has the potential for absurdities and abominations. Perhaps it is some balance to note that Winston Churchill was also saved by an inner voice telling him to move to the other side of his car just before a bomb exploded on the side where he had been.

What are the roles of these inner voices? Myrtle Heery (1989) interviewed thirty nonpathological individuals who heard inner voices. She identified three categories of messages. The first category was advice or comments that rather obviously expressed a fragmented part of the personality. Often, these were commands and demands. The messages would say things that had been suppressed or ignored and, in one example, forced the end of a relationship that the individual admitted was better ended. The second category was messages directed toward personal development or psychological growth. Rather than commands, these voices were dialog with the rest of the self. One such dialog was about accepting a job. The individual, a painter, took the advice of the voice that the job would get in the way of her more important intention to paint.

In Heery's third category were messages leading toward and beyond a higher self. These pointed the person toward training or instruction for spiritual growth. They often emphasized service to others. All the individuals in this category practiced some form of meditation on a regular basis. These people were all from California and self-selected, but the study does point out that ordinary people can have these experiences and benefit from them.

A high proportion of people having an inner voice is found among professional psychics. Charles Millar (1990) surveyed 139 persons who identified themselves as psychic practitioners. Ninety-one percent reported hearing an inner voice and judged the messages from these voices as positive and helpful. Channeling or mediumship was reported by 71 percent. The inner voice experience was significantly correlated with automatic writing.

It is a fair conclusion to say that these studies show that many people hear a beneficent mental voice occasionally or frequently. It is not an indication of mental illness, and the listener may be better for it.

Negative Voices

We should note, however, that there are negative voices. Critical voices can occur in normal people and do not mean mental illness. They may be objective comments that the person interprets as critical. Sometimes, they can be recognized as a self-critical feeling that has been ignored or repressed. On the other hand, we know of the criminal or fanatic who heard a voice which told him or her to kill, take revenge, or cleanse the world of unbelievers. These are usually heard as external hallucinations, rather than a voice in the mind. In cases where inner or hallucinated external voices are distressing, they have been treated as pathology and treated with therapy or medication. A few therapists have used the alternative model of possession in such cases, considering them to be caused by intruding spirits. They have used techniques of depossession, deliverance, and exorcism, and reported them to be effective, even when the therapist had doubts of the reality of spirits. Belief in possession is not in fashion today, yet this type of case and the effectiveness of treatment suggest that the possibility is worthy of serious study (Crabtree, 1985; Allison and Schwarz, 1980; Fiore, 1987; Wickland, 1974; Perry, 1990).

Voices, Spirits and the Other Me

Psychologist Wilson Van Dusen (1972) worked for many years in a state mental hospital and found that many patients heard both critical and supportive voices. In this setting, these voices were classed as hallucinations, of course, and indeed, the patients reported that they sounded like another person speaking. Van Dusen took the radical approach of talking to the voices and having the patients report back to him what they said. Soon, he realized that there was a lower order and a higher order. The lower order was less talented than the patient, and was attacking, critical, and threatening. The voices would threaten to kill the person, confuse his thinking, interfere with thoughts, and could even create physical pain. Van Dusen notes that they did not have a personal history or identity as we humans do (quite typical of channeled entities also), but they would provide a name (Old Timer, Jesus), to beguile the patient, which they might drop or change later. Often the voices began as friendly and then became abusive after getting the person's confidence. Some patients heard voices, some saw visions, some had a mixture. Occasionally, the voices spoke aloud through the patient. In earlier times, this phenomenon would have been classified as demonic possession. Van Dusen writes that he could sometimes, but not always, understand the relation between the voices and the emotional issues of the patient. For example, persons who had violated their conscience might be tortured by conscience-like lower order voices.

The higher order of voices was quite different. It was more knowledgeable and intuitive than the patient. It respected the patient's will, was often symbolic, and even assisted Van Dusen in the therapy. In one case, a higher order figure proved to Van Dusen's satisfaction that it had psi ability. It also had knowledge that went beyond the patient's experience and understood the implications of ancient myths better than the therapist did. This entity called herself "An Emanation of the Feminine Aspect of the Divine," and was, explains Van Dusen, "a hallucination in the head of a high school-educated, schizophrenic, not-very-gifted gas pipe-fitter" (Van Dusen, 1972, p. 159).

Van Dusen notes parallels of the negative and positive voices to the lower and higher spirits described by Emmanuel Swedenborg (1688–1772), who was a Swedish genius—scientist, engineer, statesman, and mystical visionary—a striking combination indeed. In his visions, he experienced realms of spirits and angels, of heaven and hell (Swedenborg, 1852, 1875). Van Dusen cautiously suggests that he and Swedenborg are dealing with the same matter and that the unconscious may also be a realm of spirits that can intrude into the ego (Van Dusen, 1973).

The contemporary explanation, that these are eruptions from the unconscious (rather than possession by spirits), is not satisfactory, says Van Dusen (1972). Not all his cases showed a connection with unconscious elements, nor does the unconscious model explain the giftedness of the higher order. He suggests, on the basis of the voices, and other expressions of the self, that there is an "Other Me" that lives in polar opposition to the ego. It originates in the fundamental nature of the mind, knows more than the ego, can communicate symbolically, understands that all things are related, and is concerned with the quality of the person's life. This "Other Me" is higher than the individual and lies beyond the bounds of the individual as we presently define the person. Its capabilities are quite different from the individual's own mind. There is no way, Van Dusen admits, to decide absolutely if this is part of the person in some more-inclusive sense or if it is a reflection of higher processes transcendent to the individual; he inclines toward the latter view.

Joseph Caro

A case in which critical and supportive messages are mixed is that of Joseph Caro (1488–1575), a rabbi who received guidance from a being called the Soul of the Mishnah, the oral law (Gordon, 1949). This *maggid* (spiritual teacher) spoke to Joseph through Joseph's own voice and would chastise him, call his attention to a lack of devotion, and scold him for transgressions. But it would also encourage him, tell him he was favored by God and

Rabbi Joseph Caro, who was assisted with his commentaries on Jewish law by a spiritual teacher, the Soul of the Mishnah.

the celestial council, and give excellent guidance on Talmudic and scriptural questions. Caro's code *Shulhan Aruk* and commentaries, for example, *Beth Joseph*, all done with the assistance of the maggid, are authoritative today. Like the Raj entity with Paul Tuttle, some of the *maggid's* predictions for Caro did not come true.

Psychological Aspects of Inner Voices and Guides

If we look at inner voices and guides as forms of channeling, we can first note that they are predominantly private, rather than public. The guidance of the voice is for the individual. They tend to be personal, whether practical or inspirational in content. Peck's and Tate's messages simply told them truths that transcended their ego beliefs, and they accepted them as being authoritative. One is reminded of the statement about Jesus, that he taught not as the priests and rabbis, but as one having authority.

The voices (and the constructed or evoked imaginal figures) seem to be in accordance with personal goals, but they can draw on higher goals. There is a direction toward service, truth, health, wholeness, and the relatedness of things. Heery's third category of voices with higher purposes illustrates this, as do the higher order voices reported by Van Dusen.

Some of these inner guides are constructed. Hill deliberately created his mental council. At the other extreme they can appear unexpectedly—with Tate or Jung, for example. In between are ones that are cultivated or invited. Tuttle asked for his guide in meditation. Workshops present exercises for hopeful channelers. In Rabbi Caro's time, many great rabbis had *maggids*, so this was expected.

If the self can create these figures on request, could it be that the guides and channeled voices are constructed in a similar way by the unconscious, out of building blocks of values, subliminal knowledge, and attitudes? We repress and fear higher values and spiritual impulses, it is true. If repressed guilt can erupt in a critical voice, can repressed spirituality also be given a voice? It is hard to believe that spiritual or higher purposes can have the pent-up energy that negative repressions accumulate. This idea has potential, but leaves questions to be considered.

Though inner voices by and large are beneficent, there are cases where they have not been reliable or responsible. Benjamin Creme, for example, was told that the Christ would reappear in London in 1982, the message presumably coming telepathically from a Himalayan master. The voice gave many details on how to find Christ, all of which were incorrect. Joan of Arc's voices told her that she would be freed. We have also noted that erroneous predictions were given to Tuttle and Caro. With Caro, some of these statements seemed intended to please and compliment him, for example, telling him that he would have many sons. Regarding guides in mediumship, many psychic researchers, mediums, and others, including Swedenborg, have warned that the spirits sometimes lie, are deceptive, and give unreliable advice. Thus, even with the generally positive qualities of the inner guides and voices, both the heart and head need to evaluate any communication.

We have noted that inner guides or similar parts of the self have been described in religion, channeled materials, and psychology. In Judaism and Christianity, there are the guardian angels. In Christianity, the Holy Spirit, the Spirit of Truth, the Advocate, and the Christ who dwells within have been named as inner guides. Channeled teachings have referred to the thought adjuster, Holy Spirit, and hokseda. In psychological writings this part of the self has been referred to as the deep self (Progoff), higher self (Assagioli), the transpersonal self (Vaughan), the Other Me (Van Dusen), the hidden observer (Hilgard), and the inner self helper (Allison); some of these will be discussed in Chapter 16. Most of these aspects are said to communicate through inner voices or images and may not all be the same, of course, but since models of the self from such diverse sources have included this function, there is a good possibility that there is something real that plays this role. Depending on the model, it may come from the unconscious, from a larger self, from a spiritual essence, or from an entity beyond the individual mind.

Inner voices tend to have different characteristics from channeling in which trance-speaking occurs. In trance possession, the entity has a personality, often very distinct, which interacts with the listeners. When the entities write or speak for audiences, they are much more likely to give metaphysical talks and teachings, like Seth and Ramtha (1986). The entities act the role of professor, rather than counselor. The inner voices and guides tend toward personal guidance, spiritual direction, and life decisions. Some channeling involves both, for example, Emmanuel (Rodegast and Stanton, 1985). Inner voices have the opportunity of being anonymous, though guides usually appear as an imaginal figure, such as Jung's Philemon or Joan's angels, or as a voice with an identity. The inner figures have attributes of personality, motivation, and independent intention which flavor the messages and which require that a healthy relationship be cultivated between the inner figure and the individual. Sometimes there is a transition between personal and public communication. Rajpur's dialog with Tuttle was for many months a private one, then became public. In the case of Schucman, the inner voice did dictate writing, but not initially as a public document. Often the guides evoked through a workshop or course begin as visualized inner figures for personal guidance, then move to an audience mode—answering questions and giving inspirational talks.

These personal versus public differences suggest that some inner voices may have a different origin from entities channeled in the trance mode. Some voices or guides are suggestive of the function of a higher self or spiritual essence, rather than a totally separate communicator such as an advanced master. In either event, many inner guides seem qualitatively different from the trance personality entities in their focus and content.

Quality of Inner Voices and Guides

Can we evaluate the quality of this inner guidance? Most of these cases give us reason to believe that the voice can provide superior information and direction. From a therapeutic standpoint, a positive inner voice can be of benefit to the individual or to the therapist and client. It can provide superior ideas or guidance for the person and can be an ally for personal living and growth. In many cases, it provides a bridge to understanding or commitment that the ego cannot make. Coming into the mind during times of crisis, it can bring assurance or change one's perspective. It is not a sign of mental illness. While a person might be wise not to tell friends and co-workers about hearing voices, these voices can nevertheless remain an inner resource, so long as the individual retains his or her own judgment in responding to the messages. A friend or counselor might be of assistance to help the person in evaluating the communications and connecting them with ongoing issues, goals, and decisions.

The experiences of Jung, Hill, Peck, Tuttle, and others show that the perspective of the voice comes from outside the ego personality, and it often gives a point of view that the ego could not have provided. What is also striking is that these people appropriately accepted the voice's messages. What was it that gave them the ability to do this? What source of understanding enabled them to transcend an impasse and accept the answer?

We need to learn more about our ability to acknowledge and utilize deep insights and transcendent wisdom.

There are surely many people who hear inner voices but who have not reported them publicly. Voices that are positive and pleasant but which are not helpful or wise are not likely to be reported. What publisher would market a book titled, *Dumb Things My Voices Have Said*? And perhaps there are people who hear good advice and ignore it. We can only say that we have cases in which reliable guidance has come from these inner guides, whether they were constructed, invited, or spontaneous; whether from the individual's unconscious, a higher self, or some outside source; and that the listeners found it of benefit.

CHAPTER 12

THE PROCESSES AND
DEVELOPMENT OF CHANNELING

We are now in a position to appraise the process of channeling as a human activity which has techniques, methods, patterns, and consequences. Some of the methods, for example, are more productive of good material than others, and if one were planning to become a channel, or a prophet, or a con artist, one would be well advised to select carefully the technique to be used. Similarly, if one wants to be healthy, though a channel, there are considerations to be noted in terms of relationships with the entity and human friends. We will begin with the many techniques for accessing channeled messages. You might wonder if one mode will prove to be more reliable in terms of religious inspiration, personal advice, or various other functions. Indeed, there are some consistencies that stand out.

TECHNIQUES OF CHANNELING

Ouija Board

The Ouija Board is used mostly by beginning practitioners and is probably the most popular form of beginning psychic exploration. Its use is rarely continued for serious channeling because it is very slow. The process often turns into automatic writing or mental dictation. Typical was Jane Roberts, who began with the board but, after a few sessions, began receiving the messages directly in her mind. The Michael group (Yarbro, 1979, 1986) continued to use the board for some time, and Emily Hutchins, a friend of Pearl Curran, received a novel by Mark Twain on the board. Parts of James Merrill's poetry are derived from the board.

Many people familiar with channeling have urged against using the Ouija Board. Some point out that it is very easy for subconscious negative feelings to operate the board. Others say that negative spirits and elementals are attracted to the board. Whatever the theory, it is true that the messages can be critical, manipulative, and frightening. There are some cases in which Ouija messages have persuaded people to commit various crimes, including murder (Hunt, 1985). There is no question that the movements of the

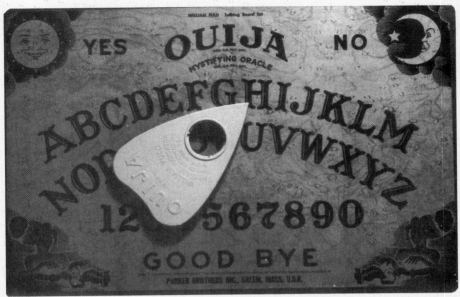

The Ouija Board is sold as a game, but it is often used by beginning channelers. Here it is about to spell out "HELLO READER."

pointer come from the persons operating the board, not consciously, but with their hands responding to dissociated subconscious direction. Usually, it is one particular person who is the essential party in the process and through whom the messages come. It is always the case that the communications are influenced by that individual. In the messages from Michael, one of the group was a student of the Gurdjieff work and, when she worked the board, the teachings were framed along the lines of Gurdjieff's ideas. When another person, interested in transpersonal psychology, was the operator, the information had a transpersonal flavor.

A disadvantage of the Ouija Board is its slow speed. The pointer must move to spell out each letter of the word, therefore the words come very slowly. In addition, the current board made by Parker Brothers contains no punctuation marks and only capital letters, so sentences and punctuation must be interpreted by the recorders. With sophisticated writing, such as poetry, this can be a problem. The poetry of Patience Worth, for example, was punctuated by the Currans, and Stephen Braude (1980), in his contemporary rendition, felt free to revise their format. Emily Hutchins' circle added punctuation marks to the board so Mark Twain could avail himself of them. They noted that Twain was not making much use of semicolons, in contrast to his usual style (when living, that is). When asked, he commented that the semicolon was near the edge of the board and he was afraid the pointer would fall off the edge every time he made a run for it. They moved it nearer the center, and semicolons returned to the writing.

In most of the cases that begin with the board, the communication moves to direct mental voice. Mrs. Curran, Jane Roberts, and some of the Michael channels received the words directly after a decent stint on the board.

Automatic Writing

Automatic writing is also fairly easy to accomplish. It is another dissociated physical activity in which the hand writes by itself, without the conscious direction of the mind. Spirit teachings, messages from spirits of those who have died, books, and other accounts have come through automatic writing. Automatic typewriting also occurs. Jane Roberts wrote a book purporting to come from William James via the typewriter. The famous *Oahspe: A New Bible* (1960) was typed automatically by John Newbrough, beginning in 1880, when the typewriter was a very new machine. It is a massive volume of about 1000 pages, telling of the doings of angels, the creation and cosmology of the universe, and how to prepare for the coming kingdom of God. One of its passages seems to describe the Van Allen radiation belt around the earth, but most of it is jargon that does not have much relation to scientific knowledge. It became the inspiration of spiritual study groups. I was told by author Colin Wilson that some of these are still active in England.

It is important to know that much material produced by automatic writing can be traced to the individual's unconscious dynamics. Anita Muhl, a psychiatrist at Saint Elizabeth's Hospital in Washington, D. C., in the 1930s, found that her patients could write and draw automatically—creating poems, statements, artwork, music, stories, and other compositions (Muhl, 1963). Some of the material discussed God and religious topics, often in paranoid style. In one case, the entities included Moses, Lincoln, Buddha, the Czar of Russia, and Enrico Caruso. Several persons produced competent art and music automatically. Some persons could write simultaneously with each hand or write upside down or backward. However, Dr. Muhl did not attribute the material to outside sources. "I have had many such subjects as patients," she writes, "and in every case where a thorough analysis was instituted, it was demonstrated that all of the automated material, bizarre and weird through much of it was, came from the subject's own unconscious" (p. 28). She found it useful in therapy and helpful to the patient. She often trained her patients to write automatically as part of therapy. It reflected traumas or conflicts, emotional reactions, undeveloped potentials, and knowledge.

Psychiatrist Ian Stevenson (1978) points out that automatic writing can tap material to which the person has been exposed, or knowledge that has been subconsciously learned, though the conscious mind may not be aware of it. This is called cryptomnesia—hidden memory. Stevenson also notes that automatic writing often has a different style of composition from the person's normal writing, but he points out that this is in the range of abilities of the unconscious and is not an argument for an outside source.

Dr. Muhl's work was with psychiatric patients, and the written material was often symptomatic of mental problems. But we know that the unconscious holds wisdom, knowledge, and positive values as well. If the unconscious can express the negative elements, it can also express inspirational, wise, and creative thinking. Indeed, Muhl reports that the automatic writing often expressed ideas, facts, aptitudes, and talents that were beyond the conscious self although she does not discuss how this might be possible. These examples raise the same questions about the sources for these capabilities that we have seen in other cases.

Automatic writing has also been studied in relation to hypnosis, since it is easy to initiate through hypnotic suggestion. It is a useful adjunct in getting memories and comments from parts of the self that are not conscious. Psychiatrist and hypnotist Milton Erickson reported cases in which he obtained automatic writing from patients' secondary personalities (Haley, 1967). Psychologist Ernest Hilgard's work with dissociation indicates (he says "strongly suggests") that the processing of information and ideas can occur outside consciousness, and tasks can be carried out by a part of the self automatically and without awareness (Hilgard, 1986). In this view, "outside" entities would be seen as constructions of another center of consciousness such as in a multiple personality.

Automatic writing is the form of dissociation that has been most studied by psychologists, therapists, hypnotists, and researchers. Their studies build a strong case that the material produced comes from the self, though perhaps from beyond the ego and personality. However, there are also some aspects of channeling that are not explained by attribution to unconscious dissociated parts. These aspects must be considered in any full view of the process and will be addressed later in this text.

Inner Dictation

When we analyze instances of inner dictation, we find the most striking productions of good quality, complex material—much more sophisticated than automatic writing or trance speaking. Inner dictation is a process in which the person hears a voice speaking mentally, and he or she consciously writes out the material (some call it telepathic dictation or clairaudience). This is the process involved in *A Course in Miracles,* in the twenty books dictated by the Tibetan to Alice A. Bailey, in the extensive writings by Geraldine Cummins, the Patience Worth writings, and William Blake's *Jerusalem.* Other poets have reported hearing words, though they have not attributed this, as Blake did, to outside authors. Rilke said that the first of the *Duino Elegies* came to him in a voice, and his *Sonnets to Orpheus* are considered by some to be inspired by Orpheus. Though it does not fit our definition of channeling, there are parallels in the writing of Richard Bach's spiritual parable *Jonathan Livingston Seagull.* The author told me that he saw it in his mind, like wide-screen technicolor, and he heard a lot of the dialog. Sometime before, he had heard an inner voice speaking the title. At one point imagery stopped, then resumed months later where it left off, a pattern we have noted in channeled dictation. This form of inner dictation must be especially suited for literary productions to have produced such an impressive body of work. The process has several striking features.

1. The material comes very rapidly. Helen Schucman said that she had to use a special, fast shorthand to write the words of the Course (a shorthand she used for recording group therapy sessions). Pearl Curran received 5000 words one evening when Patience Worth dictated the conclusion to *The Sorry Tale* and would often speak faster than the recorder could transcribe.

2. The material is presented without changes or revisions—it appears to be in its final form. The recipients say it is like the material has been completed elsewhere and now is being read off to them. In most cases, the material is reasonably well constructed and styled.

3. The content may be very complex. The Bailey books and the Course deal with complex ideas, which recur and interconnect. In the first case, there is confusion and inconsistency at times. In the case of the Course, the consistency is more even. *Jerusalem*, by Blake, is complex, personally symbolic, and somewhat a puzzle, even to Blake scholars.

4. Sometimes the material is poetically styled. This is obviously the case with poetry, but it also occurs within a prose format. Portions of the Course and *Telka* by Worth have meter and rhyme, though written in prose. The priestess of the Delphic Oracle also spoke in verse. This is not uncommon in other modes of channeling and mediumship, however, the extended poetry in the longer works is quite unusual. I have not noticed poetry within the prose of the Bailey books, but they contain prayers and invocations with poetic qualities.

Inner Voice

In using the term "inner voice," I am referring to inner guidance, as described in Chapter 11. The person is given advice, comment, and feedback by a mental voice. This seems to be a form that specializes in guidance for the person, rather than for others. We have seen several cases, as well as the research of Myrtle Heery and Alfred Alshuler which show this occurring in normal individuals, often providing useful information, inspiration, and advice.

With inner dictation and inner voices, there is the conscious presence of the person's ordinary mind, even though there may be a light trance state. The words are consciously heard and written or listened to. I think there is significant value to this. The individual remains in touch with conscious thinking and feeling, which acts as a container for the material being presented. The individual does not abandon conscious responsibility for awareness and contact with the channeled material, as would happen in automatic writing or trance speaking. It may be that this imposes some constraint or responsibility on the source of the information to communicate with the conscious mind. Further, it enables the recipient to manage surroundings and relationships during the channeling. There is a certain advantage to this!

Trance Speaking

The prophets—Elisha, Jeremiah, Muhammad, Joseph Smith, and others—tended to speak inspirationally from ecstatic or trance states. Inspirational, often charismatic, speaking comes through this mode. These prophets did not take on the personality of God, but entered into a state in which their words were the words or ideas of the deity. In other cultures, the possession trance is often an embodiment of a spirit or god, with definite characteristics. The Pythia at Delphi was assumed to be possessed by Apollo.

In contemporary channeling, the full body trance personality is usually identified with a deity, teacher, sage, extraterrestrial, group soul, or other entity. The content may be personal readings, metaphysical teachings, pop psychology, or inspired sermons. It is a form conducive to establishing a relationship with an audience, from individuals to groups, and thus conducive to transference. The purpose of the communication is often a social one, and social movements can coalesce around the channel. The personality qualities of the entity vary, including charismatic, nurturing, arrogant, feisty, sweet, and so on, and each will collect the type of audience that relates to that style. It seems that this process is a precarious one—it may lead to the heights of inspiration, or it may circle in the flatlands of adulation and entity-centricity. If the entity itself is not healthy, then it may personify repressed (positive or negative) aspects of the channel. This can lead to unbalanced points of view, fixed ideas, fanaticism, and teachings that are symbolic of inner needs rather than external reality. Anthropological linguists Dan Alford, Matthew Bronson, and Tom Condon (Bronson, 1988; Hastings, 1987) examined the speaking style of ten trance channels in the San Francisco area. The entities often spoke in a dialect, and the researchers reported that the dialects were incorrect, inconsistent, and inaccurate. The dialect of an Irish entity, Tom McPherson, channeled by Kevin Ryerson, even varied from sentence to sentence. Entities often used "we" and "us," a sort of sociolinguistic assertion of regal authority. Several names ended with -on—Ecton, Hilarion, Etherion, Jason, for example—which tended to give a technological or Biblical authority. It was concluded that there was no linguistic evidence for the autonomy of channeled entities.

The researchers also noted that several of the channels were trained in hypnosis, and the entities appeared to be speaking from a trance state. Entities often used phrasal links such as "now," "indeed," "as it were," and other repeated phrases, which could serve to stabilize the trance state. The linguists also commented that much of the channeled speech was hypnotic in its manner and content, for example: "You are what you will be, as you are what you were, for when you are in the future looking back at the person you are now, you are the same person only older." Channeled discourse, they conclude, has its own jargon that bespeaks a set of values, a subculture, and a way of being, as does all language.

Another linguistic analysis, by Sarah Thomason of the University of Pittsburgh, similarly found that there were inconsistent dialects, contradictory elements, and incorrect usage (Thomason, 1989).

Overall, in relation to method, it appears that the best quality material from the channeling process comes through inner voices and dictations, from people who themselves have balance and ego strength. However, good material has come through all these forms of channeling; the converse is also true: trivialities and platitudes know no constraints and make themselves at home in any mode.

LEARNING

Channeling begins in many ways—from spontaneous emergence to deliberate cultivation. Often, there is a need to develop, refine, and improve the process and content. Few contemporary channels have engaged in deliberate training to refine and stabilize their channeling. Since channeling is found throughout history and in many settings, we can look at ways that have been used within specific contexts to develop this ability.

Historical Training
The Delphic oracle, with its eleven-century span, surely used various methods of selection and training of the priestesses, but we do not know what they were. We do know that the priestesses were selected from ordinary families and had no ability to prophesize outside the oracular state. As an earlier chapter described, a ceremony was used to frame and induce the state; this is a good practice for any channeling session. The priests surrounding her were in charge of managing the ceremony, asking the questions, and recording the answers.

With shamans, now and probably going back into prehistory, the training was by apprenticeship and inner transformation through dreams, guided imagery, psychedelic substances, chanting, and so on. As discussed by

Mircea Eliade, Michael Harner, and others, the shamans' intensive studies include visionary states and journeys. In these visions, they may contact the spirits of the tribal tradition—deities, nature spirits, supernatural forces. These are channeled by the shaman for information and healing. In *The Spirits of Shamanism*, Roger Walsh (1990) discusses the psychological and spiritual aspects of these practices.

In the time of the Hebrew prophets who reported, "It is Yahweh who speaks," prophecy was a profession which was studied by aspirants. There was a Brotherhood of Prophets, with schools in various communities (see Kings II, 2, for example). Usually centering around a leader, the students would practice to learn the method of inspirational speaking (James, 1958).

Contemporary Religions

In spiritualist churches—the contemporary religion that formalizes mediumship for religious and personal guidance—there are training courses and programs for ministers. Intuition, psychic skills, and voicing of spirit personalities are taught. I recall one session I attended in a spiritualist church, in which a minister was just learning to channel an Indian maid named Moonchild. He stuttered and spoke haltingly, and the words came out in Pidgin English: "Me come to bring greetings," and so forth. The congregation was encouraging and supportive, saying, "Hello, Moonchild," and "Welcome." To my perception, it seemed to be an attempt to help a character develop along expected lines in a kind of dramatic way, rather than discovering someone inside oneself who wants to communicate.

Several contemporary religious or personal development organizations cultivate channeling in their work. Eckankar followers report that they receive teachings from masters on the inner planes. Students in Astara may make contact with a being called Zoser. Students of the Bailey writings are taught by inner-plane adepts. These communications are for personal guidance within the teachings, rather than public presentations.

Eileen J. Garrett's Training

The training of Eileen J. Garrett illustrates some important elements for an individual learning to channel. She was trained in mediumship work at the British College of Psychic Science, now the British College of Psychic Studies, by James Hewat McKenzie. Putting Mrs. Garrett into deep trance states (with mesmeric passes, by the way), he literally educated her spirit controls in how to behave in her mediumship trances. Uvani was taught to protect her from questions, demands, and pressures by acting as the manager or "master of ceremonies" during sessions. He described himself as the keeper of the gate, to protect her from being overwhelmed. McKenzie guided Uvani in moving through Mrs. Garrett's mind by using spatial metaphors, telling him to go upward, downward, inward, deeper, and so forth. He felt that the control personalities were limited, and they needed help and training to function at a high level (Hankey, 1963; Garrett, 1949). The control served as the medium's alter ego in the trance state; most channels in current times do not have this perhaps useful assistant.

With Mrs. Garrett herself, much of the training consisted of her learning not to be attached to the trance messages. She realized that if she desired to give a happy message to a couple who had lost a son, or wished for approval and appreciation from her sitters, her channeling would be biased by these ego needs. She had to learn to do the trance channeling, but not have expectations about the results. Probably the quality of her work owes much to this fundamental training. McKenzie was a confirmed believer in spiritualism, while Mrs. Garrett was more skeptical and psychological in her views, but she recognized that the training he gave her was invaluable.

SOCIAL CONTEXT

All these methods of learning and refining channeling, from shamans to mediums, have in common a setting (a tradition, religion, society, and so on) which gives a particular role to the channel. The purpose is clearly defined, there is a social ceremony or setting, and the training orients the channel to carry out a defined role. Thus, there is an understanding about what questions can be asked and a consistent metaphysical view about what is happening, thereby avoiding the unconstrained and contradictory metaphysical assertions that are current today. Further, this channeling has an accepted place in the society or subgroup. It fits in with the norms and receives social support. Admittedly, some of the Hebrew prophets were not always well received by the rulers, but that has to do with their messages, not their prophetic profession.

Most of the channels in the current phase are not characters within a context. The advantages of broad social support are not theirs, and their role is more often that of an eccentric, at least in relation to the mainstream, even though there is interest within various subgroups of society. An advantage of this position is that there is more independence and creativity possible outside a conditioned social role. The disadvantage is that the channeler cannot draw on social resources for education, training, ethical values, and protection.

Problems of Social Exclusion

Because of the lack of social acceptance, channels are susceptible to a variety of status maladies, such as these:

1. From the mainstream point of view, channelers may be seen as frauds, self-deceived, or mentally disturbed. Messages of value may be ignored or discounted by others. Personal and social insights may be overlooked. The channel may be rejected personally or socially ostracized.

2. The person who is channeling can feel isolated and different. There may be worries about being crazy or mentally unbalanced. This is true whether the person is channeling for the public or is simply hearing a private inner voice. It is true even when the person is functioning well, is mentally healthy, and the messages are helpful and positive. Psychologist Alfred Alschuler (1987) describes his personal alarm when he began hearing an inner voice, "I was worried this might be the beginning of a breakdown." It wasn't, but he had to continually remind himself that he was not psychotic and that he was doing his job effectively. The fears themselves can lead to mental distress and defensiveness. They may also motivate the channel to compensate with feelings of being special, chosen, and beyond others. But this, of course, is simply another form of separation from others and does not provide interpersonal support.

3. The channel may be seen as a gifted visionary by his or her audience, a group which can turn into "groupies." These folks can become true believers, attributing to the channel special knowledge, powers, insight, and cosmic connections—without good cause. The group becomes an elite, privy to special knowledge. Idiosyncratic views of the world can be promoted that are socially or personally unhealthy. In these situations, the dynamics of groups and individuals are well known. People give the leader emotional authority. There is a transference reaction—feeling that the channel or entity is like a parent or a grownup to a child and knows more, can do more, and holds the power of approval and disapproval. This projection is similar to reactions to many people in positions of prominence—rock stars, statesmen, sports stars, professors, physicians, ministers, TV evangelists, Nobel prize winners, and others who are often given credence for comments far outside their area of expertise. It is one of the reactions that usually has to be addressed in psychotherapy for the person to develop personal self-esteem, freedom of choice, and good judgment.

4. Egocentric reactions and inflated feelings of self-worth can result from the dynamics described in Number 3. Coexisting with these feelings are feelings of insecurity and vulnerability. The channel is surrounded by a group of followers, many of whom are serious, professional, and respected community types, who give positive comments and

strokes. He or she rarely receives objective feedback or honest criticism, and the desire for these is ambiguous at best. It is no wonder that they may think of themselves as being super special (just as do some rock stars, statesmen, professors, and other authority figures). This may lead to unfortunate consequences. On a grand scale, the channel may take the group to Montana in preparation for Armageddon, announce the coming of Christ in London, or plan for UFOs to arrive in Los Angeles. On a lesser scale, an in-group develops, like a cult. If a channel or entity appears to be genuinely spiritually wise, certainly one should respect this, but there are enough cases of gurus and religious leaders who have fallen prey to money, fame, and sex to show that uncritical deference does not serve their integrity. These are hard lessons for channels, entities, and followers alike.

CONTEMPORARY APPROACHES

There are today a few channeling development programs in a public format offered by private "psychic centers" or individuals. They are at an introductory level and usually purport to teach how to channel, which may mean contacting inner guides, speaking in the voice and role of an entity, or using intuition or psychic functioning (which is not channeling in the usual sense). The programs rarely give attention to quality control, that is, the level of the material, the attitudes of the participants, and the training of the entity.

Books are also available describing how to learn channeling. J. Donald Walters (1987), a spiritual leader in the yoga lineage of Paramahansa Yogananda, takes the position that other beings and realities outside the ego exist and can be channeled. But he rightly cautions that uncritical belief and ego-satisfaction can mislead and lead to dependency. The entities do not communicate spiritual discipline, nor do they have a sense of how to be a spiritual teacher. His theme is that higher truth can only come if a person cultivates spiritual development and motives. He recommends communicating any inspiration as a way of testing and exploring its value, not as a way of imposing the truth on others.

A similar perspective is developed by Carla Rueckert in *How to Channel*, a well-written and professional discussion of the personal qualities and preparation needed for being a channel (Rueckert, 1987). She urges meditation, self-understanding, and an honest consideration of one's motives. Desiring to be special or to get the admiration of others are temptations. The motive for the best channeling is a desire and willingness to be of service to humanity. Do not try to learn it by yourself, she says, but work with a teacher or group. Reuckert does not present specific techniques for learning the process—it's easy enough, she says, but should be learned directly from a teacher.

The book *Opening to Channel* by channels Sanaya Roman and Duane Packer (1987) presents a how-to-do-it approach using guided visualization in a relaxed trance state, presumably something the person can do in his or her own home, alone or with a partner. The authors suggest the imagery of a doorway through which one imagines the guide coming. "Sense this guide," they write. "Feel his or her love for you. Be open to receive. Feel your heart welcoming this guide. Feel the response. Believe that it is really happening!" (p. 81). The authors believe that the imagination is the person's closest ability to channeling and that this is the easiest connection the guide has to the person. Whatever imagination might be in this case, it is certain that this type of visualization process can produce independent figures in the mind, with information and ideas that are different from the conscious ego.

Meditation, prayer, and inner work have been precursors for many persons' initiation into channeling. This is true for many spiritual leaders such as Joseph Smith and Muhammad, and for others, such as Paul Tuttle and the third category of persons in the study of inner voices by Myrtle Heery, described in an earlier chapter. Some contemporary channels experienced spontaneous beginnings, but usually these come to a person who is already interested in psychic matters. One channel was driving on a freeway in Los Angeles when a voice in her head told her to pull over to the side of the road and get out a pen and paper. The voice repeated this three times before she paid attention to it. When she followed the instructions, her hand began to write automatically. The message was that she was being prepared to channel. This woman had taught psychology in a community college, was interested in psychic matters, and considered herself unsatisfied with the answers she had found. However, she had not cultivated an interest in channeling, and this was a surprise to her.

Stages of Development

Most channeling does not happen all at once, coming out of the blue to a person hitherto oblivious. In her research on thirteen mediums, that is, channels, Margaret Chandley (1986) found that there was a general, though not absolute, progression of understanding and skills. She interviewed trance-channels—people who are professional mediums—ranging in age from 30 to 50 in the Los Angeles and San Francisco areas. Interviews and a questionnaire enabled Chandley to group the development of channels into seven phases.

The first phase she describes is one of conceptualization. This is simply the person recognizing that there is a nonphysical reality. This may come through hearing voices, out-of-body experiences, psychic abilities, contact with a deceased person, and the impact of images, fantasies, and dreams. These often occurred in childhood. The average age for these experiences was 14.8 years in Chandley's survey. For these mediums, the experiences were accepted as indicating a nonphysical reality, whereas in ordinary cultural norms, these experiences would recede in importance.

The second phase is a stage of preparation in which the nonphysical level is nurtured through meditation, visualization, psychic studies, hypnosis, voice dialogue, and other methods that seem to prepare the mind to accept the nonphysical dimension of the psyche. This is a more intentional activity and may involve work with teachers who are mediums or channels. Chandley noted that emotions, including anger and grief, often arise at this stage. It is also at this stage that issues of ego control and grounding arise.

The next phase is described as gestation in which, Chandley says, the energies activated are taking form in the unconscious. During this phase, there arises the issue of responsibility for bringing through the energy to be channeled. Twelve of the thirteen cases Chandley studied had experiences of physical symptoms such as changes in body sensations, sounds, lights, pains, chakra activation, and vibrations at this point in their development.

Phase four is the recognition of the energy, which at this point becomes imagery or form, that is, an entity, guide, and so on. Chandley does not say why the individuals develop channeling rather than psychic abilities or healing, for example. This phase is a choice point for mediums, who must decide either to continue to interact with the channeled energy or to return to the gestation phase and work with the emotional system. Here, the mediums interviewed commented on the sense of purpose, the desire to teach and assist others, and feelings of harmony, peace, and love.

The fifth phase is that of activation, where there is a full identification of the entity or energy source as separate from the medium's own personality. With Chandley's subjects these were classified into three realms: spirit (including the unconscious level of self), archetypal or angelic, and extraterrestrial. The person is presenting himself or herself as a channel and is continually attuning and adjusting in relationship to the entities.

In the sixth phase, integration with the energy, there is a trust and comfort that develops between the medium and the nonphysical energy. This trust facilitates the transmission of information that is self-empowering and inspiring. Each individual carries out this integration with his or her own unique methods of expressing and utilizing the experience.

Maturation is the seventh phase that Chandley postulates. During this phase, there is a movement toward a unified final personality, a whole of self-actualization in which the channeled energy is not necessarily separate from the self. There is a perspective on purpose and value that is more objective and may more fully be at transpersonal levels. Chandley is more tentative about this stage of unification, but I know several examples of individuals who moved from channeling to a more unified personality state. One person channeled an entity named Galileo for several years, then stopped. She told me that she felt the purpose of the channeling was to move her mind past its limits. Another, previously mentioned, who channeled a source named Pleiades, felt that she had incorporated their functions into her own capacities, which was one of the purposes intended. Suzanne Kluss Malkin (1989) wrote of her personal experiences, first in channeling, then in realizing the information was serious and real, and finally in coming to the realization that she was accessing her own source of information and wisdom, which she called Spirit. In this last phase, she said that channeling would have felt like an artificial barrier between herself and the insight that was available to her from some level of her own self.

Chandley also notes that several of the mediums had difficult childhoods, some of them abusive, but she does not speculate whether this is a factor in their development. This does suggest a similarity between trance channeling and a secondary or multiple personality, since almost all multiples have experienced abusive childhoods, and this was a factor in their personality splitting. An earlier study of mediums showed the same occurrence of emotional trauma. Alain Assailly (1963) reported that of ten mediums he studied, four had violent fathers, and many had emotional problems with their parents, difficult adolescence, and unhappy marriages. Earlier we noted that there was emotional abuse in Jane Roberts' childhood.

Chandley's point of view is that there are physical and nonphysical energies that go through processes of development, and the "mediumistic personality" is developed through the phases she describes to handle and integrate the nonphysical energies. Her studies were of contemporary, professional channels, so I would not expect them to apply equally well to those who are amateurs, historical figures, or those who experience inner voices. Many channels may have quite different processes of development. Chandley's analysis makes clear, however, that there can be preparation and development of the channeling capacity, and there are psychological issues to be addressed in the process.

Some other studies suggest that channeling abilities tend to manifest in adulthood. Joy Young (1986) found that for twenty-six respondents in the U.S., and an equal number in England and Scotland, the greatest number had their initial channeling experience between the ages of twenty-two and thirty-five. This would probably be in the fourth phase in Chandley's model. In the study of psychics by Charles Millar (1990), 86 percent reported they first experienced channeling as an adult. The percentages of initial channeling experiences during the teen years was low. Seventy-nine percent experienced automatic writing and 44 percent experienced inner voices initially as adults. However, 43 percent indicated they first experienced inner voices as a child.

CHAPTER 13

CHANNELS AND ENTITIES

It should be evident that the person who channels is not a disinterested agent in this whole matter. In addition to the social difficulties outlined in the previous chapter, there are problematic issues that arise in all forms, and more so with trance-speaking and public channeling. In discussing these issues, it will be useful to speak of the entities and channels as autonomous, separate personalities, which they are, regardless of the origin of the former.

THE ENTITIES SPEAK ON CHANNELS

We can get a useful perspective if we ask how an *entity* might view the responsibilities of the person who is channeling him or her. We will indulge in a bit of fantasy channeling! I seem to be channeling the notes from a committee meeting of entities, held in some transpersonal region of the imagination. Let's find out what they recommend for the training of those who channel them.

Resolutions

Be It Resolved that the Entities Committee on the Training and Development of Channels recommends the following:

1. *That persons desirous of learning to channel should have a "real" job, so their livelihood does not depend on our presence. [Unanimously passed, with the question of fulltime prophets and the Delphic priestess referred to a subcommittee.]*
2. *That channels should read, study, and in many ways improve and broaden their knowledge, ideas, language, and experience so that their minds are available to express the clearest and best messages we can communicate. [Adopted with applause.]*
3. *That they do something about their own biases, emotional conflicts, and other personality difficulties. Otherwise their problems color our messages. [Several members of the committee asked if entities should also be free from emotional bias, present company excepted, of course. The chair pointed out that this should be referred to the Entity Quality Control committee.]*

4. That channels should learn to reduce their desire for approval, fame, or specialness as a result of channeling. The committee recommends that they cultivate nonattached receptivity. [One entity objected to this as irrelevant and was accused by another of being codependent with his channel. A scuffle ensued and both were ejected into lower level time-space dimensions of the repressed unconscious.]

5. That if they use us for guidance, they learn to test and judge what we say, so they retain their own choice and power. [What, asked a group entity of teachers, about the value of ego surrender; what about accepting an answer that goes beyond their own rational thinking? After discussion the committee added the phrase, "except in cases that appropriately transcend the self," which caused demands for definitions and comments that it was worse. Barely adopted with a recommendation for further study.]

6. That they keep their friends from asking questions about real estate, changing jobs, their soulmate, and whether a past life has got them into this mess. [That's the only fun I ever get, said one member, who was hooted down by the others.]

7. That they refrain from believing that we are omniscient even if we believe it ourselves. [Committee comment: We know this is true.]

8. That channels develop their own regular inner practice that enables them to develop higher motives and spiritual values, and that they cultivate friends and relationships that go beyond their channeling role. [Unanimous approval.]

9. That they learn when to stop channeling and go to the next stage of intuition, growth, and relationship. [Adopted without dissent.]

10. That channels stop asking who we are, thus causing us to fabricate an impressive name and biasing our character. [Some members disagreed, saying they thought it was useful to play Socrates or Commander Astara. Others indignantly said they were Socrates and Commander Astara. Resolution passed on a split vote.]

11. That channels develop the wisdom to know when these resolutions apply and when they do not. [Adopted unanimously.]

The entities have said it well. If I were to oversimplify, they focus on three themes, ones that human observers have also noted. The first is that the channel should have emotional health and balance. The second is that the channel will gain by elevating and stabilizing his or her values, mental control, and spiritual level. The third is that the channel should have a separate identity and should have a healthy, communicative relationship to the source or entity—not one of dependence or passiveness. On this latter point, one has only to review the discussions held by Moses and other prophets with God to know that one can have one's own sense of self, even in a relationship with the Other.

Another identity problem for the channel is becoming caught up in the fame of the entity, becoming a devotee or subordinate to its authority. Personal identity is difficult enough for some people without it depending on some spooky spirit that talks out of their mouths. Another concern might be that the state of dissociation involved might lead to psychological instability. However, the cases of channeling I have seen do not suggest this result. Rather, there is often an opposite effect of too little dissociation, in which the messages of the entity reflect elements of the person's desires or complexes, and the person and others give them undue authority because the messages activate these elements in their psyches. This is another cause that leads to cult formation, rigid belief systems, and emotional dependence on the part of the devotees. Channels and entities in this kind of relationship often seem to develop a charisma that appeals to their followers' need for certainty.

THE MEDIUM CONTRIBUTES TO THE MESSAGE

Most channels say that they "transmit" the messages from the entities without any changes or alterations. Phrases like "pure channel" and "I just get out of the way" are often heard. I recall asking one channel if she was sure that the message was from the entity (Christ, in this case). She stopped for a moment and then reported that she had asked . . . and received the confirmation that the message was from the entity not from her. This is like reading the newspaper a second time to confirm that it was right the first time. One cannot take the word of the entity that it is correct or that the source is outside the mind of the person.

The evidence suggests that the person is not purely a vehicle in this process. Whether the entity is from inside the self or from outside, its messages are certainly influenced, even skewed, by the language, beliefs, personality dynamics, and experience of the channel. I have not encountered a channel, contemporary or otherwise, that did not have an influence on the channeled material.

Carla A. Rueckert, herself a knowledgeable and experienced channel, says that as much as 25 percent of the material comes from the person. I think this is a conservative estimate; Bailey's Tibetan said that only 15 percent of the channeled teachings overall came from discarnate teachers. One of the entities communicating through Geraldine Cummins in Great Britain identified himself as the psychical researcher Frederic Myers and insisted that the medium should be considered an interpreter, not a conduit. He commented that the spirits had to impress thoughts and ideas on the person's mind at a subconscious level. These are then clothed in words and concepts supplied by the person. In addition, any strong point of view held by the medium is likely to intrude into the content. Said the channeled Myers, "You should study the medium, and if you perceive any very strong prejudice expressed, you will know that it comes from the subconscious overflow, and not from the poor shade who has the greatest difficulty in contending with any fixed ideas in the medium's deeper mind" (Cummins, 1932, p. 182).

This interpretation process sometimes occurs at a more conscious level. David Spangler says that his channeled messages come as a complex bundle of meaning and feelings, which he then has to put into language. (This reminded me of Patience Worth, who said that she rolled her meaning up into a golden ball and threw it into Mrs. Curran's mind.) Once, when I was apparently communicating with entities in a light trance state, I sensed their message in a kinesthetic way—which I then had to describe to myself or put words to. It was like the experience in which one says, "I know what I want to say but I have to find the words to say it." There is a felt sense which has to be unpacked into language, and one knows when the words and feeling are congruent. Perhaps a similar case is Joseph Smith, who, when "translating" the Book of Mormon, said that he would see in his mind the symbols from the gold plates and then the translation. A revelation to a friend said that the method was to "study it out in your mind," and if the words were right, "it will cause that your bosom shall burn within you" (*Doctrine and Covenants*, 1949, p. 18).

LANGUAGE, CONCEPTS, AND EXPERIENCE

In all cases, the messages are put into the language and concepts of the channel. These are learned in childhood and become automatic. Language always has assumptions about the world built into it and, even without knowing it, the channel's messages are framed within those assumptions. English, for example, includes assumptions about objects being separate, linear causes and effects, natural polarities, and sequential time. Any message in English has these implicit assumptions. At the next level of semantics, the message must be in the vocabulary of the channel. The words the channel knows determine the building blocks of the message. Here again the channel influences the message.

At the level of knowledge and experience, the channel supplies the raw material for the message, and a naive or uneducated channel (intellectually and/or emotionally) is unlikely to enable complex messages. Tam Mossman reports a comment from a colleague about a trance channel he was trying to assist. "Last night, her entities more or less threw in the towel. They want to deliver some really important and helpful information, but she won't read the books that will give her the vocabulary they need. Until she makes some effort to educate herself, there's nothing they can do" (Mossman, 1986, p. 14).

PREDISPOSITIONS AND EMOTIONS

Often a channel's emotional predispositions, more than just the language and concepts, will influence the attitude and advice coming through the entity. I collected accounts of several personal readings with one particular channel, and the theme that emerged was "Do what your heart's desire is; don't give in to social conventions." The entity (Christ) advised questioners to drop out of school, change jobs, and said that they knew better than those who disagreed with them. It was not difficult to recognize the consistent theme of the messages, which would resonate with feelings the individual was having and usually was conflicted about. But I also knew that the person channeling had, after inner struggle, decided to drop out of school herself. Giving similar advice to others would reflect her need to justify her decision. One can see in Seth's discussions of God the reflection of concerns that Jane Roberts had about her Catholic childhood. The revelations of both Muhammad and Joseph Smith were criticized, especially the later ones, for catering to the prophets' personal viewpoints and political needs. Perhaps an example of cultural influence is in Edgar Cayce's health diagnoses and remedies, which were largely within the folk remedy and home treatment medicine of the South, where he lived.

Emotional reactions of the channel can intrude into channeled communication. Joy Young (1986) asked eleven therapists who considered themselves channels about difficulties in using channeling in counseling. Most of them pointed to the problem of projection—the emotional issues and problems of the counselor being projected into the channeled information about the other person. The channel needs to have worked through his or her own shadow issues and conflicts. If a channel is not trained to be detached, as Eileen J. Garrett was trained, then the pressures of performance and need for approval will influence what is communicated.

These cases show that the channeled messages are affected by the feelings, language, and point of view of the channel. Any message is a translation, even a partial construction by the channel, influenced by the personality of the channel and drawing on the deeper dynamics of the mind. The channel is rarely aware of this and often rejects the idea. From the point of view of the entity as a separate ego, this situation becomes a barrier to communication because emotional pressures prevent objective perception.

COMMUNICATION PROBLEMS AND SOLUTIONS

Channeled communication is difficult enough anyway. The entity Frederic Myers, speaking through yet another channel after his death, said, "The nearest simile I can find to express the difficulties of sending a message is that I appear to be standing behind a sheet of frosted glass which blurs sight and deadens sounds—dictating feebly to a reluctant and somewhat obtuse secretary" (Johnson, 1955, p. 161).

I have come across several instances in which the communicating entity had to resort to ingenious tricks to get a word across to the channel, not because of emotional bias, but for some unknown reason. Raj, trying to get a word through to Susan Tuttle, knew that she was a seamstress. He showed her a mental picture of cloth interface material. "Interface?" she said. She did not know the relevance of the word, but the person she was talking to, a computer operator, understood immediately. When Pearl Curran was writing one of her novels, Patience Worth could not get her to receive the name of a character. Patience got Pearl to think of Christmas, then Christmas carol, then "Carol," the name itself. One of Geraldine Cummins' communicators was trying to dictate the initials D.I., and had to associate them with D-Day for her to get them. In another instance, the entities told a medium that they had worked subconsciously on her mind to prepare it to comprehend some of the concepts they needed to communicate.

Still, some channeled messages do go beyond what the channel knows or has experienced, and this is certainly true of the more extraordinary cases. Patience Worth used words and gave information not available from Mrs. Curran, and the same is true of the writings of Geraldine Cummins. Also, we have seen cases in which channels produce inspirational material, art, metaphysics, and channeled advice that transcend at least their conscious and perhaps unconscious abilities. It is as though a higher level of ideation or ability is functioning, although it uses the words or physical body of the channel. These cases raise provocative questions. They can be considered evidence for outside entities, for complex telepathic ability of the channel, or for the existence of extraordinary abilities in the subconscious or superconscious mind. Whatever the origin, the material does not come purely from an independent entity, but is colored by the person doing the channeling.

PARTNERS

Many channels have a partner in their work, a human one, that is. Often this is a spouse or close friend who is involved in their life and their channeling activities. This is true of several well-known channels—Jane Roberts, Alice A. Bailey, Helen Schucman—and of lesser known ones as well. The role of the partner seems to be emotional support, assistance in the practical necessities of channeling, engaging with the entity, and often providing feedback for the process. I do not know of any duo who jointly channel—rather, one is the channel, and the other is a companion in relation to the work of the channel.

Jane Roberts' husband, Robert Butts, was an integral part of communicating with Seth. Butts supported and reassured Jane and, at the same time, probably provided some focus and containment. He talked with Seth, took down in writing the dictation and statements of Seth, and maintained the continuity of the record. As a professional artist, he painted an intuitive portrait of Seth, adding a visual dimension to the process. (Seth commented that it did look like him.) The writings by Jane show a warm, close relationship between her and Robert; they shared much beyond the Seth experiences.

The husband of Pearl Curran was a key figure in her channeling of Patience Worth. He took full responsibility for recording the sessions with Patience Worth. Dialog, poetry, epigrams, and table talk were all carefully noted and typed, with information about participants, accounts of discussions, and occasional comments such as noting that the party adjourned to the dining room for refreshments or that they had seen an interesting motion picture which stimulated a poem or message. We do not see much of his personality in any of the transcripts, but the meticulous recording shows dedication to Mrs. Curran and her channeling. His dedication must also have been social and financial, since the Currans never took money for hosting the many seances, guests, researchers, and reporters in their home.

John Curran died in 1922, after keeping the records for seven years. Others took over, but without his attention to detail. There are gaps of time, no reporting of dialog, and mostly just the bare words of Patience. The context of the words, so important for understanding, is not recorded. Reading the record, my distinct impression is that the intensity and quality began to decline at that point. Although Mrs. Curran had friends, there was none who was a partner with her.

Alice A. Bailey met Foster Bailey, her husband to be, while working for the Theosophical Society. They were both interested in Theosophical teachings and worked together in the Society until politics and disagreements caused them to go their separate way. It was just about the time they were married in 1921 that the first of the Tibetan books appeared, and they were teaching classes on Theosophy together. Foster seemed to fill the role of "production manager" for the public activities which, it was said, he carried out in love and service, making the work his own. He was instrumental in founding the Arcane School for study of the teachings, and in establishing the Lucis Trust, which publishes the A.A.B. writings. So far as I can tell, there is no indication that he helped in his wife's writing or channeling. When A.A.B. died in 1949, he continued with the organizations that disseminate the teachings.

The relation between Helen Schucman, scribe of *A Course in Miracles,* and her partner, Bill Thetford, was not marital. They were academic colleagues in a psychology department. Their personal chemistry was intense. They argued; they rubbed each other the wrong way. But they highly respected each other, and there clearly was an emotional bond. In Course lore, they are referred to as Helen and Bill, as though they were the twin co-authors.

Indeed, it is likely that the material would not have been written without both of them, for the symbiotic relation was necessary for the support of Helen in her writing. Helen was frequently frightened as she took the dictation for the Course. She was afraid of the content and alarmed at hearing the voice. When she brought in her shorthand transcript, she would read it aloud for Bill to copy. She was sometimes so distressed that she became temporarily blind and could not see the page during the reading. Bill would reassure her and work with her until the vision cleared. Bill was the supporter, the one who was curious about the material and the meaning, and the one who encouraged and comforted Helen throughout the writing.

Both of them thought that the Course had been given for them personally. Thus, Bill was not simply an outside colleague, but was a cause and evoker of the material, and they felt it was directed to him as well as Helen. I would expect that some of the contents and ideas were of particular relevance to Bill. Bill was more interested than Helen was in the metaphysical aspects of the material and how it fit into other spiritual teachings. He began to read books and attend lectures on metaphysical, psychic, and spiritual topics. In a discussion that he and I had, he recommended to me Robert Crookall's book *The Interpretation of Cosmic and Mystical Experiences*, which analyzes information from channeling, psychic perceptions, and mystical experiences in order to map the levels of transpersonal consciousness (Crookall, 1969). He often took Helen to lectures, much against her desires. In going to one lecture, he said that he had to "literally" drag her kicking and screaming up the stairs; she was protesting all the way. At that lecture they met Eileen J. Garrett, who showed great interest in the Course material.

Thetford was also more comfortable with teaching and presenting the Course. Helen was ambivalent, but Bill took it as a matter of course (he could. since he hadn't channeled it!). In a way, he could do what she could not in accepting the material as authentic. It was as though each represented half of a whole; one holding the doubt, the other the acceptance.

There are other cases in which a partnership is involved. W. B. Yeats' wife was a medium and received material for him through automatic writing. The "spirits" said "We have come to give you metaphors for poetry." It was a collaboration, with Yeats managing the sessions while his wife was in a trance, writing or speaking and responding to his questions. He developed the material into a system of human types, historical cycles, and oppositions, based on metaphorical phases of the moon. It took form as his book *A Vision* (Yeats, 1938).

Also in the literary mode, Pulitzer Prize recipient James Merrill's poetry includes many lines spelled out by a Ouija Board—printed in capitals—presented often as a dialog with the author. The board was worked jointly by Merrill and a friend, D. J. In the introduction to *The Book of Ephraim*, Merrill says he will write "The Book of a Thousand and One Evenings Spent / With David Jackson at the Ouija Board / In Touch with Ephraim Our

Familiar Spirit" (Merrill, 1982). The board discusses both Merrill and Jackson, and it seems clear that Jackson is an important partner in the process. The writing is more personal and introspective than the work by Yeats. The spirits—Mirabell, Ephraim, and others—write both blank and rhymed verse quite well; Merrill has received Bollingen and National Book awards for his work.

Another case of partnership is with an entity called Gildas, channeled by Ruth White in England. Her associate is Mary Swainson, a psychotherapist, of whom she was once a client. The two talk together with Gildas and conduct group sessions. Gildas was quite active in helping them learn to have a dialog with him, encouraging them to ask questions without hesitation and to follow intuitions (White and Swainson, 1971). Another example is Pat Rodegast, who presents a being called Emmanuel and who leads group sessions with her friend Judith Stanton. The work with Emmanuel has involved both of them.

The partners answer the needs of the channel for protection, support, and balance. These are necessities whether a channel has a partner and associates or works individually. One can observe many ways besides having a partner that these needs have been met. The priestess of the Delphic Oracle had the priests who trained her, structured her role, and handled all the inquiries and procedures. Carla Rueckert, who channels Ra in a small study group, is carefully eased into the channeling state in quiet surroundings and privacy, with a specific ritual. Paul Tuttle, channeling Raj, travels with his family, and they run seminars together. Eileen J. Garrett received intensive training and feedback from J. Hewat McKenzie of the British College of Psychic Science; later her spirit guides Uvani and Abdul Latif managed the trance state. Edgar Cayce always had a conductor run the session—his wife, son, or a close friend. Ken Carey moved, with his family, to an isolated country location and wrote *Starseed Transmissions* while in seclusion.

DIFFICULTIES WITH ENTITIES

Not only should the channeler work with his or her own process, but the entity should receive some training. The uncritical assumption made by most who channel is that the being is in a state of spiritual elevation, higher consciousness, and omniscience. Often the entity says so or implies it (just like some earthbound ministers and gurus). However, it is my conclusion that, whatever their status, they can benefit from feedback from human personalities. These beings are not all-knowing and make mistakes, mislead individuals, and often speak that which they do not know. Their ESP, as was noted in earlier chapters, is not 100 percent accurate; in fact, it is about the same as ESP levels in the normal personality. Their comments often contradict each other, especially on metaphysical topics such as karma, reincarnation, UFOs, and the nature of reality. Spiritually, few are in the realm of transpersonal or transcendent states. Their egos are usually well established. They are often very desirous of attention from their audience. These characteristics are true of many entities, and have been observed by many objective researchers, scholars, and spirit mediums.

Yet many channelers are in awe of their entities and give them free rein. As we noted, Alice A. Bailey said that she never changed a word that was dictated to her and, in my opinion, the writing suffers. The same need for editing shows in the books dictated by Seth, though to Jane Roberts' credit, she wrote books of her own on Sethian topics which were more focused in content and style. If the masters are so egocentric as to insist that every word is a perfect pearl, then they need help from us, rather than the reverse.

USEFUL FEEDBACK FOR ENTITIES

What kinds of dialog would be useful for channeled entities? I would suggest these.

1. *Feedback on personal information.* Like any therapist, teacher, or psychic practitioner, the entity can benefit from feedback on the accuracy and relevance of the information. Planned feedback on readings, predictions, personal advice, and so on, should be given.

2. *Questions, discussion, editing, and critique of written or spoken materials.* Some entities are impervious to this—Patience Worth brooked no trifling with her writing, and Helen tried to alter some words of the Course but found she had to change them back for the material to be consistent. However, a considerable amount of channeled writing and speaking is poorly phrased, disorganized, jargonish, and stays at one level of abstraction. Editing and questioning will be instructive for the entity, if it is willing to take commentary, and will develop healthy independent judgment on the part of the channel.

3. *The entity and the channel must learn to respect each other's needs.* The relationship must be one in which each can communicate and be respected. Negotiation and dialog can be learned by each. The needs of each personality must be understood by the other. Lawrence LeShan was once monitoring a session with Eileen J. Garrett, in which the personality of a very talkative doctor was communicating through her body. LeShan realized that the session was going on so long that Garrett would be exhausted and tried to get the doctor to leave. He refused and insisted that, as a doctor, he could tell how things were in the medium's body. LeShan would have none of it and told the doctor that if he did not leave, he would not be allowed to return; the doctor finally agreed.

Channels and entities need to discuss when and where channeling can occur, which topics are all right and which (if any) are not, the emotional needs of the person, the ethics and responsibilities of the entity, the impact on the everyday, practical life of the channel, and other issues.

4. *Explorations of specializations.* There needs to be an awareness of any special topics or abilities of the entity. Just as some TV stations focus on religion, others sports or news, the entities tend to have particular interests. It may be that personal counseling or guidance is the major interest, or social and environmental concerns. Inspirational preaching or development of consciousness and compassion may be a strength. Once recognized, the focus and quality of the material can be strengthened and developed. But other possibilities can also be explored. For example, Jane Roberts tested Seth for psychic functioning. Our present channeling trends are mostly in the areas of psychological and spiritual concerns, but there may be potentials for channeling artistic creativity, inventions, technological ideas, literature, physical skills, and other human potentials.

5. *Responsibilities of the entity.* I wonder if there should not be some awareness of ethical responsibilities. I don't know if the Order of Ancient, Present, and Future Channeled Entities has set up an ethics committee, but channels need to be clear that the entities need to be responsible in terms of human relationships and ethics.

PROBLEMS OF ENTITIES

While entities may claim to be angels or masters, it is obvious that many have not left their personalities behind, or else they are reflecting the personality aspects of the channel. They have reactions, traits, and attitudes that are problematic, just as they would be with humans. It might be helpful to identify some of these pitfalls.

1. *Desires for approval, dependency, fame, and money.* I met one entity who told me he was going to make his hostess famous. She did not object. This did not seem like a good sign to me! (It didn't happen, so much for omnipotence.) Other entities, usually with the agreement of the channel, seem to encourage followers to give them total emotional belief and attention. These tendencies are ego traps in entities as well as humans. Sometimes they are subtle and may reflect the desires of the channel coming through the personality of the entity. When the channel's income depends on the entity, there are usually difficulties. Expectations and needs are likely to be imposed on the entity, where independence and mutual rights should hold.

2. *Giving authority to the personal needs of the channel.* The media reported that Ramtha was at one time recommending that followers buy horses bred and sold by J. Z. Knight, who channels him. Other entities have given direct support to the private life of the channel. The later revelations of Muham-

mad often fell in line with the personal and political desires of the prophet, a fact noted by those around him and especially those who did not agree with him. The Mormon prophet, Joseph Smith, also received channeled revelations that authorized him to have multiple wives, but this revelation was kept secret for several years. Returning to current times, one can pay a hefty fee and dine with one channel and his entity.

3. *Self-aggrandizement.* Claims of enlightenment, higher evolvement, and superiority are red flags with entities, just as with ordinary humans. One current entity announces that he is a god and that he is here to teach the rest of us to be gods. His manner is more of a warrior king than a god, with the rest of us as his subjects. Higher wisdom and values should be self-evident, not self-proclaimed. If an entity cannot shift from a condescending attitude, it is not likely to develop healthy relationships with those who attend to it.

4. *Misuse of the channel.* Some unconstrained entities do things that abuse the person who channels them. They may stay in the body for long periods of time, exhausting the person, or insist on coming through so frequently that the person has no time of her own. Jane Roberts often seemed consumed by her channeling. I have heard of an entity that occupies the channel's body and eats and drinks, leaving the channel with a hangover and a few pounds heavier. There must be negotiation between the entity and the person to respect the needs of each.

5. *Metaphysical speculations.* Some entities are enthusiastic about metaphysical talk—other realities, levels of consciousness, karma, and grand schemes of the universe. Some talk of little else; their *raison d'etre* is to explain these matters to us. For example, the *Urantia Book* and *Oahspe* include much metaphysics. I take a dim view of these, because the ideas are so far away from outer or inner verification. There are, after all, experiences of mystics and visionaries, and scientific and philosophical analyses of the external world which lend themselves to questioning and disciplined consideration. The metaphysical material of the entities is flat assertion, laid out authoritatively. Unfortunately, there is usually no reasoning or data given in support of these theories. At one of my lectures on channeling, a member of the audience commented in a puzzled way that the entities did not agree with each other in descriptions of metaphysics and often were contradictory. I was not puzzled at all, because it seemed evident that they were making it up or doing the best they could without definite information.

Belief in these metaphysical vistas comes from the emotional or intellectual thrill of the assumed knowledge or the grand scope of the systems or ideas. It does not come from their applicability to worldly affairs or personal transformational work. It may be that some of these systems are projections and symbols of inner reality. Many channeled works such as Blake's *Jerusalem* are, and this might account for some of the attraction at an unconscious level. Others, such as the revelations of the prophets or the Koran of Muhammad, are attractive because they seem to hold answers to the mystery of the universe and, in this sense, some are religious systems, though with more limited social impact.

Unfortunately, questions about these matters are often urged on the entity by the channel or others, because they want to know the truth about these topics that so interest them, and they assume that the entity—being an advanced being—must know. Few entities can ignore the opportunity to respond, but they should be encouraged to resist the temptation. Patience Worth was exemplary in this respect; she never talked about spirits, the levels of heaven, or psychic phenomena. She usually applied her sharp tongue to those who asked questions about them.

6. *Poor-quality messages.* Throughout this book, it should be evident that many channeled messages are lacking in content, and it is only the emotional tone and the assertion of coming from disembodied space beings, or whatever, that give them appeal, usually to persons who have not learned to be emotionally or intellectually critical. Dennis Stillings says it dramatically: "I have watched rooms full of goggle-eyed channeling groupies listening slack-jawed to an hour of the most hackneyed drivel imaginable" (Stillings, 1986). When famous people are channeled, such as Einstein, Tesla, Swedenborg, Washington, even psychologist and psychic researcher William James, the character and level of their thinking goes down so far that one historian commented, "If the great minds of this world degenerate so much in the next [world] the prospect for lesser fry is bleak indeed" (Gauld, 1968, p. 18). James, *in vivo,* quoted a Connecticut congressman, Sidney Deane, who said, "The names of scholars and thinkers who once lived are affixed to the most ungrammatical and weakest of *bosh.* . . ." (Murphy and Ballou, 1960, p. 51). This description also applies to many messages from not-so-famous scholars and thinkers.

It is not worthwhile to listen to this level of message, or even to offer the entity a self-improvement course. It is important to learn to detect channeled nonsense through educated judgment, knowledge about these topics, and a reduction in emotional dependency. In this book, I have tried to give enough varied cases of channeling for readers to develop caution along with curiosity. Do not put one's full weight on any message, but keep a part of one's commitment in reserve. Of course, a side benefit of this approach is that it also could protect us from propaganda, sales pitches, religious fanatics, and politicians on the human side of things. Perhaps we could practice on channeled entities, since sometimes they are more obvious.

CHAPTER 14

OVERVIEW

Now let us step back for an overview of what we have learned about channeling. We have defined it as receiving coherent, purposeful communications from a source other than the conscious mind, a source that appears to have a personality or consciousness. We have found some form of this process in every period of history, though the name given it has varied: oracle, prophecy, inspiration, revelation, possession, mediumship, channeling. It is found in many cultures even today. Our overview will set the stage for discussing possible models for the source of these communications and for evaluating the significance of contributions of channeling to human society.

WHAT HAS COME THROUGH CHANNELING?

First, there is the consideration of the kinds of messages or expressions that have come through channeling. The following list indicates the major subjects and the forms they take, with the caveat that their quality varies.

Poetry, novels, short stories, plays, essays, poetry embedded in prose

Musical and artistic performances

Written music compositions

Mathematics, scientific concepts, cosmology

Governance and political decisions

Social commentary, utopian models

Community organization and development

Military strategy and tactics

Psychological theories, personality typologies, therapies, and consciousness-expansion practices

Advice on daily life decisions, including finance, health, family matters, jobs, and so on

Personal guidance and advice, self-knowledge, therapeutic in-
terventions, character and personality readings; insight into
psychodynamics, emotional conflicts, psychological and
spiritual issues

Information on karma, past lives, life purpose, and so on

Diagnosis and treatment of illness and medical needs

Horticultural advice on preparation, planting, and cultivation
techniques

Revelations, prophecy, inspiration

Religious and spiritual teachings, practices

Metaphysics

Messages from spirits of the deceased

Characteristics of the Messages

Several consistent patterns are found in these channeled messages, or can
be inferred from the data. The following list contains the ones based on the
cases previously described.

Symbolic forms such as imagery and metaphor are frequent in
literary works and messages of personal guidance.

The entities often have skills at conversation, interpersonal
communication, teaching, public speaking, and humor (but
not dialects).

Messages concerning personal guidance are usually concerned
with healthy emotional and mental states, service and care
for others, self-esteem, higher values, and other elements of
healthy individual development.

Most messages and entities are beneficent.

Creative works are communicated in final form without apparent developmental processes or practice. Written material
can be dictated with a rapidity beyond the capacity of
ordinary mental composition. The process can be stopped
and resumed with precise continuity.

The information, ideas, conceptualizations, and counsel found
in the communications may be beyond the knowledge,
skills, and capabilities of the person doing the channeling.

There is evidence of psi (ESP) ability in the communications,
including telepathy, clairvoyance, and precognition, which
appear to be at the level of human ability and are likely to
come from the channel's own psychic abilities.

The predispositions and dynamics of the channel influence the form of the entity or source, the language, and the contents of the messages. The communications draw from the language, knowledge, and ideas of the channel and culture.

The substance of the messages varies from trivial to reformulation to innovative.

Channeled communications have served the purposes of advising, persuading, authorizing, inspiring, setting values, and giving information to individuals and social groups.

The channeled messages are directed to audiences in particular settings, times, and circumstances. They address the needs of the channel, individuals, and society. Nevertheless, the entities come with their own concerns and urgings and may attempt to influence the channel and audience to accept their agenda.

The social context is often one of crisis in which there is a lack of authority or adequate information for individual or social decisions.

In the past, the messages have come as oracles or prophecy from God and lesser deities. Recent times have found channels receiving from sources who are in the roles of sages or teachers.

CHAPTER 15

MODELS AND THEORIES OF CHANNELING: Outside Entities

We now turn to the question of where these messages originate. Do they come from entities or beings communicating to the mind or through the body of the channels? Is it God who speaks through the prophets, a spirit teacher through a channel, an ascended master dictating to a writer, or a UFO crewmember warning of a coming cataclysm? Many people have accepted the reality of the beings who say they are communicating. However, given our knowledge of psychology and the materialistic assumptions of current science, others today believe that these entities are secondary personalities constructed out of the unconscious by the mind. Another view would class channeling as fraud and deception. These and other theories have their advocates, and there is enough variety in documented channeling cases to provide evidence for each point of view. In the next two chapters, we will consider the major theories, the cases that support them, and what the implications are for each one.

We will begin with a description of the cases in which the source seems to be an outside being communicating through the channel. This being appears to have an autonomous ego and personality which is coherent, consistent, and persistent. In short, it seems to be a person, though without a body of its own (except for those who borrow the body of the channel). It is like a person who visits intermittently, or someone with whom one speaks over the telephone.

This channeled being rarely has a personal biographical history, unless it claims to be a spirit of a deceased human; nor does the entity seem to reside anywhere when between appearances. The kinds of beings that communicate through the channeling process are congruent with the time, culture, and circumstances. The following list contains examples of past and present beings from the lore of channeling who presumably have communicated through this process. The range is impressive and, given various circumstances, the being can evoke worship, awe, inspiration, and other responses.

Gods and deities: Yahweh, Christ, Zoroaster, Apollo, Ishtar, Adonis, Zeus

Angels: Michael, Gabriel, Raphael, Metatron, Uriel, angels in
  general

Spiritual figures: Saint Catherine, Saint Margaret, Soul of the
  Mishnah, Padmasambhava, Holy Spirit, Saint John

Advanced masters: Saint Germain, Moyra, Hilarion, Sananda,
  living humans

Energies and forces: Logos, Creativity, Limitless Light and Love,
  Pleiades

Extraterrestrials: space brothers, UFO occupants, guardians,
  Ashtar, Hatonn, Ra, Semjase, Ramonsara

Discarnate teachers: Seth, Ecton, Bartholomew, Emmanuel,
  White Eagle, Rector, Zen Tao, Gildas, Orin, DaBen, Etherion

Nature: devas, spirits of plant families, Pan, dolphins

Spirits of deceased humans

This list could be expanded; but what is the possibility that these beings
really exist and are communicating through the channels? We will begin
with two explanations that reject the existence of these entities.

FRAUD

One of the obvious questions is whether the channels are fraudulent; that
is, consciously acting out the character of the entity or pretending to hear a
voice. In the cases that I have studied, this has occurred very rarely. I know
of one channel who was observed going in and out of the entity role as she
talked with one group and then turned to another; the suspicion was that
the shift was entirely a performance. I have seen other trance channels who
appeared to be simply acting out the role of an entity and acting it not very
well. There are some channels who speak impromptu or intuitively and
consider this channeling. This may be self-deception, but would not be
normally considered fraud. However, if channeling can make a person
famous, or admired, or prosperous, there certainly are motives for deception, and some people will do it for those reasons. There were many
documented examples of fraud among mediums in the spiritualistic movement. In short, while not common, fakery should not be ignored in looking
at particular cases.

On the other hand, there are many examples of channels who gained
little from their work or for whom it was a burden. It is not likely they would
resort to fraud to continue this. Irving Litvag, the biographer of Mrs. John
Curran and Patience Worth, interviewed many people who had known the

Currans. He told me, in 1987, that no one questioned Mrs. Curran's sincerity, a conclusion with which W. F. Prince also agreed. Greek and Roman writers agreed that the Delphic oracle was genuine. In one instance, an inquirer tried to force the priestess to prophesy. She tried to pretend, but could not speak in the hoarse and special voice that was used by the god, and the inquirer knew she was not in her oracular state. Scholars feel that this is a point against fraud at Delphi.

SCHIZOPHRENIA OR MENTAL DISTURBANCE

Graham Reed (reported in Metzger, 1989) suggests that channeling is similar to schizophrenia, though he notes that the person can control the delusions. This is not unreasonable to consider, since one of the forms of schizophrenia is the hearing of voices. Anita Muhl's work with automatic writing showed that conflicts, psychological repressions, traumas, and so on, were expressed or symbolized in the writing. This explanation fits some cases of voices or inner figures, especially with persons who have other mental disturbances. The material produced in these cases gives evidence of these disturbed elements. Such cases usually do not get recognized publicly, and few of them show up in the genre of channeling literature.

There are many cases that do not fit the schizophrenic model. We have noted that Joan of Arc, with what might today be called flamboyant hallucinations, was considered quite sane by George Bernard Shaw and F. W. H. Myers, in contrast to those who thought her visions were signs of madness. Alschuler's and Heery's work shows that inner-voice experiences happen to people who are psychologically normal. As far as I know, there has been no actual diagnosis of mental illness relating to channels, and blanket assertions of this by critics are irresponsible.

OUTSIDE, SEPARATE BEINGS

At the other extreme from fraud or schizophrenia is the position that some or all of the entities are spirits from beyond the individual. This belief that there are discarnate beings—whether gods or spirits—is held in many cultures, all religious traditions, and by many of those who listen now to channels, though not without ambivalence. Technically, it is not possible to absolutely prove that channeled entities are separate beings, simply because there is no independent, consensual verification that such separate beings exist. For example, we can agree that a mother and her daughter are separate beings because they can be observed in physical space. However, we do not yet have such perceptual agreement for mental space. Perceptions of spirits by a medium, for example, may be projections of his or her mind, and there is very little consistency in such perceptions among several mediums. Even if there is agreement, there is the possibility that it is the result of telepathy between the persons, rather than the existence of outside beings. Philosophers and theorists have wrestled with the arguments for discarnate beings and their identity, and how consciousness could exist without physical embodiment, but without finding any satisfactory conclusions (Wheatley and Edge, 1976; Williams, 1964; Flew, 1964). Roger Walsh (1990) says this is a case of ontological indeterminacy, in that there can be many interpretations of the cases, but we have no way of determining which interpretation is best. In other words, these outside beings may exist, but given that they are experienced through the mind, it is difficult to establish unequivocal evidence for them in ways we usually accept as conclusive. This does not deny their reality. It simply means that there are always alternative explanations to the cases that we have, even the good ones. We will have to be satisfied with evidence that suggests and implies outside beings, without absolute proof. Ultimately our choice of a theory will have to be a matter of belief, not proof. Other explanations of outside sources have been suggested, such as abstract information accessed by the channel, vibrations and resonance with facets of reality, and ideas that everything has consciousness. Because these are so speculative, this discussion will focus on cases that involve personified entities.

The Entity as a Distinct Personality

There are three lines of reasoning usually given for believing that the entity originates independently of the channel. The first is that the entity has a distinct personality and is quite different from the channel. The entity may have different interests, beliefs, and personal mannerisms. Its beliefs or concerns may be so different that the channel is upset or unable to accept them. The character traits are consistent over time, and the entity may communicate in a quite different way with people interpersonally. In short, he or she appears to be a person quite separate from the individual doing the channeling. While it might not be the person it claims to be, it is nevertheless a person and, if the entity appeared in its own body, it would be clear to us immediately that its personality was different from that of the channel. I know of a few unpublished studies in which brainwaves have been compared for channels in their normal state and the channeling state. There have been distinct differences. These studies show that the brain is in a different state when channeling, though no one is yet prepared to say what this means. Also in support of this position are the cases of ostensible possession and negative voices, which suggest the presence of an outside force. In religious traditions, the angels, deities, or spiritual teachers that are experienced on the inner planes (for example, in Yoga, Eckankar, and the Alice Bailey works) appear to be beings that are independent of the person and are contacted rather than imagined.

Several times, Edgar Cayce's self-hypnotic trance was interrupted by an entity. Once, the angel Michael took over Cayce's voice and roared, "Who will approach the Throne that ye may know that there is no one that surpasses the Son of Man in His approach to human experience in the material world" (Carter, 1972, p. 63). Given Cayce's insistence that he used his own mind in his readings, this suggests the intervention of an outside being who was different from his own self.

We should note some critiques of this line of thought. First is that the entity does lack a physical body, and this is one of our usual standards for considering someone to be a person and to have an identity that is separate from other individuals. By definition, discarnate spirits do not have a body; this means that they appear only through another's mind, so their independent existence is indeterminate. A second consideration is that we know that distinct, autonomous personalities can be produced in the minds of individuals through guided imagery and also by persons who have multiple personalities. These figures also have characteristics that are quite different from the primary personality, but there is no doubt that they come from the human being involved. With the multiple-personality syndrome, the alter egos occur as a result of trauma, which is not necessarily present in channeling, and they are clearly related emotionally to the overall life of the person (one may be an angry character, another idealistic). While some channels have had difficult childhoods, there is no indication that the channel/entity relationship is psychologically similar to that of multiple-personality relations. Philosopher Stephen Braude (1988) has compared mediumship with cases of multiple-personality syndrome, and he found that the parallels give reason to question the hypothesis of disembodied spirits. In summary, the fact that the entity is very different from the channel is suggestive, but not proof of a separate being. We should also note that if there are outside beings, such entities could actually be quite similar in interests or mannerisms to the host, just as friends have similar interests, because the entity draws on the conscious and unconscious resources of the host.

Skills Not Possessed by the Channel

The second reason given for believing the entities are independent beings is that they show abilities that are beyond those of the person channeling them. We have seen several cases of this sort, and the reasoning is that if the human being does not have the writing skill or artistic ability shown in the channeling, then it must be coming from the entity. This is more persuasive than the presence of a different personality alone. The question that has to be addressed from a contemporary scientific framework is whether the person could have learned the ability subliminally and brought it to light through the channeling. Many persons (skeptics and objective researchers alike) have attributed channeled skills and talents to the operation of the unconscious (Stevenson, 1978). This is not unreasonable, since we know that some people have talents—poetry, music, inspiration—that seem to come from unconscious levels via dreams, imagery, words, and so on. Poets, writers, and artists use conscious talents to revise and work with these creative inspirations. There are also cases called cryptomnesia, where an unexplained piece of knowledge turns out to have been observed but consciously forgotten. However, in the case of many channeled works, the conscious mind of the channel clearly does not have the ability required. To explain the skill as coming from some exceptional self-developed unconscious ability is circular reasoning, since the only evidence that the unconscious mind has the ability is the skill itself, and it is not known that it comes from unconsciously learned skills. Proving that it comes from an outside entity is equally difficult. The most we can conclude is that it is unlikely that the channel had the particular talent at conscious or unconscious levels; therefore, the implication is that it came from the outside. We will look at some cases that particularly suggest the presence of outside entities in this way.

Pearl Curran and Patience Worth   Perhaps the most striking support for an outside entity comes from Pearl Curran, who channeled Patience Worth. As described earlier, Patience wrote novels, poetry, and other literary compositions. All who studied the case agreed that this was beyond the skills of Mrs. Curran. The use of language, the realistic details, the obscure Anglo-Saxon words and locutions, and the craftsmanship showed writing ability of which Mrs. Curran had none, nor did her education and experience give her any chance to develop these, even in the unconscious mind. Patience also showed a grasp of philosophical ideas and thinking which were expressed throughout the writing and which were foreign to Mrs. Curran. There were also writing feats of multiple compositions, rapidity of dictation, lack of revision, and improvisational writing. Mrs. Curran simply could not have done any of this herself, the researchers agreed.

Could Patience have been developed from Mrs. Curran's unconscious mind? Some observers thought that Mrs. Curran should be psychoanalyzed to find out. Neurologist Morton Prince (not the same as W. F. Prince) and Professor Charles Cory believed Patience was a subconscious personality and suggested that hypnosis would get to the bottom of the matter (Prince, 1927, pp. 428–436). Mrs. Curran quite properly declined these offers. Patience was amused, and said of Cory: "I be a-tickle. It be such a queerish task for to sit aside the day and see man strut forth with his barb o' learning and plunge it at the breast of God's wisdom, swaggering hence with a chucklin' o' satisfaction, without lookin' ahind for to see be it a kill!" (p. 237).

Cory's point was that Mrs. Curran could have a dissociated co-conscious personality which, freed of the necessities of running the body and taking care of life's activities, could devote itself to writing. However, he acknowledged that Mrs. Curran's experiences and knowledge would not have given the Patience personality the knowledge and compositional skills with which to work in this regard and says this is a problem to be considered. A related view was given by the prominent American authoress Mary Austin, who contended that the writing process of Mrs. Curran was the same as that of many authors. She suggested that it was the result of unconscious composition combined with the use of ESP to get information and language that was not known by the conscious mind (Prince, 1927). In all, no one explained how Patience, as a part of Mrs. Curran's mind, could have gained the writing skills of style, plotting, narration, and characterization that she evidently had. Such skill in writing normally requires practice, feedback, and revision. Yet Patience's poems, stories, and novels came through from the beginning at a good level of craftsmanship. And where would the unconscious have obtained such detailed knowledge of the Holy Land or Victorian England? Patience herself did not give much to go on regarding herself. She claimed to be the spirit of an English girl who immigrated to America, but gave little historical background, so her existence could not be confirmed historically.

Mrs. Curran's reading was minimal—mostly ladies' magazines of the time. The Currans' library was studied by Prince and found wanting, at least in regard to this question. I wondered if a possible source for some material could be motion pictures. D. W. Griffith's *Intolerance* came out in 1916, and C. B. DeMille's Biblical epics *Ten Commandments* (1923) and *King of Kings* (1927) would have shown scenes relevant to her novel of Biblical times, *The Sorry Tale*. But Patience was already dictating the book in 1915. Lew Wallace's *Ben Hur* was published in 1880, but there is no indication that Mrs. Curran had read it. There were apparently no sources from which Mrs. Curran, even at a subliminal level, could have learned what Patience was writing about. Here we have a case in which the channeled material goes far beyond the conscious *and* unconscious experience and learning of the channel. An outside entity is plausible.

It is important to realize that this does not explain how Patience herself had this literary ability. Even if a personality is in a nonmaterial reality, we presume that it still must have sources for its knowledge and ways to develop its skills. Cayce, for example, said his subconscious mind received health information from the subconscious minds of other persons and the past-life readings from actual records in space-time. Patience gave no explanation for what she could do. When asked if she thought about the stories between sessions, she commented, "Doth the spider think o' web?" (Litvag, 1972, p. 67).

It is easy enough for critics to say that this was all done by Mrs. Curran's mind, creating another personality and carrying out all the preparation and writing process at unconscious levels. If so, one must be willing to give the unconscious part of the mind extraordinary qualities and show that these are coming from the mind, not from somewhere else. Walter F. Prince clearly recognized that this was the choice and, after a ten-month investigation, he came to the following conclusion about Mrs. Curran and Patience:

> Either our concept of what we call the subconscious must be radically altered, so as to include potencies of which we hitherto have had no knowledge, or else some cause operating through but not originating in the subconsciousness of Mrs. Curran must be acknowledged (Prince, 1927, p. 8).

Channeled Music   A case in which artistic skills are demonstrated is that of Rosemary Brown, the medium who channels musical compositions (mostly piano) from Liszt, Chopin, Schumann, Schubert, and other deceased musicians. To the listener, the pieces are very much in the style of the named composers. These compositions have been put in print by reputable music publishers and have received attention from performers and musicologists. Two issues are relevant: first, are the compositions comparable to the music of the composers while living; and second, does Mrs. Brown have the ability to do the composing herself?

The most thorough analysis of the music has been done by Ian Parrott (1978), Professor of Music at the University College of Wales, who is sympathetic toward the conclusion that the compositions originate with composers. Parrott writes that the Brown pieces have harmonic progressions, key changes, tonal qualities, chording, and compositional styles that are characteristic of the presumed composers. One piece, *Grubelei* by Liszt, was written at a BBC television session and was complicated enough (simultaneous 5/4 and 3/2 time) that Mrs. Brown could not play it herself. Living composer and Liszt scholar Humphrey Searle said that the chromatic harmonic style and design were typical of Liszt and that the markings were in Italian and French, which was also characteristic. He noted one bar that had chording similar to Liszt's *Liebesträume* and concluded that it was "the sort of piece that Liszt could have written, particularly during the last fifteen years of his life when he was experimenting in new directions" (Brown, 1970, p. 4).

However, there is also disagreement regarding the music. A review by Kenneth Mobbs (reported in Parrott, 1978) of Mrs. Brown's first printed album (1974) criticized frequent weaknesses in the material—awkward progressions, problems in chording, naive accompaniment patterns, too frequent modulation, and poor formal balance. In a BBC television special, André Previn states that some numbers were only third-, fourth-, or fifthrate Liszt. One pianist said the music was a pastiche. Another claimed to find errors in a Brahms waltz.

Actually there are few passages in Mrs. Brown's compositions that are close parallels to compositions by the composers in question, so the creations are not pastiches of bits taken from the original works. The numbers are themselves original in their themes and typical of the composers, though they are mostly short and midlevel in quality—not up to the best of their composers' works. Classical pianist Julian White observed to me in 1988 that many of the pieces were not fully developed, as though they were first drafts or communicated with difficulty. Such qualities would not speak against their spirit origin, since transmitting musical composition information is more complex than say, dictating literary messages. Giving composition instructions under difficult conditions to an untrained transcriber might require simpler and less elaborate pieces. Mrs. Brown acknowledges the problems and reports occasional uncertainty in the notes or elements transmitted (Brown, 1971, pp. 31–32). This is typical of channeled communication. For these reasons, I think it is not a telling criticism that the numbers are not equal to the best of the composers, works. *Grubelei* (Brown, 1970) seems to be the most notable of the transmitted compositions. To my knowledge, there have been no well-designed studies in which Mrs. Brown's numbers were judged by persons not knowing their origin or compared against compositions of similar level by the claimed composer. The analyses and critiques all come from persons who know the circumstances and are bound to be influenced by their predispositions to believe or be skeptical. However, taken overall, there seems to me to be sufficient data to say that the compositions have the qualities, style, and character of pieces by the composers named.

The next question is whether Mrs. Brown has the skills to compose such pieces consciously or unconsciously. Mrs. Brown has experience as a medium but, insofar as her musical education or exposure is concerned, the answer appears to be no. From her account, she had a year or two of lessons as a girl, two terms as a teenager, and a year when she was married. She says that she rarely went to concerts or listened to radio classical music. She had no lessons or training in composition, which is a difficult art. She took some piano lessons after Liszt began to communicate music to her, but then stopped to concentrate on receiving the composition. Her own performance skills are limited and she can play only the simpler pieces that she writes. Some musicians with training and experience can compose in the style of a composer, but Mrs. Brown does not have training, experience, or extensive musical knowledge. It is difficult to grasp how some nonconscious part of her mind could have developed this ability from her limited musical exposure. Certainly, there are natural musical geniuses, such as Mozart, but they functioned at conscious levels and generally had performance talents. What would it mean to be an unconscious musical genius? How would one know the skill was coming from the person and not from outside the mind?

So, there is evidence in this case for reasonably good musical composition coming from outside sources. The entities claim to be spirits of the composers. Like many of the guides in channeling, they have their own independent personalities which are similar, at least, to the composers in question. I have not here considered the cases of musical mediums who perform music they say is inspired by deceased composers or the harp music of Joe Andrews, said to come from various discarnate masters. These individuals already have performance skills, and it is difficult to distinguish objectively between their own performance ability and outside musical influences.

The Paintings of Gasparetto   We will now look at other cases of channeling that are illustrative of the hypothesis of outside entities. These cases are not proof of the model, but would fit within its theory. The artwork of Luiz Gasparetto is claimed to come from the spirits of deceased painters; Gasparetto says that Toulouse-Lautrec and other artists take over his hands and carry out the art (Dubugras, Gasparetto, and Espiritos Diversos, 1979; Gaetani, 1986). The drawings and paintings show the stylistic qualities of the various artists and some of these paintings are respectable, though not masterpieces. The paintings have not been evaluated objectively for similarity to the artists. Gasparetto began automatic drawing at the age of thirteen. He had some art training, but his spirit paintings show different (and more talented) qualities in comparison to his own work (Long, 1986).

What about the possibility that the material comes from his own hidden capabilities? The art of Gasparetto could be similar to that of "quick sketch" artists, who do rapid drawings in the styles of famous artists. Many of his techniques (extreme rapidity, upside-down drawing, use of nondominant hand) have been recently used as techniques for getting nonartists to improve rapidly in drawing skills, suggesting that this is a way of bypassing the ego and drawing with less habituated, more intuitive responses. However, from the point of view of this model, these techniques could also be a way to get Gasparetto's conscious ego out of the way to enable outside entities to work through the body. A technique, using hypnosis, that appears similar to Gasparetto's process is reported by psychologist Stanley Krippner (1980) and writers Ostrander and Schroeder (1970). They report that artistic skills have been enhanced through hypnosis by Soviet researcher Vladimir Raikov, who tells entranced subjects they are Raphael and other artists. The subjects' artistic skills are said to improve over several sessions, and one subject observed by Krippner even signed her paintings "Raphael." Raikov calls this "artificial reincarnation" and uses the technique for improving musical skills as well. Thus, while Gasparetto's work would fit the model of outside entities, there are other explanations. There have been other paintings presuming to come from spirit sources, and, again, they are suggestive, though not possible of total proof.

A Course in Miracles   *A Course in Miracles* was dictated by an inner voice that eventually spoke of itself as Christ. The writing speed and complex composition placed it outside the conscious ability of Mrs. Schucman, who wrote it down. While it has similarities to other writings in psychology, religion, and philosophy, it was dissimilar to Mrs. Schucman's own academic work and temperament. The metaphysical content was alien to her belief system and created extreme conflicts for her. All this would fit into the model of an outside agency. On the other hand, the Course was psychologically oriented and used techniques of logic and analysis that would be consistent with Mrs. Schucman's knowledge and concepts. An outside being might draw on her knowledge in this way so as to communicate the ideas most effectively to her understanding, or it could be seen as an indication that the source of the writing was in her own mind.

Mediumship   Many instances of classical mediumship provide strong evidence for an outside entity—usually identified as a spirit of someone deceased. Researchers have documented cases in which presumed spirits gave private messages, exhibited personal mannerisms, and communicated information not known to the medium that identified the spirit as a particular individual. For discussions of cases and issues in this area, see Gauld (1977), Cook (1987), *Journal of the Society for Psychical Research,* and *Journal of the American Society for Psychical Research.*

What are called the cross-correspondence cases provided especially good evidence for outside entities (Murphy, 1961; Heywood, 1959). These involved many messages coming through several British mediums. These messages were like pieces of a jigsaw puzzle which were individually meaningless, but when several from the various mediums were put together, the meaning became evident. It seemed that the best explanation was that there were spirits on the other side managing the communications in a way that was beyond the capacities of the mediums.

Paranormal Information

A third reason that suggests the presence of an outside personality is the presence of information of a paranormal nature. There is an assumption that if the entity can give telepathic, clairvoyant, or precognitive information, the entity must be in a different dimension or beyond space and time. There is a tendency to attribute psi skills to some transhuman ability. Our cases of psi in channeling have shown that the paranormal abilities are at about the same level as those of humans, and it is likely that the source of psi lies in the psychic abilities of the person, not the entity. That is, the ego of the person and the ego of the entity both draw on the same sensitivity, presumably in the unconscious of the individual. An independent entity might have its own psi ability, but we do not have cases that illustrate this. It would seem that whatever an entity might be, it has to function through the capabilities of the channel, in both sensory and parasensory modes.

IMPLICATIONS OF THIS MODEL

We see that the evidence of several cases implies that the presence of an outside entity is a plausible hypothesis. In fact, this theory would fit most cases of channeling, in the sense that an outside being could be communicating the messages. However, the conclusion is not certain because there are alternative interpretations. So, if one accepts this model, it has to be as a choice rather than on the basis of complete proof. We might look at what happens if one chooses to believe this model as an explanation of channeling, mediumship, prophecy, and the other occurrences of this process. If one accepts that there are outside entities involved in channeling, there are significant implications for our assumptions about reality and knowledge.

1. There is a nonphysical realm populated by various discarnate beings. These may include gods, angels, spirits, teachers, group entities, and perhaps abstract qualities and principles of other dimensions of reality or consciousness. Each of these suggests potential relationships and responsibilities.

2. Humans can contact these beings through mental communication and trance states, and these beings can themselves initiate contact with humans. People can attune to higher or lower levels in regard to qualities of the communicators.

3. The entities have, or can adopt, personalities with intentions, perceptions, thoughts, emotions, memories, and other characteristics. Some of the characteristics may originate with the channel.

4. Many of the beings have talents in literature, mathematics, musical composition, performance, painting and drawing, and various fields of knowledge. These talents appear to be present without developmental processes or practice. There may be other abilities of which we are unaware.

5. The entities can access knowledge or information that is not bound by the known laws of time and space.

6. Information, decisions, advice, inspiration, ideas, and artistic creations can be given by the entities for individual and social purposes.

7. Individuals can be assisted by these entities toward physical health, emotional health, practical accomplishment, insight, and spiritual values and development.

8. These beings can assist society toward humanistic and transpersonal attitudes, justice, compassionate treatment of those less fortunate, attention to global problems, and promotion of peace.

9. The beings may have agendas and desires of their own, which they urge or impose on the channels.

10. The entities may be deceptive and unreliable in terms of valid information and responsibility. There is no acknowledgment on their part of these aspects, and discernment must be learned on the part of humans.

To accept the theory that there are outside entities involved in channeling clearly has significant consequences for our ideas about realms of consciousness, the presence of other beings whom we can contact, and the possibility of expanded sources of information and knowledge.

There are psychological attractions of this theory besides the evidence for it. It is appealing to those who want to have a source of authority from which to obtain assistance and security and for those who value advice on the many choices of life that must be made in circumstances of uncertainty. For those concerned about the welfare of our planet, the idea of beneficent and concerned beings holds out the hope of help to deal with the problems that ordinary human entities have created. This is not to say that the entities, should they exist, would satisfy these hopes or whether they might suggest that the solutions lie within our own hands and hearts.

CHAPTER 16

MODELS AND THEORIES OF CHANNELING: The Unconscious and the Transpersonal

ANOTHER PART OF THE SELF

We next turn to the idea that channeled material comes from the mind of the individual rather than any outside source. This model assumes that the unconscious mind formulates messages to serve various needs of the individual and communicates them to the conscious mind in the form of a voice or entity. As an actor might construct a character with awareness, ideas, feelings, and actions, the personality of the entity is put together by some process outside the person's ego; that is, it develops its own consciousness. From this consciousness, the entity can send thoughts into the mind, control Ouija Board movements, write automatically, and take over the body when the normal personality goes into a trance.

Several motives and purposes would facilitate this sprouting of other selves. A repressed emotional conflict may surface as a voice or figure asserting the repressed ideas and feelings. In shamanistic societies, trances in which the shaman is possessed by deities or spirits are often motivated by social conflict or a problem that cannot be mediated within the group. The channeling occurs in order to transcend the social level and provide an answer that will be accepted by all. Like dreams and divination, the message comes from a sacred space that holds authority for the group.

The same process may be occurring now regarding global social problems, values, and conflicts. There may be feelings of community concern arising at unconscious levels. Perhaps these are suppressed by the individual, or the individual feels frustrated in being unable to address the issues. The unconscious formulates responses to these feelings and puts them in the mouth of an authoritative being who will command social attention. Similarly, in current societies, a person might feel inadequate in terms of religious or spiritual values, yet express his or her ideals through the creation of a spiritual being or voice.

From the point of view of the self, the conscious personality may need certain ideas, information, or motivation for healthy growth, decisions, motivation, and life goals. If the ego cannot get this information through its own efforts, the unconscious can provide it through the channeled mode.

The unconscious mind often appears to have more knowledge and wisdom than the conscious mind, and channeling can become a method for the unconscious to communicate this wisdom to the primary ego in a way that will command attention. Some part of the unconscious thus becomes an inner teacher.

This model is consistent with the guided-visualization technique for learning to channel and with the imaginal figures of authors, which are presumed to come from within the mind of the person. The person essentially gives the mind instructions to create an inner image with certain characteristics and this image is generated by the unconscious. The figure takes on some level of consciousness (though how this happens is not known), thus becoming autonomous.

Beyond the Conditioned Ego

Though autonomous, the imaginal figure is not just an automaton. The being has its own conscious ego and can draw on the unconscious mind's vast range of information, ideas, and capabilities. It is outside the primary ego structure, so it is not limited by many of the assumptions and values that the ego has developed in adjusting to social reality. The conscious mind has roles, emotional parameters, limiting beliefs, fears, and other conditionings. The inner figure can be formed without these limitations and can have a perspective that transcends the ego's blind spots. It can also be unbalanced because it does not have those experiences, responsibilities, and controls. It can draw on information acquired subliminally by the mind or can acquire it through psi. Presumably, it can direct the performance of complex skills and creative work and devise systems of complex ideas.

Simulations of Channeling

The first line of argument to support this model is to compare channeling with situations in which figures or guides have been consciously created. In these cases, there is no reason to believe they come from an outside source.

Napoleon Hill's mental advisory council of Lincoln, Emerson, and others is an example. Their characters were created by Hill based on their biographies; once they were imagined, then Hill's unconscious mind continued to develop their personalities autonomously.

Such scenarios can be created through hypnosis. Thomson J. Hudson (1970) reports an experiment in the late 1800s in which a hypnotized subject was told that the spirit of Socrates was before him. The subject discussed philosophy for two hours with Socrates, who explained a system of spiritual philosophy so persuasively that some of the group listening to his report believed that it was actually the spirit of Socrates or some other high intelligence. As proof, they pointed out that many of the answers contradicted the subject's own beliefs. In subsequent sessions, other spirits were suggested with the same results. However, one of the "spirits of the deceased" was found to lie about a fact of his life. Even more telling was the hypnotic instruction to hallucinate a philosophical pig (said to be a Hindu incarnation) who gave a learned discussion of reincarnation and Hindu philosophy. The subject was knowledgeable about these subjects through his own reading and was delighted, Hudson said, to find the pig confirmed his reading.

The "artificial reincarnation" method used by Raikov in the U.S.S.R. is an example of using hypnosis for improving artistic skills through identification with the artist. Milton Erickson (Haley, 1967) reported a case in which a painting of good quality was produced at enhanced speed as a result of hypnotic suggestion. Both of these cases suggest that many skills can be evoked from the unconscious mind.

Another example of a parallel to channeling is reported by Jean Houston (Klimo, 1987). She and her father paid a personal visit to Edgar Bergen, the ventriloquist. They found him talking with his ventriloquil figure, Charlie McCarthy. Bergen was asking questions about love, virtue, and life, and Charlie was answering with beauty, elegance, and brilliance. "A regular wooden Socrates," says Houston. An embarrassed Bergen said that Charlie knew much more about these topics than he (Bergen) did, and that he did not have the faintest idea what Charlie was going to answer (p. 229).

These instances show that channeling types of experiences can be created or can occur out of the inner resources of the individual without requiring an outside agency. The implication is that other cases of channeling are also coming from the individual's own mind. We should note that these cases include messages of good quality, going beyond the capabilities of the conscious mind. We are clearly not talking about the Freudian unconscious, with repressed impulses and traumas, but one with higher levels of knowledge and skill. We should not equate an origin in the unconscious with less valid or spurious information. We should acknowledge also that we do not know how the unconscious mind cultivates wisdom, produces creative art, writes, and so on, so we are explaining one unknown by suggesting another unknown.

Clinical and Psychological Studies

A second reason for concluding that channeling and similar phenomena are from other parts of the mind is that the messages express the emotional feelings and motives of the channeling individual. We have already noted that Anita Muhl's studies of automatic writing give great weight to this mode. She claimed that the extensive writings she had seen could all be traced back to personal psychology. She suggests a model of the mind that has seven levels and also suggests that automatic writing comes from a layer of the active personal unconscious below the focus of attention and conscious awareness. This level contains the records of all the experiences of one's life, remembered consciously or not. Stevenson (1978) and Rawcliffe

(1959) review automatic writing cases in which the most plausible source is the subconscious of the individual. Stevenson says that the Patience Worth case is the only one that raises the question of an outside agency.

The neo-dissociation theory of Ernest Hilgard (1986) would say that a channeled entity is a personality system that is separated from the main personality, but which can draw on basic language, knowledge, and behavior for its own use.

Julian Jaynes (1976), in *The Origins of Consciousness in the Breakdown of the Bicameral Mind*, makes an extensive analysis of oracles, prophecy, inspired writing, and hallucinated voices from ancient times to the present. His model of explanation holds that the right hemisphere of the brain is the source of these communications. In an autonomous way, it takes the role of organizing, planning, and guiding and communicates this to the other side of the brain, where it is heard as voices attributed to God, spirits, deities, muses, and other supernatural figures. At the beginning of human civilization, he suggests that there was an almost complete dissociation between these two hemispheres. In our time, there is more or less coordination but, under stress, the right side of the brain can speak separately to the left hemisphere, which is where the sense of identity is located for most people. Jaynes discusses practices from ancient and classical cultures that demonstrate how prevalent channeling and its parallels were in those times. His review of research on voices in schizophrenia emphasizes their negative qualities but, as noted by Van Dusen, there is not an obvious link to the psychological issues of the patients. A critique of Jaynes' position is that the right hemisphere does not have the capabilities that he attributes to it, at least according to current research. It has minimal linguistic skills, certainly less than that exhibited by muse-inspired poetry, prophecy, or the oracular utterances of the Delphic priestess. And, as Jaynes points out, it is not clear how these voices would turn into full-trance possession by the deity. If one speaks of the unconscious mind in general, there is more reason to accept that it has complex linguistic and personification skills, but there is still the question of how the mind has the qualities of understanding, wisdom, and guidance that the muses, gods, and voices communicated.

The psychiatrist C. G. Jung (1977) investigated many mediumship cases that we would call channeling. These included teachings on metaphysical levels of the universe, messages from the deceased, and visions. He was open to the possibility of discarnate spirits, but to him it was likely that the entities could be constructed by, and from within, the unconscious. In referring to possessing spirits or spirits of the dead, he said, "Spirits, therefore, viewed from the psychological angle, are unconscious autonomous complexes which appear as projections because they have no direct association with the ego" (p. 116). He noted that this does not settle the question of whether spirits exist in themselves, only that complexes can behave like spirits. He said in a letter (Klimo, 1987) that the hypothesis of spirits gave better explanations in the long run, though he was skeptical of individual cases.

These theories assert that the unconscious mind is the origin of channeled entities and communications. Except for Jaynes and Hilgard, their conclusions tend to be based on pathological cases where the messages can be traced to psychological problems. Their application to more healthy cases with positive messages needs to be considered. The theories give no explanation as to how the unconscious puts together these constructions. Neither are there explanations addressing the frequent religious and spiritual themes. As with the entities model, the theories leave many gaps, and the unknown of channeling is explained by invoking another unknown—the unconscious mind.

Cases of Channeling

Some cases of channeling fit this model very easily. Many Ouija Board messages can be cited as reflecting inner fragments of the self. The daughter of a friend of mine was at college and began playing with a Ouija Board with friends in the dorm. It began giving messages and announced that it was the spirit of one girl's father, communicating while he was sleeping (he was still alive). The amazed girl asked if he had a message for her. The board spelled out, "STOP SMOKING." It is not difficult to see this as a message coming from a guilty part of her self. More tragic have been many cases in which the board urged persons to commit crimes, kill spouses, and destroy themselves through malicious advice. These can be understood as psychic eruptions from repressed feelings, coming out in automatisms.

Even exceptional cases of channeling can be viewed from this model. In the case of Joan of Arc, the great psychical researcher Frederic Meyers believed that there was no reason to assume that the voices and figures were other than from her mind. But he noted that it spoke well for Joan to be able to use them for greater skills than she herself had. Here is another case in which the qualities of the material transcended the capabilities of the individual.

Edgar Cayce is a confirming example, since he himself said in his trance state that the health readings came from his subconscious mind. I have been told of a group of channels in the Los Angeles area whose trance personalities said they were from the unconscious minds of the channels. Seth, channeled by Jane Roberts, did not claim to be an outside entity. He said at various times that he was an energy essence personality, an advanced form of her, Jane of the future, and that he and Jane were part of the same overall entity. His discussions of God and expansion of consciousness paralleled her own interests and suggests that he was from her own self. With the case of Ramtha, various observers have suggested that the entity comes from J. Z. Knight's own mind, if indeed it is not deliberately acted out.

Many of the channeled entities are reluctant to give any identity or explain their origin. Early in their experience with the Ouija Board, Robert Butts, Jane's husband, asked if it was Jane's subconscious talking. The answer given was, "Subconscious is a corridor. What differences does it make which door you travel through?" (Roberts, 1976, p. 15). When Paul Tuttle asked Rajpur, "Am I making you up? Am I making up the words?" Rajpur answered, "Yes and no" (Tuttle, 1985, p. 1). When the Curran circle asked early on who was sending the messages, the board spelled out, "Should one so near be confined to a name? The sun shines alike on the briar and the rose. Do they make question of a name?" (Litvag, 1972, p. 15). While these instances do not mean that the messages come from the self, they do indicate that the identity may go through a process of development in response to the insistence of the sitters. Certainly they are compatible with the model of unconscious personification.

One may also see the voice of the unconscious in the commonality of the messages. Some of the main themes of channels in the last decades of the twentieth century are messages of a common inspirational nature. They speak of such subjects as the true self, love for others, caring for the earth, "cleaning up our act," cultivating inner spirituality, expansion of consciousness, a coming new age, and concepts of karma, reincarnation, Christ consciousness, and past lives. Their commonalities are reminiscent of a century ago, when William James noted that 50 percent of the spirit teachings seemed to be written by the same person. Not only are they similar to each other, but there is little that could not come from the unconscious and be put into the mouth of a constructed character whose function is to inspire and motivate. Some of the material is unsophisticated, disorganized, inconsistent, and emotionally driven. Some of it is focused, pertinent, and persuasive. It is not pathological, but it does suggest that messages from the unconscious are being called out by idealism, dissatisfaction, and, of course, the demand characteristics of the times. ("Demand characteristics" is a term used in hypnosis to refer to the implicit assumptions on how to behave in a trance situation.)

This model is an effective explanation for many of the cases of channeling that we have reviewed. Besides the ones mentioned above, it would apply to some that have become well known in recent years, with entities such as Lazaris, Emmanuel, Bartholomew, Ramtha, Mafu, Rafael, Orion, Orin, and many others. In some of these instances, there is remarkable material being presented, but it does seem to be within the range of human creativity. In effect, there is little need for any other model for the cases of channeling that are current, a conclusion also reached by others (Anderson, 1988).

Critique

While the conclusion is persuasive, we should remember that the model does not have a good explanation of how this process works, how a personality is built by the mind, and what it draws on for its sense of self and function. How is it that the mind turns an attitude into a visual image of a person, dressed in a particular way, and with a distinct accent? How is it that Lincoln began always to arrive late for Napoleon Hill's council meetings? What is it that gave Scott Peck's mind the words "the only real security in life lies in relishing life's insecurity"? The voices speak, no doubt, but when you get down to the nitty-gritty, there is no explanation of how the mind does it. Relegating the process to some place outside conscious awareness does not explain how it is done. The assumption is that, in some way, the entity arises from somewhere within the individual self, even though that place is not in ego awareness. Sometimes, one can see the connections between what is said or written and elements in the overt personality, for example, similarity of interests, expression of biases, and complexes. However, there are cases where similarities are less evident, Pearl Curran and Rosemary Brown for example. What is the conclusion then? Even in cases where the channel and the entity have similar interests, Alice A. Bailey for example, there is no proof that the entity and the person are within the same self. The conclusion that an autonomous other comes from the same self is valid only on a case-by-case basis. We do not know concretely what it means to say that there is a larger mind than our ego and that there are other ego personalities within it. We cannot conclude that our larger mind stops at some point or knows directly what is beyond our conscious experience. Even if the channeled material is within personal capability, this does not preclude the possibility that it is produced by an outside entity.

For some people, ascribing channeling to the unconscious is a handy way to discount it. However, placing the source in the unconscious should not be construed to deny the personal and social importance of the material that comes through the channels. What we will have to acknowledge is that this model implies that extensive knowledge and capabilities reside in the unconscious mind and that they can be made accessible through the channeling mode.

Implications

In Chapter 15, I suggested several implications of the belief that outside entities are the source of channeling. The attributes given to those beings would be applied to the unconscious mind in terms of this present model. That is, if the material comes from the mind of the individual, then the mind has the capability of paranormal perception, unconscious creativity, spiritual teachings, personal guidance, social concerns, and so on. It will be useful to list the capabilities of the mind implied by the data of channeling.

1. Personalities can be constructed by the mind without historical development or behavioral experience. This is a re-

markable feat. The Seth personality, in only a few weeks,
was speaking through Jane Roberts. Patience Worth un-
folded very rapidly in her English accent and manner. The
observed extent of the personalities ranges from inner verbal behavior to full interactive behavior in the body. Possibly there are potentials here for therapeutic change through
the creation of alternative or healthy selves. There is perhaps a suggestion that people can experience almost immediate changes or "transformations." There may be a parallel with religious conversion experiences.

2. Some part of the human mind can be aware of information
   without the use of the recognized sensory channels, that is,
   psi. This can come to consciousness in channeled modes of
   writing or speaking.

3. Some human beings, perhaps many or all, have the capacity, from apparently unconscious sources, for talents and
   skills for which they have little or no training; that is, they
   can perform far beyond their knowledge or education. The
   skills are accessed through the channeling mode rather
   than the ego state. The skills include painting, music, poetry, creative writing, political decision-making, planning,
   spiritual teaching, therapeutic techniques, health diagnosis,
   and inspirational speaking. We do not know that every individual can channel some of these skills, but it is true that
   the individual's overt personality in most cases shows no
   sign of the talent that is there while channeling. Sometimes
   the person can direct these talents, such as with Cayce,
   and at other times they come with their own agenda, such
   as with Pearl Curran.

4. Complex material in final form, verbal, symbolic, and artistic, can be produced systematically and without conscious
   planning, preparation, or ego processing. The creation can
   be interrupted and later resumed without interference with
   the material.

5. Some part of the mind outside the ego can have knowledge, information, and perspectives that are superior to the
   conscious ego. The ego can learn to engage in dialog with,
   or relate to, this other part.

6. It appears that skills and qualities are acquired without a
   developmental process. Perhaps information or ideas can be
   assimilated without much effort, but it is hard to imagine
   sophisticated writing or compositional skills springing forth
   "like Athena from the brow of Jove," though that is what

seems to happen. There is no explanation of how this occurs.

7. To produce sophisticated channeled material may require the separation of the creative process from the primary ego consciousness, thus enabling something other than the ego to do the work. The cases do not show that these capabilities of the mind can be gained by directly contacting them with the ego. Few of the channels were able to take over the creative process themselves. In clinical and therapeutic work, there is an assumption that integration of the self is desirable, the goal being a unified self under the direction of a healthy ego. Perhaps we have an alternative suggested here. We have noted that Mary Watkins (1986) suggests that the presence of the imaginal other should be honored, rather than co-opted. A similar position is explored by Douglas Richards (1990), who suggests that "dissociation" can be a path to creativity, personal growth, and transformation of the self. Some of the channeling cases show that the separation enables access to material that is superior to what can come from the ego of the person, even a healthy one. The separation of part of the self from the constraints of the ego personality may enable a broader perspective, a specialized skill, or a deeper level of insight. The ego's belief system might be inconsistent with the material or fixated in a restricted framework and thus be unable to produce the material within itself. Rather than trying to co-opt these talents, our role may be to learn to relate to them as consultants, friends, and advisers, giving them whatever status they deserve and demonstrate.

8. In a social context, there may be some messages that can be heard only if they come from the outside. Ideas and perspectives may be channeled from the individual or collective unconscious that could not be generated within the social belief system or would be blocked from acceptability if they came from one of the members. Perhaps the authority of a transcendent being is necessary, even if that authority is a projected one. Jungian scholar Marie Louise Von Franz has suggested that we project our wisdom onto the forms of gods, then take it back as we integrate those qualities. Such transcendent or authoritative sources can resolve disputes between competing parties. They may provide a path to enable movement where action has been blocked. They may instill overriding values or principles into a culture.

TRANSPERSONAL LEVELS OF CHANNELING

It is obvious that religious and spiritual themes are predominant in channeling, from oracles and prophets to New Age entities. This has puzzled some observers who believe that the channeled material is coming from the unconscious and wonder how to account for its frequent religious interest. Some ideas of the human unconscious are modeled after Freudian psychology, giving the unconscious mostly sexual and aggressive impulses, fantasies, and repressions. A different perspective is offered by transpersonal psychology (Walsh and Vaughan, 1980; *Journal of Transpersonal Psychology*, 1969—), which suggests that there are aspects of the personality, conscious and unconscious, that involve intuition, creativity, purpose and meaning, higher values, transcendent experiences, and spiritual concerns. These are understood to be healthy and a part of human development. It appears that the channeling mode can express or tap into these levels of the self. We will review their relevance for the models we have discussed.

The Superconscious or Higher Unconscious

Roberto Assagioli (1965) identified in the mind a higher unconscious as well as a lower unconscious that includes the Freudian repressions, drives, complexes, and pathology. The higher unconscious consists of the processes of intuition, inspiration, creativity, ethical impulses, altruism, humanitarian, and heroic impulses. See diagram, p. 181. Others have noted these characteristics of the mind. Frances Vaughan's (1979) *Awakening Intuition* describes four levels of intuition and ways of refining the process. *Higher Creativity*, by Willis Harman and Howard Rheingold (1984), presents creativity as an innate capability of the unconscious. Thus, it would appear that if the source of channeling is in the unconscious, these functions could be available. Many creative works could come from this level of the mind, whether they are directed by an outside being or an inner figure of the self.

The Higher Self

Discussed briefly in Chapter 11, the higher self is said to be a distinct part or function of the individual. It is an entity in itself, with consciousness or awareness like the ego, and it is assumed to be a part of everyone (Vaughan, 1986). It witnesses the person's experiences. It is nonpunitive, objective, and nonjudgmental. Its orientation is toward higher values, life purposes, healthy emotional and mental development, and spiritual qualities. Jungian psychologist M. L. Von Franz (1964) refers to it as an "inner guiding factor." In therapeutic work with multiple personalities, something similar is found, referred to as an Inner Self Helper (Allison and Schwarz, 1980; Damgaard, 1987). The therapists report that this helper is nonpathological. It tells them that it has always been present, and it is concerned with the survival and healthy growth of the person. Its advice is exceptionally useful. Often it has

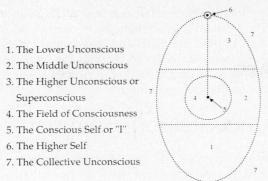

1. The Lower Unconscious
2. The Middle Unconscious
3. The Higher Unconscious or
   Superconscious
4. The Field of Consciousness
5. The Conscious Self or "I"
6. The Higher Self
7. The Collective Unconscious

Roberto Assagioli's diagram of the mind, with the superconscious and the higher self.

a religious or spiritual quality. It expresses only love and goodwill. This helper can communicate through inner voices, visions, speech, and writing. As was noted in Chapter 11, several religious and psychological systems hypothesize the presence of a part of the self or a spiritual essence that functions as a guide. This could be the source of many channeled communications.

Archetypes

Archetypes, as defined in the psychology of C. G. Jung, refer to forms or structures that, throughout history, repeat themselves in the human psyche as roles or relationships, for example the Great Mother, Witch, Healer, Prophet, and Trickster (Singer, 1973). Earlier in this book, I have suggested that there is an archetypal pattern in prophecy. Jung felt that archetypes came from the human collective unconscious, the experience of all people shared by everyone, which is beyond the individual. Archetypes have energy of their own in shaping how they are made concrete and in maintaining themselves. In channeling, a person may connect with archetypal energies and personify the pattern as an entity. There are dangers in this. When a person's psychic energy is attracted to, and caught up in, an archetype, it is amplified and the pattern becomes dominating. This can lead to being overwhelmed, to having inflated self-esteem, and to other imbalances.

Archetypes are often called out by the demands of the times. Prophets tend to arise in times of social crisis and value confusion. The Hebrew prophets, Muhammad, and Joseph Smith are examples. The contemporary Elizabeth Clare Prophet channels messages on the dangers facing the United States and its destiny. The Warrior or Hero archetype is not common in channeling, but can be seen in Joan of Arc. The contemporary channeled entity Ramtha claims to be a warrior king from 35,000 years ago. His teachings are not about war, but some have felt his manner fits his claimed role. Brad Steiger (1988) suggests that Semjase, a UFO entity, personifies the Great Mother. The predominant archetypes of current channeling are those of the Teacher and the Healer. Seth and Emmanuel (1985) are teachers. *A Course in Miracles* is in the healer form. Perhaps the increase in channeling is another way the collective unconscious has of communicating with us and bringing forth the archetypes needed for our times.

TRANSPERSONAL PRINCIPLES

Transpersonal experiences and values appear to be an intrinsic part of human nature. It is becoming evident that they can be studied objectively as a psychology of consciousness and human development. Transpersonal experiences are often interpreted as religious and can occur spontaneously or through meditation, prayer, experiencing natural beauty, sexuality, and other experiences. They include inspirational or peak experiences in which the universe is perceived as harmonious and unified. Opposites are transcended, and qualities of goodness, beauty, and meaning are experienced directly. They may give direct contact with what is described as the consciousness of God or the divine. Psychologist Abraham Maslow (1964) found that from such experiences, and with growth toward self-actualization, the person becomes motivated by higher values, which he called metavalues. Examples of these are wholeness, truth, beauty, aliveness, goodness, order, harmony, uniqueness, justice, and playfulness. Also, at these transpersonal levels of the self, one can experience primary energy qualities such as compassion, power, sexuality, intelligence, love, wisdom, and creation. Like the archetypes, these transpersonal principles and experiences are part of a larger reality of which the individual is a part. They have been described by Ken Wilber (1980), Stanislav Grof (1985), Lawrence LeShan (1976), Charles Tart (1975), and others. Indeed, these transpersonal ideas are so prevalent that Brad Steiger (1973) humorously suggested that it was as though there was a cosmic broadcasting station sending out the same program all the time, and the channels tune in to it. I am suggesting, rather, that there are transpersonal levels of reality in, and beyond, the self that are articulated in channeled discourse.

Frank Haronian (1974) observed that we can and do suppress these spiritual feelings, which then have to find means of expression. Higher states and spiritual values can be just as taboo or embarrassing as aggression and conflict. Perhaps in the channeling mode these qualities can be articulated and given emotional charge and inspirational charisma. Depending on the channel, they may be repetitive platitudes or inspired imagery, a one-note theme or a wide-ranging exposition. If the person is channeling these from his or her own psyche, it may be possible for them to be expressed more strongly or fully than would be possible from the ego, thus giving the fire of prophecy or the certitude of higher wisdom.

In the model involving independent entities, these levels of reality may also be expressed by channeled beings, whether gods, angels, wise figures, or inner voices. This does not mean that channeled beings (from inside or outside) are enlightened when they discuss religious or transpersonal matters, rather, that the transpersonal levels of consciousness can influence the purpose and content of channeled communications. Like human religious teachers, there is a wide range of channeled teachers. Yogi Donald Walters (1988) says that few of the channeled entities have skills as spiritual teachers. Some know the words, but seem not to have experienced transpersonal states or seem to have slid off into paranoia and fanaticism. Again, the best policy for us is to develop our sensitivity to recognizing transpersonal qualities.

If the superconscious, higher self, collective unconscious, archetypes, and transpersonal experiences are acknowledged, the boundaries of the unconscious must either be expanded or made more permeable. If the origin of channeling is in the personal unconscious, it can still draw on a wider perspective that goes beyond the limited self and the encapsulated personality level. There may be cases in which the channeling process expresses both personal qualities from within the self and transpersonal qualities from a larger independent reality. Ira Progoff felt that this was the case with Ramah, channeled by Eileen J. Garrett. Transpersonal realities might be personified, and archetypes contacted, through the channeling process. These may come from outside the self, though the self collaborates in their manifestation.

CONSIDERING THE SOURCE

Each model of channeling fits some cases very well and leaves out others. If the models are applied case by case, several models have to be used. Many cases of channeling can be best understood as coming from some more-inclusive self of the individual and drawing on the knowledge and skills presumed to be in the unconscious mind. Some cases distinctly suggest outside beings who are contacting, or being contacted by, the individual. Many cases clearly point to the presence of ESP abilities, exceptional talents, knowledge, traits, insights, and transpersonal consciousness that go beyond the conscious personality of the person. In some cases, these appear to originate within some larger mind of the person; in other cases, they appear to have their reality beyond the individual.

With our present knowledge, it does not seem possible to derive one master theory that will account for all cases without awkward cutting and pruning of some of the data. We do not know enough to prove completely that channeling comes from spirits, the mind of the individual, other levels of reality, or from some other source. Almost any theory about channeling can be supported by some cases and contradicted by others. Accepting one or another theory seems to be a choice, a preference rather than a logical conclusion. It is what we choose to believe. Studies in psychology and sociology show that people adopt a belief for many reasons, not just evidence. They may misinterpret, create, or imagine evidence to justify a belief that they want to hold. Therefore, even if we believe that a theory about channeling is the right one, and have cases to prove it, it is probably healthy to remember that nothing is certain just because we have honored it with our belief. We do not have enough understanding of the mind and its reaches to say with certainty what is possible and what is not. Our beliefs should be open to change as we learn more. We can still come to conclusions for practical purposes and test their value by how useful they are in understanding experience and guiding action. The models we use should be steppingstones for further exploration.

CHAPTER 17

THE SIGNIFICANCE OF CHANNELING

It should be evident that the process we know as channeling is not an aberration. It is an activity that has occurred throughout all recorded human history. It has significantly affected the course of events. Forms of channeling have been actively cultivated in many societies, and a role has been created for the person who channels. At this point, we can begin to suspect that it is natural. Could it be desirable? To get a sense of its contributions to society, we will look at the effects of channeling in several areas of human endeavor and consider how it may be of relevance now.

RELIGIONS

The religions of human beings have been more powerful in shaping cultures and societies than any other social institution. Channeling has played a central part in three major religions and minor parts in others. The traditions originating in the Near East can be characterized as religions of revelation in which prophecy, a form of channeling, plays a major role. Judaism now encompasses 18 million people, Christianity 1.8 billion, and Islam 880 million. This is a total of 2.7 billion people or over one third of the world's population. In addition, there are forms of channeling in the major Eastern religions of Hinduism, Buddhism, and Taoism, some minor Western religions, and in perhaps half the tribal religions of the world.

Judaism
In Biblical Judaism, the prophets were spokesmen for God. We have seen that there were brotherhoods or groups of prophets (see I Kings and I Samuel) and their communication was clearly a mode in which they experienced God speaking through them. Jeremiah says he felt God touch his mouth; phrases are used such as, "It is I, Yahweh, who speaks," and "The mouth of the Lord has spoken." The prophets were conduits through which God could speak to man. The early prophets spoke their messages to kings and individuals; the later prophets spoke to the people, as a whole, of the need for social justice. Religious philosopher Huston Smith (1958) attributes to the prophets our Western attitudes that the future of a people depends on

the justice of their social order and that individuals are responsible for the condition of their society as well as their personal lives. The prophets also defined the relationship of the Jews to their God. Their oracles (as their statements are often described) announced that the troubles of the people were a warning from God and established the meaning of suffering as a teaching experience, a perspective that is held by many today. Their messages created a social sense that stabilized the Jewish people and preserved their relation to Yahweh in troubled times.

In post-Biblical times, reliance was more on written tradition, and prophecy had to be within the bounds of the Torah, so it declined. However, rabbis in the Middle Ages often had a spiritual teacher, a *maggid*, that assisted them in their studies and teaching. We have mentioned Joseph Caro (Gordon, 1949), whose *maggid* spoke through his voice. It introduced itself as the soul of the Mishnah (the oral law) and also as the celestial mother and the Divine Presence. The *maggid* gave Caro advice on his commentaries, which are still authoritative references. The famous rabbi Ari (the Lion) and others also had *maggids*.

In contemporary channeling, there are few Jewish teachings. One is *An Introduction to the Keys of Enoch,* by James Hurtak (1975), which includes extraterrestrial vistas, pyramid energy, prophecies of catastrophes, and references to the secrets of science, in the language and concepts of Jewish mysticism. This is not the sort of teaching that is likely to have much impact on contemporary Jewish thought. However, the contribution of Biblical channeled prophecy to Jewish identity and Judaic beliefs has had lasting effects on Western culture.

Christianity

In Matthew 10:19–20, Jesus tells his disciples not to worry about what to say when they are arrested: "When the time comes, the words you need will be given you; for it is not you who will be speaking, it will be the Spirit of your Father speaking in you." In the gospel of John, Jesus said that the Advocate, the spirit of truth, would speak through his disciples. In early Christianity, the Holy Spirit was assumed to be the fulfillment of this statement. Theologian Morton Kelsey (1964) says, "It was believed that the Spirit could speak directly through the man whom it had indwelt. It could speak aloud, and in two ways, intelligibly or unintelligibly—'in the tongues of men or of angels.' The first of these ways was known by the early church as prophecy" (p. 15). The churches, at first, only allowed prophets filled with the Holy Spirit to speak in the services. Paul said that prophecy was the greatest of the gifts of the Holy Spirit, because people in the church would know their hearts had been read, judged, and their secret thoughts laid bare. This suggests that it was similar to a channeled reading involving some kind of psychic awareness. However, the Corinthians were apparently feeling too competitive about individual gifts of the spirit. In the first letter to the Corinthians, Paul admonished them that, whether one spoke in tongues or prophesied or had any other gifts, the most important quality to have was love.

The New Testament book Acts of the Apostles tells of Paul and other apostles traveling from place to place, giving the experience of the Holy Spirit by touching believers. This was one of the definitive practices that created the early church. Kelsey notes that most of the sermons recorded in Acts were spoken from the inspiration of the Spirit. Also, in these early days, various channeled books such as *The Shepherd of Hermas* were written and were considered authentic Christian doctrine, though they were not included in the Bible.

In the second century, a prophet named Montanus claimed to be speaking with the voice of the Holy Spirit and founded a pentacostal-like movement. He prophesied the imminent coming of Christ, laid down a rigorous moral code, and opposed the hierarchy of church organization that did not allow for more revelation from the spirit. At first supportive, the Roman Catholic Church excommunicated Montanus about 177 A.D., but Montanism continued as a separate Christian movement until at least the fifth century.

As the church became more institutionalized, the liturgy became fixed, and there was no room for prophetic speaking, just as happened in Judaism. The church took the position that prophecy was demonic. There is no contribution now to contemporary Christian doctrines by channeling. Prophecy and revelation are assumed to have ceased. However, as we have noted, there are many channeled teachings coming from a Christian orientation. We will look more at these later as candidates for new religious movements.

Muhammad and the Koran

The revelations of Muhammad became the chapters of the Holy Koran, the foundation of the third major Near Eastern religion, Islam. They were remarkably attuned to the Arabic people and culture, and they also addressed the practical concerns of Muhammad as ruler of Medina in later years.

The initial revelation of Muhammad involved a vision as well as a channeled transmission. He was praying in a cave about 610 A.D., when an angel, traditionally Gabriel, appeared before him and ordered him to read (or recite). He protested that he could not read. Three times the angel insisted and at last spoke:

Read: In the name of thy Lord Who createth.
Createth man from a clot.
Read: And it is thy Lord the Most Bountiful
Who teacheth by the pen,
Teacheth man that which he knew not.

(Surah 9, 1–5, Pickthall, n.d., p. x)

The Prophet Muhammad (at right) with his son Ali and grandsons Husein and Hasan. His revelations make up the Koran.

For later revelations, Muhammad would speak after going into a trance state. His words were considered revelation only if they were made from a trance state, and his followers would observe him closely to be sure the signs were there. He would be covered with sweat, seized with violent shudders, and would often lie unconscious for an hour. He said that he often heard the sound of chains, bells, or rushing wings. Mostly, he felt an inward inspiration at those times and, when he recovered, he would speak the words that he had heard or that he read from a heavenly tablet called the Mother of the Book which was the will and expression of God's truth. Sometimes, he would experience inner visions or voices; occasionally, he saw an external angel whom his companions did not. His followers recorded his words; later these were collected into the Koran.

Muhammad's earliest revelations were short, rhymed or poetic, and often disjointed. The early surahs (chapters) are associated with his time in Mecca and are more lyrical, terse, and imagistic. Later, when he was in Medina, the character of the surahs changed. They were longer and more practical. They would denounce the enemy, reassure the armies, give rules, and mobilize people to action. They played an important role in his rule of the city and his followers. This is an example of the channeling process developing according to the needs of the circumstances.

An important contribution of the Koran was to establish an appropriate spiritual revelation for the Arabic peoples. Many prophets and religious groups had been active in that part of the world, and there was familiarity with the religions of the Jews and Christians, including the stories of Noah, Abraham, Moses, Jesus, and other figures. Both the Jews and the Christians had sacred books that spoke of God. However, people of those faiths looked down upon the Arabs, and, for their part, the Arabs were reluctant to join a religion that was someone else's faith. However, the revelations of Muhammad spoke directly to the Arabic peoples, making a direct contact between them and God and providing a sacred book in their own language. Islam included the Jewish and Christian revelations, but went further with the words of Allah to Muhammad. The Koran speaks of one God, Allah, all powerful and with all transcendent attributes, who created and rules the universe.

The doctrine of one God is an important change from the polytheism and religious indifference that was present among Arabic peoples (though Muhammad belonged to a group that was monotheistic). It reflects the archetype or metavalue of unity, or oneness. The relationship to this supreme unity will tend to create a unity of identity for the people as a whole.

The requirement of submission to Allah (Islam means "submission") can be an important transpersonal process, in both sacred and secular settings. For the fiercely independent, clannish, tribal peoples of the desert, the act of submission would be a powerful transformative experience. It is not just obedience to the laws of God, but total submission to his will. This establishes Allah as the basis of life, law, decisions, and action. The appeal of this, and the leadership of Muhammad, created a religion that appeals not only to the people of its origin, but now to many people worldwide.

Hinduism

The oldest scriptures in Hinduism are the Vedas, channeled poetic hymns from the gods, that are traditionally said to have been heard by the sages. Later Hinduism and the practice of yoga emphasize personal experience rather than revelation, but some of the methods are much like channeling. In particular, Guru Yoga is a practice of learning to experience one's guru inside as an internal teacher. This may be a representation of one's actual living teacher, a master who is no longer physically living, or an advanced being such as a deity. Both J. Krishnamurti (Alcyone, 1970) and Sri Aurobindo, influential contemporary Indian teachers, transcribed material that they received from discarnate masters. One of the current movements in the Hindu tradition, Brahma Kumaris, is based on continued channeled teachings from nonphysical masters.

Buddhism and Taoism

In Tibetan Buddhism, spiritual teachings continue to be transmitted through a channeling process. The guru Padmasambhava, who traditionally brought tantric Buddhist practices from India to Tibet in the eighth century, is said to have developed teachings for later discovery when the time was appropriate. Some of these are physical scrolls, hidden in statues or caves. Others are said to be mental teachings and were placed in the minds of his disciples. They are found by later incarnations of these disciples through meditative states (Thondrup, 1986). Tibetan Buddhist teachers also receive transmissions of teachings directly from deities and other discarnate beings.

Tibetan guru Padmasambhava, who transmitted teachings called hidden treasures, to be discovered through meditation and inspiration by later followers. The statue is said to have been made during his lifetime.

The best known of these discovered hidden treasures is the *Tibetan Book of the Dead*, but there are many others which give meditative practices and prayers. These serve to connect the doctrine with its origins and yet provide new energy for the contemporary religion. As in the Hindu tradition, Buddhists also use forms of Guru Yoga to invoke the inner presence and embodiment of deities and teachers.

In Taoism, many scriptures have been received by revelation. The Mao-Shan sect uses trance states to channel deities who write in calligraphy through the priest. In 1987, American meditation teacher Shinzen Young told me that the Taoist Order of the Red Swastika uses a divination procedure in which a deity gives meditation teachings through automatic writing by priests holding a stylus in a box of sand.

Latter Day Saints and Other Religions

Probably the most significant religious movement that has originated in the United States is the Church of Jesus Christ of Latter Day Saints, the Mormon Church. Joseph Smith, Jr. (1805–1844) was said to have translated scriptures from records inscribed on golden plates found by him through the guidance of the angel Moroni (*Book of Mormon*, 1920).

The prophet Joseph Smith, Jr., translator of the Book of Mormon.

In the actual translation process, Smith gazed at a polished stone in a dark hat and visualized the writing and English translation. As we noted, a revelation said he was to study it out in his mind, and God would cause a burning in his bosom if the words were right. If the words were not right, there would be a stupor that would cause him to forget them (*Doctrine and Covenants*, 1949, p. 13). Many revelations came through Smith. Some of these added to church doctrine and encouraged believers, but many were related to governance. They appointed elders, named officers, made church policy, and gave other instructions. Today, Mormons number 4.2 million, and church leaders are said to continue to receive guidance from angels and church fathers in nonphysical realms.

There are a few other religions in which processes similar to channeling are significant. One of the practices of the Society of Friends, the Quaker Church, is cultivating the still inner voice of God for inspiration and guidance. The National Spiritualist Church lists about 5,000 members in America, and other spiritualist church groups add more to that number. The Swedenborgian church, based on the channeled teachings and visions of the Swedish genius Swedenborg, lists 2,500 American members and more abroad. Worldwide, shamanistic religions involve about 12 million persons, and probably half of these involve possession states.

RELIGIOUS SIGNIFICANCE

In relation to formalized religion alone, the influence of communication from beyond the individual, accepted as coming from God or a spiritual source, has been essential. This form of revelation or channeled prophecy has spoken to doctrines and interpretation, ceremonies, spiritual practices, relationship with God, and church organization. About half of the world's religious population belong to religions in which channeled revelation and prophecy has been, or is, a primary aspect of the religion; in many others, it is accepted or plays a role. It is fair to say that much of Western religion would not exist without this form of revelation. The influence of these religions on world events, science, economy, values, and culture is substantial, probably more than any other social institution. Within the institutions themselves, there are the heights of inspiration, ethics, and values, and the depths of Inquisitions, Holy Wars, and intolerance. This underscores that it is not just the message, it is how the message is understood and responded to that makes the difference.

POLITICS AND GOVERNANCE

Besides religion, the institution with the longest history of channeling is governance. In the Near East, the Delphic oracle was a strong political force for the first six or seven centuries of its existence. This was a time of small

Greek city-states, warring kingdoms, and unorganized populations. Though the Greeks prized rationality, they also accepted the need for transrational decisions from the oracle (Dodds, 1963). There was literally no major decision made without consulting the Pythia. The oracle inspired and directed Greek colonization throughout the Mediterranean area. Such colonies included Istanbul, Asine, Claros, Magnesia, Ephesus, and others, with lasting effects on the culture of Europe even to our times. The oracle told which laws to enact; it either gave or approved the constitution of the city of Lycurgus. It told communities to appoint governors and named the persons. The oracle gave its sanction to kings. It gave battle plans and advised on wars. It explained the causes of plagues and famines. It told of the best trade routes and approved new cults and festivals. Delphi was the closest institution to a central government for the Mediterranean area. Says historian Harry Carter (Herodotus, 1958), "The power wielded by the priests at Delphi . . . was the only power in the nature of a federal government of Greece" (p. xix). In this regard, it is irrelevant as to whether the Pythia was possessed by the god or drew on psychic abilities in a trance or whether the oracles were made up by the priests. The oracular authority and its continued success gave Delphi its power.

Channeling affected politics in another way, through the military campaign of Joan of Arc in the fifteenth century. She mobilized the French army in a time of crisis and led them to defeat the English forces and restore the French crown to Charles VII. This proved to be the turning point in the Hundred Years' War. She did this in response to communication from voices and inner guides, who, we note, were high figures in the spiritual realm of Christianity. The Archangel Michael is the Prince of the Armies of the Lord and the one who defeated Satan, casting him from heaven. How appropriate!

In the nineteenth century, the British utopian socialist Robert Owen (1771–1858) was influenced in his later years by spiritualism. He incorporated ideas from the messages into his social and educational philosophy, though he was a reformer and humanitarian long before he encountered the spirits.

Another political activist was Victoria Claflin Woodhull (1838–1927), who in the late 1800s in America championed free love, woman's suffrage, socialism, and the Greenback movement. She was a clairvoyant and medium and channeled teachings on these topics from diverse spirits. She was the first woman to run for president (on the ticket of the Equal Rights Party) and was influential in social and humanitarian movements. The American novelist Henry James attended some of her lectures and fictionalized her and other spiritualist speakers in The Bostonians (Kerr, 1972).

Theocratic governance has had assistance from channeling. We have noted that the prophet Muhammad was a capable and successful political and military leader in his own right, and the channeled messages supported this role. Tibetan Buddhism continues to use traditional possession oracles for advice on matters of state decisions and policy, as well as religion, as was described in Chapter 4. Similarly, many of the activities of groups around channeled leaders are governed by the messages. The movement of the Mormon Church from New York westward was helped through revelations.

I do not know of any contemporary political leaders who are channels or aficionados of channeled communications. Other than during the period of the ancient oracles, there is no record of major political decisions that have been submitted to channeled sources for determination. If anything, the influence has been on individuals. Usually they have been predisposed toward the themes of the teachings such as Owen, but sometimes they have simply taken them as good advice, for example, the messages to Lincoln from Nettie Coburn Maynard. The ascended masters channeled through Elizabeth Clare Prophet (1976) include several who are quite nationalistic. They contend that the United States was organized on a spiritual basis and must fulfill its destiny of becoming a democratic and spiritual utopia. They militantly urge their listeners to oppose Communism and the Soviet Union. Channels occasionally bring through messages from political figures. George Washington spoke on the occasion of the bicentennial, for example. The messages from political leaders that I have seen offer little more than inspirational platitudes fit, perhaps, to be read into the *Congressional Record*, where they will take their place with similar expressions from politicians still in their bodies.

Nevertheless, channeling has potential for relevant political commentary, drawing as it may from outside perspectives, collective concerns, or unconscious personal perceptions. Earlier, I have noted the theme of social and global issues in channeled discourse.

CHANNELING AND NEW RELIGIOUS MOVEMENTS

A case can be made that contemporary channeling is both reflecting and expressing a new religious spirit. The spiritual themes in channeled messages are persistent and pervasive, and, since there are thousands who channel and many more who listen or read, it appears that the ideas are resonating with a significant minority of the Western culture.

Some sense of public response can be obtained by looking at the sales of spiritually oriented channeled books. *The Impersonal Life* (Brenner, 1949), first published in 1941, had 321,000 copies in print by 1983. *The Urantia Book*, published in 1955, sold 140,000 copies by the mid-1980s. *A Course in Miracles*, published in 1976, had 700,000 copies in print by 1990. *The Starseed Transmissions* (Carey, 1982) sold 100,000 copies from 1982 to 1988. The Seth books have sold several million copies altogether since their beginning in 1970. With the exception of the Seth books, these sales have been with little or no advertising.

Among contemporary channeled works, *A Course in Miracles* has created a social reaction very similar to a religious movement. Publications, teachers, seminar leaders, and study groups have grown around the Course. The followers, though not organized, are probably larger in numbers than Quakers, Christian Scientists, and other small denominations which are based, to some extent, on inspired messages. The Course has the most systematic belief system of any of the channeled teachings. While the Course does not have the usual religious metaphysics such as historical stories or supernatural forces, it does have a set of principles about spiritual states and transformation. Like many principles of other religions, they are directed toward personal goals and states. Interest in the Course is likely to continue, if its message continues to speak to individuals or if a prophet arises to give it personal charisma. In that case, it may develop into a religious movement with its own religious organization.

The Alice A. Bailey material has also attracted many students. The Meditation Group for the New Age, one of several organizations involved, has a mailing list of 10,000. The Arcane School and other groups undoubtedly have students in the tens of thousands. The A.A.B. material has had the benefit of organization and multiple centers, but the disadvantage of thereby becoming a somewhat closed system: an esoteric teaching dispensed by the official groups. This is perhaps intentional, with a view toward protecting the integrity of the practices, but it also historically has led to rigidity in institutions.

Followers of the Seth material publish newsletters and periodicals such as *Reality Change* (1980–), hold conferences, and meet in study groups. The flavor is less religious or esoteric and more in the vein of consciousness expansion and exploration of personal awareness. There are also groups that have formed around the teachings of Michael, *Oahspe, The Urantia Book*, and Ramtha; and around the channels Elizabeth Clare Prophet, Ruth Norman, and probably hundreds of others throughout America and Europe. The inescapable conclusion is that interest in these materials is having a social impact and seems to be in response to a need for religious revitalization. The personalities involved are preachers of a new faith, though one not yet codified and institutionalized.

Channeled Religious Revitalization

These preachers and teachers seem to be emerging from the dissatisfaction and ferment that began in the 1960s. Such social destabilization often calls forth "revitalization movements," a term coined by anthropologist A.F.C. Wallace (1961) to refer to deliberate, organized attempts to construct a more satisfying culture. Wallace noted that a successful social revitalization movement goes through several stages, beginning with an increase in individual stress and dissatisfaction and attempts to make the system work (probably along with attempts to deny that it is dysfunctional). At some threshold, there emerges a new code of ideas, values, beliefs, myths and practices. This is a transformative vision and holds promise of an ideal society. "Not infrequently," says Wallace, "the code, or the core of it, is formulated by one individual in the course of a hallucinatory revelation;

such prophetic experiences are apt to launch religiously oriented movements, since the source of the revelation is apt to be regarded as a supernatural being" (p. 148). The channels are bringing in what Wallace calls a
new code, which is indeed often visionary and ideal. As described in the
chapter on prophecy, there are channeled critiques of social ills, prophetic
warnings, and visions of a new age. *The Starseed Transmissions* (Carey, 1982),
New Teachings for an Awakening Humanity (Christ, 1986), and David Spangler's *Revelation: The Birth of a New Age* (Spangler, 1976), are examples of these.
The prospects of the 1990s are explored by Jon Fox, Kevin Ryerson, and
other channels in *Intuiting the Future* (Krantz and Branon, 1989) which
includes political, economic, and educational forecasts.

Emphasis on Psychological Process

There is an increasing emphasis on psychological change as a path toward
spiritual growth such as in *A Course in Miracles, Emmanuel's Book* (Rodegast
and Stanton, 1985), Seth, and others. This is a recent and new theme in
channeled material. It suggests to me that the collective unconscious and/or
channeled beings are beginning to make connections between our knowledge of psychological processes and the higher life purposes that have
traditionally been a part of the spiritual domain. This is a significant shift in
channeled discourse, and I would expect it foretells a similar shift in many
mainstream religions.

Loss of Meaning

I think that the channeled spiritual themes are getting more than usual
interest because of a loss of meaning in traditional religions as well as
concern for destructive social and political practices. For many people,
religions, as they are practiced, have lost their resonance with deeper feelings and fail to provide a felt relationship with the universe. They do not
evoke spiritual values for many people. They do not meet the psychological
needs for religion. The messages of the channels, from platitudes to pro-
fundities, are trying to express these inner needs. The same factors are at
work in the many cults, new religious movements, and modern forms of
traditional religions that are springing up. Any religion will be satisfactory
only if its outer form (myths, beliefs, practices, and so forth) links with some
inner state, thus releasing that energy into the life of the person. That link
may be on the basis of emotionally comforting beliefs or deep transpersonal
levels of being. Many of the messages of contemporary channels give ideas
and ideals that meet these inner needs.

Channeling has not yet provided a new religious synthesis. It is one
movement among many that are expressing similar themes. There are many
channelers, but no one has emerged with a transcendent vision and
formulation that would serve as the nucleus for a movement. Given a
formulation, there would still need to be social communication and organ-

ization of the vision. Contemporary channels are teachers and transmitters rather than social leaders. The emphasis tends to be on the sources, the entities, rather than the channels, who are more passive, which is the best state of mind for receptivity. Most contemporary channels are more passive than Joan of Arc, Muhammad, and the prophets and shamans who have led revitalization movements. We have noted a few groups or quasi-cults built around channels but, generally, the channels (and entities) are not organizers or social activists. There may yet be a leader who will invoke channeled revelation as a vision for religious or social renewal. It could be through his or her own channeling, or it could be through incorporating channeled themes in a new religious synthesis.

WHEN CHANNELING IS SIGNIFICANT

We can now see several kinds of social conditions in which channeled messages have had significant impact. These usually occur during times of instability when channeled messages fill the need for information, decision, meaning, and authority.

1. There may be no central human or institutional authority, as with the first seven-hundred years of the oracle at Delphi or Arabia in the time of Muhammad. Here, the communication commanded allegiance through its position of authority or established a doctrine which became a unifying mythology or system of belief. The pronouncements at Delphi were highly influential in raising the moral values of the culture.

2. There may be a social crisis, as in fifteenth-century France when Joan was inspired by her angelic guides to lead the army.

3. There may be a disintegration of meaning in, and dissatisfaction with, cultural symbols. This is seen by many as the state of contemporary religion and contemporary values. In this situation, movements, some involving channeling, revelation, and so on, may arise to meet the need for a transformative vision. Depending on the content of the vision, the leaders, and the social organization, a change in the culture may result.

4. Channeling can also be called upon when a society encounters a conflict that cannot be resolved within the regular norms or behaviors of the group. An answer is required that transcends the level of authority held by those in disagreement. Channeled information or judgments then settle the matter. The disputes brought to Delphi or actions urged by the Hebrew prophets illustrate this. God speaks, and the matter is settled. This also occurs in tribal societies, where the tribe resorts to divination when there is a failure to resolve a conflict, often using the procedure of a possession trance in which a deity or spirit is consulted.

5. A society also may be stymied by an issue or need that cannot be managed within normal cultural perceptions, beliefs, or behaviors. Channeling may bring in alternative ways of perceiving the situation, new

information, or new directions. For example, the successful gardens at Findhorn were reliant upon channeled advice, some of which was contrary to ordinary gardening customs. The advice to the Liparians by the Delphic Oracle, to fight with as few ships as possible, is not what the ordinary naval strategist would advise.

In summary, forms of channeling have had enormous significance on a societal level. They have led to the colonization of the Mediterranean area, founded one religion with 880 million followers and contributed essential elements to several others, enabled military victories in the ancient and medieval worlds, affected local decisions, and influenced public beliefs and values in many cultures including virtually the entire Western world.

In contemporary American and European societies, one does not see official recourse to spirits, deities, or other channeled sources. There are few public policymakers who have channeled advisers or who speak as prophets in other than their own person. Our times are more skeptical, and the messages we have heard are not socially that powerful. Only a small number of the channelers are socially active. Nevertheless, we would be wise not to close off this source of ideas and vision. Whether these communications come to us from our idealistic repressions, from outside entities who want to "put in their two-cents worth," or from our collective unconscious speaking to us in one of its many ways, at least some of the messages are signs of the times and attempts to remedy global and individual problems with visions that go beyond our conscious limits.

SIGNIFICANCE IN PERSONAL LIVES

In our times, channeling appears to be most active in its impact on personal lives. While its significance cannot be evaluated on a large scale, its contributions can be illustrated.

1. *Personal decisions.* Questions on practical matters have always been asked of channels, from the times of ancient oracles to the present. These are stimulated when circumstances are ambiguous or when the decision must go beyond the data and principles available. Sometimes, the inquirer was famous and powerful, and his personal decision might have resulted in a war. At other times, the inquirer might have been a common citizen asking about an ordinary challenge of life. It is human to ask from a source presumed to be more knowing, having access to greater information, or better able to judge what is best, whether that source is a human expert or a disembodied entity. Sometimes, as we have seen, the channeled entity can indeed give relevant and accurate information.

2. *Therapeutic information.* On the wall of the Temple of Apollo at Delphi was the phrase "Know Thyself." In those times, this probably was a philosophical knowing. Now, we think of knowing oneself in psychological terms. Therapy and the desire for self-understanding have increased in importance since the beginning of the twentieth century and will probably

continue for decades. Responding to these needs and drawing on the collective knowledge that appears to be available in the channeling mode, the communications provide psychological descriptions, insights, and therapeutic practices for the individual. Channeled modes may be used by therapists in some cases, or individuals may seek out channels in furtherance of their own self-understanding. Channeling in the form of inner guides or voices seems to be particularly helpful for insight and personal growth.

3. *Inspiration and authority.* Channeled messages have often served to inspire and motivate. The communications seem to draw upon resources beyond the individual. They may come at critical moments and create a sense of certainty, understanding, and assurance. They may provide motivation for a cause or service beyond the self. Prophetic messages may lift the spirit to higher values. Many times, the message serves to authorize commitment or action which is carried out in private life or public roles.

4. *Reassurance.* The major role of the mediums in the beginning of the ninteenth century was to bring messages from the spirits of those who had died. These were essentially messages of reassurance and comfort and, as with most of our present cases, there was little attempt to confirm more than superficially the identity of the spirit. Some might think that these messages are no longer needed, but death is still a loss, and people still reach for an answer. While most channels do not carry out this function, those who have some mediumship inclinations receive requests for information about friends and relatives who have died. Rosemary Brown, in the middle of a film session with the BBC, was asked by one of the producers to contact his mother. In a drawing session that I attended with Luiz Gasparetto, one person asked him to contact a friend who had recently died. Such sessions were typical for Eileen Garrett, since she was known as a professional medium. The reassurance of these messages is often remarkable in reducing emotional grieving.

The personal services that come through channeling are not in the form of public statements; they are responses to individual struggles with life. There is evidence that channeling can give useful information at least some of the time. Seeking the aid of a channel is no different from contacting an expert, a therapist, or hoping to see a departed loved one in a dream. However, we have noted that the emotional dependence on a channel, or the giving over of authority, is often a problem. Another problem is that some people can get the most astute insight or the best advice and neither recognize it nor follow it. Channeling information should be tasted and tested, the same as for information from more ordinary sources.

PERILS AND RISKS

An obvious risk in channeling is that the information presented can be inaccurate, misleading, and deceptive. The authorization may be spurious. Many entities proclaim that they are not 100 percent correct, but one is not sure that they want to believe it. Listeners or followers often assume, uncritically, that the channeled material is true, relevant, and authoritative. We have noted that these are emotional beliefs that may be encouraged by the entity or the channel.

The Delphic oracle was known for its ambiguous answers. Plutarch said this was to be diplomatic when the answer was disagreeable to the inquirer. One might think it could also be to avoid giving a definite answer that might be incorrect. In fact, the Pythia urged the Greeks not to resist the invasion of the Persians. The Greeks did resist and won, and the oracle never recovered its original credibility.

Specific catastrophic prophecies of contemporary entities are disconfirmed with great regularity. Yet prophecies of calamity or of imminent landings of spacecraft seem to link with emotional fears or hopes of some groups. Several cults have formed in these circumstances, reminiscent of the groups that formed around adventist preachers who predicted the end of the world in the 1840s.

Even with a channeled being whose messages appear to have some correct psychic information, there is no guarantee that other information is correct. Channels and entities apparently have no way to tell if the information is accurate psi, analytic interpretation, or wishful thinking. Total discrimination is not possible even with the most experienced human psychics—those with training and integrity—and it is even less likely with untrained discarnate beings. When the channeled messages consist of metaphysics, past-life information, and other assertions that cannot be confirmed, there is no way to know their validity.

A further concern occurs with personality readings. Inquirers are often in a vulnerable state, perhaps a light trance, and will frequently accept statements as relating to them specifically, when the description is actually common to many people, such as "You usually try to be pleasant to people, but you can dig your heels in when you are pushed too far." A collection of these statements can create the illusion of an astute personality inventory but with no basis in actual knowledge of the person. In the world of fraudulent psychics and mediums, this is called a cold reading.

Again, in the state of listening to a channel, pronouncements about far-off past lives and karma, or realtime relationships, motives, problems, and so forth, are often taken very seriously. The reality perception of the individual can shift to accept these characterizations just as if he or she were responding to hypnotic suggestions. People will actually shift their perceptions of themselves or the external world to conform to the descriptions given by the entity. This can be disastrous, as channeling sources are usually not very sophisticated as psychologists or spiritual teachers. Of course, this is not limited to messages from channels, but happens with psychologists who tell patients what's wrong with them, doctors who describe the side effects of drugs, and many other authority figures.

PROBLEMS WITH GROUPS

When groups form around channels and entities, the problems are multiplied. Freud noted that a group mind can develop in emotionally based groups. The group essentially takes over the superego function of the individual, determining what is right and wrong. With channeling groups, there is a tendency for belief to grow because of the novelty of the experience, the link with unconscious needs of the individuals, and the support of the other members of the group. These belief systems seem to become much stronger when the group is geographically centralized and isolated. Ramtha requires that all followers come to a ranch in rural Washington for trainings, and only those who have taken the introductory sessions can move on to the advanced levels. Elizabeth Clare Prophet and several thousand followers moved to a ranch in rural Montana where they stockpiled food, built bomb shelters, and collected weapons in preparation for a nuclear war. Most channeling is done in more permeable social settings where people return to everyday life and a variety of points of view. Again, the need for discernment is evident, a skill that is useful in more than just evaluating channeled material.

SURVIVAL OF DEATH

The current wave of channeling provides almost no evidence of survival after death. Generally, this needs to be established by proof that the spirit communicating is the same as the person in his or her life. One can't take fingerprints, but the spirit can give facts, personal memories, and behave characteristically to prove that he or she is a surviving personality. As was noted, some studies of mediumship turned up plausible evidence of this sort. However, the New Age channels do not host spirits of this genre but, rather, presumed advanced beings who have long been out of the body, groups of entities, and other types of beings, some nonhuman. The few who were once on earth show little interest in proof though, as noted earlier, the spiritualist mediums still channel messages of reassurance. The entities make ample statements that consciousness survives death, but these are made metaphysically rather than evidentially.

PHILOSOPHY, PSYCHOLOGY, AND RELIGION

Many current channeled beings claim that they are from other realities or levels of consciousness, but do not describe these with consistency or specificity. It is as though there is a different metaphysical framework for each one, or each one is making up something that satisfies his or her own experience, the notions of the time, and ideas gleaned from the minds of listeners. In the times of the founding of religions, the transhuman realities were described in terms of God, angels, and heavenly kingdoms. In nineteenth- and twentieth-century spirit teachings, there were ideas of progression to higher and higher levels. Robert Crookall's (1969) book, *Interpretation of Cosmic and Mystical Experiences*, shows that psychic and channeled material from this period is roughly consistent with reports of mystical experiences.

Contemporary channeled messages often touch on these themes, but they are not equivalent to the literature of mysticism which focuses on salvation in Christ, union with God, or merging with the absolute. Contemporary messages tend to be in the intermediate realm of human striving to manifest qualities of love, charity, spontaneity, wisdom, truth, spiritual purposes, and values. Some channels and entities refer to Christ consciousness or returning to what they call the Source, God, All That Is, or the True Self. Seth emphasized that consciousness can be expanded beyond the conditioned social ego to intuitive and creative levels. Few of the current channeled beings show familiarity with the mystical traditions or mystical experiences, at least as they have been described by mystics and practitioners. The presentation of most current channels is a popular and inspirational one.

The *Urantia Book*, *Oasphe*, and the Alice A. Bailey writings describe hierarchies of angels, masters, and other beings. They include Christ, but are otherwise diverse. Many channeled messages discuss karma, reincarnation, and spiritual stages, though they are not expounded. Meditation is often recommended. The theme of evolutionary development of consciousness frequently appears, a concept that was introduced into the stream of Western metaphysics in the 1800s in the Theosophical literature channeled by Helena Blavatsky.

By analyzing the channeling processes and communications, one might identify some metaphysical and psychological hypotheses. This is what Crookall did in noting that psychic experiences often paralleled mystical ones. Lawrence LeShan (1966), after working with Eileen J. Garrett, suggested that the nature of reality depends on the assumptions held about it and that mystical and clairvoyant realities stem from axioms that are different from those of ordinary reality. There are other useful principles and hypotheses that can be derived from a study of channeling.

Some of the psychological systems that have come through channeling are well worth studying, as noted earlier in this book. These include the seven-ray model, the enneagram, the Michael typology, Seth's exercises in consciousness, and the Quadrinity process. Channeled spiritual and religious ideas should be of interest to scholars as well as practitioners. There are some well-developed myths, belief systems, and practices that may influence future religious ideas, either directly or by cultural assimilation.

THE POTENTIALS OF CHANNELING

So, we find that channeling is natural in human experience and, even more, it has made desirable, positive contributions. Channeling is of service to humanity. It is a contact point between human personality and a source or sources that can be transcendent, wise, practical, and inspirational. The study of channeling can remind us of this contact and can point to exceptional capabilities that are open to the human mind and heart. These are most striking when the person involved does not have the talents, yet demonstrates them in channeling. It does not matter whether we assume these potentials come from the personal unconscious of the individual, are brought by a visiting outside entity, or draw on transpersonal levels of the self. They are there, and one access to them is through the mental and physical processes of channeling.

Many provocative questions are raised by acknowledging these processes. For example, how many of these abilities can be directed from a conscious level using a channeling mode? Often, the communications and communicators come with an agenda of their own. Can the process be intentionally directed toward specific creativity, writing, higher levels of wisdom, decision-making, and other talents? Would the other entity be integrated into the personality or eliminated in these activities? If so, the conscious self would be in command of a vast range of potentials.

On the other hand, it may be that there are advantages to separating these skills from the conscious ego. Perhaps an outside entity, or the construction of one, is essential to bypass the habits, assumptions, defenses, and so on of the mind, which would block the access and use of these superior abilities. If so, the relationship between the ego and the other entity should be honored. It could be explored more fully using what we know about trust, intimacy, and responsibility in interpersonal relations. This could result in a partnership, with mutual respect, through which the benefits of channeling could be developed.

Perhaps there are many more potentials to be encountered through channeling than have appeared in the documented cases. There may be skills and talents, social commentary, and ideas that move us beyond present limitations. Further, it is quite possible that serious training can refine and expand the skills and quality of the communications.

Equally important is learning to avoid the dangers and perils of channeling. Some of these are human personality issues, such as dependence, inflation, and lack of balance. Others have to do with the communicators, when they are negative, malicious, demanding, or deceptive. Psychological health is called for, along with a combination of self-discipline and open-mindedness.

The title of this book emphasizes that information, ideas, and talents are worthless unless they are used in the context of love. This is not just a sentimental idea, but one which is echoed by the the best channeled communications and highest spiritual traditions throughout history. A consistent theme in channeling from Delphi, revealed religions, Patience Worth, and contemporary channels is the value of these higher qualities: justice, wisdom, righteousness, humility, compassion, service, knowledge, self-respect, understanding, and love. People and civilizations are judged by such qualities. Whether the tongues of channeling are from the minds of men and women or from the angels, their messages often remind us of those values. We should take these messages seriously, so that the knowledge that comes to us from channeling, or any source, will be used in wisdom and love for the benefit of people and the world.

REFERENCES

Alcyone (Pseud. of J. Krishnamurti). (1970). *At the feet of the master*. Wheaton, IL: Theosophical Publishing House. (Original work published 1910).

Allison, Ralph, & Schwarz, Ted. (1980). *Minds in many pieces: The making of a very special doctor*. New York: Rawson, Wade.

Alschuler, Alfred S. (1987). Recognizing inner teachers: Inner voices throughout history. *Gnosis*, No. 5, 8–12.

Alschuler, Alfred S. (1990). Revelation and renewal. Keynote speech at the National Convention of the American Association of Counseling and Development, Cincinnati, Ohio, March 17, 1990.

Anderson, Rodger. (1988). Channeling. *Parapsychology Review, 19*(5), 6–9.

Andrews, Joel. (1989). *A harp full of stars*. Ben Lomond, CA: Golden Harp.

Assaily, A. (1963). Psychophysiological correlates of mediumship faculties. *International Journal of Parapsychology, 5*, 357–374.

Assagioli, Roberto. (1965). *Psychosynthesis*. New York: Hobbs, Dorman.

Assagioli, Roberto. (1973). *The act of will*. New York: Penguin.

Bailey, Alice A. (1922). *Initiation: Human and solar*. New York: Lucis.

Bailey, Alice A. (1934). *A treatise on white magic or the way of the disciple*. New York: Lucis.

Bailey, Alice A. (1936–1960). *A treatise on the seven rays*. (Vols. 1–5). New York: Lucis.

Bailey, Alice A. (1936). *Esoteric psychology, vol. 1: A treatise on the seven rays*. New York: Lucis.

Bailey, Alice A. (1944). *Discipleship in the new age*, vol. I. New York: Lucis.

Bailey, Alice A. (1951). *The unfinished autobiography*. New York: Lucis.

Bailey, Alice A. (1955). *Discipleship in the new age*, vol. II. New York: Lucis.

Bailey, Foster. (1954). *Changing esoteric values*. New York: Lucis.

Blavatsky, Helena P. (1966). *An abridgement of* The Secret Doctrine. London: Theosophical Publishing House. (Original work published 1888).

The book of Mormon (Joseph Smith, Jr., Trans.). (1920). Salt Lake City, UT: Church of Jesus Christ of Latter Day Saints. (First edition 1830).

Braude, Stephen (Ed.). (1980). Selected poems of Patience Worth. In J. Laughlin (Ed.), *New directions in prose and poetry 40* (pp. 155–166). New York: New Directions.

Braude, Stephen. (1988). Mediumship and multiple personality. *Journal of the Society of Psychical Research, 55*(813), 177–195.

Brenner, Joseph. (1949). *The impersonal life*. Los Angeles: DeVorss. (Original work published 1941).

Bro, Harmon H. (1970). *Edgar Cayce on religion and psychic experience*. New York: Paperback Library.

Bronson, Matthew. (1988). The voice of the "other": Linguists consider channeling. *New Eyes: The Quarterly Newsletter of the Center for Applied Intuition, 4*, 3–6.

Brown, Rosemary. (1970). *A musical seance* (phonograph album). Phillips PHS 900-256. With album notes.

Brown, Rosemary. (1971). *Unfinished symphonies: Voices from beyond*. New York: Bantam.

Brown, Rosemary. (1974). *Immortals by my side*. Chicago: Regnery.

Brown, Rosemary. (1977). *Music from beyond: Seven pieces for piano solo* (music album). Eastwood, England: Basil Ramsey.

Brown, Rosemary. (1978). *Intermezzo in A flat for piano* (Inspired by Brahms) (Sheet music). Eastwood, England: Basil Ramsey.

Brown, Rosemary. (1980). *An album of piano pieces for children of all ages* (music album). Eastwood, England: Basil Ramsey.

Caddy, Eileen. (1976). *Foundations of Findhorn*. Forres, Scotland: Findhorn Publications.

Carey, Ken. (1982). *The starseed transmissions: An extraterrestrial report*. Kansas City: Uni-Sun.

Carey, Ken. (1985). *Vision*. Kansas City: Uni-Sun. Introduction by Jean Houston.

Carey, Ken. (1988). *Return of the bird tribes*. Kansas City: Uni-Sun.

Carter, Mary Ellen. (1972). *My years with Edgar Cayce: The personal story of Gladys Turner Davis*. New York: Harper and Row.

Cayce, Edgar. (1934). Transcript 507-1, Association for Research and Enlightenment, Virginia Beach, VA.

Cayce, Edgar. (1970). *Individual reference file*. Virginia Beach, VA: Association for Research and Enlightenment.

Cayce, Edgar Evans, & Cayce, Hugh Lynn. (1971). *The outer limits of Edgar Cayce's power*. New York: Harper and Row.

Cayce, Hugh Lynn. (1964). *Venture inward*. New York: Paperback Library.

Cerminara, Gina. (1950). *Many mansions*. New York: New American Library.

Chandley, Margaret Ruth. (1986). *A psychological investigation of the development of the mediumistic process in personality function*. Unpublished doctoral dissertation, International College, Los Angeles, CA.

The Christ. (1986). *New teachings for an awakening humanity* (Virginia Essene, Chan.). Santa Clara, CA: Spiritual Education Endeavors.

Clifton, Chas. (1987). Changing channels. *Gnosis*, No. 5, 13–16.

Cook, Emily Williams. (1987). The survival question: Impasse or crux? *Journal of the American Society for Psychical Research, 81*(2), 125–139.

Cosmic Awareness speaks. (n.d.) Seattle, WA: Servants of Awareness.

A Course in Miracles: Vol. I, text (Helen Schucman, Chan.). (1985a). Tiburon, CA: Foundation for Inner Peace. (Combined volume edition, with pagination identical to the original work published 1975 in three separate volumes.)

A Course in Miracles: Vol. II, workbook for students (Helen Schucman, Chan.). (1985b). Tiburon, CA: Foundation for Inner Peace.

A Course in Miracles: Vol. III, manual for teachers (Helen Schucman, Chan.). (1985c). Tiburon, CA: Foundation for Inner Peace.

Crabtree, Adam. (1985). *Multiple man: Explorations in possession and multiple personality*. Don Mills, Ontario: Collins.

Crookall, Robert. (1969). *The interpretation of cosmic and mystical experiences*. Cambridge: James Clarke.

Cummins, Geraldine. (1932). *The road to immortality: Being a description of the after-life purporting to be communicated by the late F.W.H. Myers*. London: Psychic Press.

Damgaard, Jacqueline A. (1987). The inner self helper: Transcendent life within life? *Noetic Sciences Review*, No. 5, 24–28.

Davis, Andrew Jackson. (1875). *The principles of nature, her divine revelations, and a voice to mankind* (34th ed.). New York: A. J. Davis. Original edition published 1847.

Delaney, Gayle. (1988). *Living your dreams*. New York: Harper and Row.

The doctrine and covenants of the Church of Jesus Christ of Latter Day Saints. (1949). Salt Lake City, UT: Church of Jesus Christ of Latter Day Saints.

Dodds, E. R. (1963). *The Greeks and the irrational*. Berkeley: University of California.

Dubugras, Elsie; Gasparetto, Luiz Antonio; & Espiritos Diversos. (1979). *Renoir, e voce?* (Trans. E. Dubugras) Sao Paulo: Federacao Espirita de Estado de Sao Paulo.

Earth changes: Past, present, future. (1963). Virginia Beach, VA: A.R.E. Press.

Ebon, Martin. (1968). *Prophecy in our time*. New York: New American Library.

Ebon, Martin. (1971). *They knew the unknown*. New York: New American Library.

Eggenstein, Kurt. (1973). *The unknown prophet Jakob Lorber: A prophecy and warning for the near future* (Violet Ozols, Trans.). Bietigheim, Germany: Lorber-Verlag.

Elkins, Don, & Rueckert, Carla. (1977). *Secrets of the UFO*. Louisville, KY: L/L Research.

Elkins, Don; Rueckert, Carla; & McCarthy, James Allen. (1984). *The Ra material: An ancient astronaut speaks*. Norfolk, VA: Donning. (Original published as book I of *The law of one*.)

Ellwood, Robert S., Jr. (1973). *Religious and spiritual groups in modern America*. Englewood Cliffs, NJ: Prentice-Hall.

Evans, Hilary. (1984). *Visions, apparitions, alien visitors*. Wellingborough, Northamptonshire, England: Aquarian.

Eyer, Kenneth M. (1987). *Channeling: An emerging rationale*. Seattle: Kairos.

Festinger, Leon; Riecken, Henry W.; & Schachter, Stanley. (1956). *When prophecy fails: A social and psychological study of a group that predicted the end of the world*. New York: Harper and Row.

Findhorn Community (W. I. Thompson, Ed.). (1976). *The Findhorn garden*. New York: Harper and Row.

Fiore, Edith. (1987). *The unquiet dead*. New York: Doubleday.

Flew, Antony (Ed.). (1964). *Body, mind, and death*. New York: Macmillan.

Fodor, Nandor. (1966). *Encyclopaedia of psychic science*. New Hyde Park, NY: University Books.

Fox, Matthew. (1983). *Original blessing: A primer in creation spirituality*. Santa Fe, NM: Bear & Co.

Gaetani, Vera Regina Marcallo. (1986). *Gasparetto, nem santo, nem genio, médium*. Sao Paulo: Aquarela.

Garrett, Eileen J. (1949). *Adventures in the supernormal: A personal memoir*. New York: Creative Age.

Gauld, Alan. (1968). *The founders of psychic research*. New York: Schocken.

Gauld, Alan. (1977). Discarnate survival. In Benjamin B. Wolman (Ed.), *Handbook of parapsychology* (pp. 577–630). New York: Van Nostrand Reinhold.

Glass, Justine (Pseud, of Alice E. Corrall). (1969). *They foresaw the future: The story of fulfilled prophecy*. New York: G. P. Putnam's Sons.

Gordon, Hirsch Loeb. (1949). *The maggid of Caro*. New York: Pardes.

Govinda, Anagarika. (1966). *The way of the white clouds*. London: Rider.

Grady, Harvey. (1988). Castor oil packs: Scientific tests verify therapeutic value. *Venture Inward,* 4(4), 12–15.

Grof, Stanislav. (1985). *Beyond the brain: Birth, death and transcendence in psychotherapy.* Albany: State University of New York.

Grof, Stanislav, & Grof, Christina (Eds.). (1989). *Spiritual emergency: When transformation becomes a crisis.* Los Angeles: Tarcher.

Haley, Jay (Ed.). (1967). *Advanced techniques of hypnosis and therapy: Selected papers of Milton H. Erickson.* New York: Grune and Stratton.

Hammond, David. (1975). Unpublished recorded interview with Helen Schucman.

Hankey, Muriel. (1963). *J. Hewat McKenzie: Pioneer of psychical research.* New York: Helix.

Harman, Willis & Rheingold, Howard. (1984). *Higher creativity: Liberating the unconscious for breakthrough insights.* Los Angeles: Tarcher.

Haronian, Frank. (1974). Repression of the sublime. *Synthesis, 1,* 125–136.

Hastings, Arthur. (1983). A counseling approach to parapsychological experience. *Journal of Transpersonal Psychology, 15*(2), 143–168.

Hastings, Arthur. (1987). The study of channeling. In D. H. Weiner & R. D. Nelson (Eds.), *Research in parapsychology* (pp. 152–153). Metuchen, NJ: Scarecrow Press.

Hastings, Arthur. (1988). Exceptional abilities in channeling. *Noetic Sciences Review,* No. 6, 27–29.

Hastings, Arthur. (1990). Psi and the phenomena of channeling. In Linda Henkel (Ed.), *Research in parapsychology, 1989.* Metuchen, NJ: Scarecrow.

Hawken, Paul. (1975). *The magic of Findhorn.* New York: Harper and Row.

Heery, Myrtle W. (1989). Inner voice experiences: An exploratory study of thirty cases. *Journal of Transpersonal Psychology, 21*(1), 73–82.

Herodotus. (1958). *The histories of Herodotus* (Harry Carter, Trans.). New York: Heritage Press.

Heywood, Rosalind. (1959). *The sixth sense: An inquiry into extra-sensory perception.* London: Pan.

Hilgard, Ernest R. (1986). *Divided consciousness: Multiple controls in human thought and action* (Expanded edition). New York: John Wiley.

Hill, Napoleon. (1960). *Think and grow rich.* New York: Fawcett Crest. (Original work published 1937).

Hillman, James. (1983). *Healing fiction.* Barrytown, NY: Station Hill.

Hillman, James & Dunn, Barbara. (1989). *A Course in Miracles:* Spiritual path or omnipotent fantasy? *Common Boundary, 7*(5), 9–12.

Hodson, Geoffrey. (1968). *The seven human temperaments.* Adyar: Theosophical Publishing House.

Hoffman, Bob. (1979). *No one is to blame: Getting a loving divorce from Mom and Dad.* Palo Alto, CA: Science and Behavior. (Original work published 1976 as *Getting divorced from Mother and Dad).*

Hudson, Thomson Jay (1970). *The law of psychic phenomena: A working hypothesis for the systematic study of the vast potential of the human mind.* Monterey, CA: Hudson-Cohan. (Original work published 1893).

Hunt, Stoker. (1985). *Ouija: The most dangerous game.* New York: Harper and Row.

Hurtak, J. J. (1975). *An introduction to the keys of Enoch.* Los Gatos, CA: Academy for Future Science.

James, William. (1958). *The varieties of religious experience.* New York: New American Library. (Original work published 1902).

Jaynes, Julian. (1976). *The origin of consciousness in the breakdown of the bicameral mind.* Boston: Houghton-Mifflin.

Johnson, R. C. (1955). *Psychical research.* New York: Funk and Wagnalls.

Journal of the American Society for Psychical Research. (1907-to date). Vols. 1–.

Journal of the Society for Psychical Research. (1884-to date). Vols. 1–.

Judah, J. Stillson. (1967). *History and philosophy of the metaphysical movements in America.* Philadelphia: Westminster.

Jung, C. G. (1959a). *The basic writings of C. G. Jung* (Violet Staub de Lazlo, Ed.). New York: Modern Library.

Jung, C. G. (1959b). *Flying saucers: A modern myth of things seen in the skies.* New York: Harcourt Brace.

Jung, C. G. (1968). *Analytical psychology: Its theory and practice.* New York: Viking.

Jung, C. G. (1973). *Memories, dreams, reflections* (Richard and Clara Winston, Trans.). New York: Random House.

Jung. C. G. (1977). *Psychology and the occult.* Princeton, NJ: Princeton University Press.

Kahn, David. (1970). *My life with Edgar Cayce.* Garden City, NY: Doubleday.

Kautz, William H., & Branon, Melanie. (1987). *Channeling: The intuitive connection.* San Francisco: Harper and Row. Foreword and forecast by Kevin Ryerson.

Kautz, William H., & Branon, Melanie. (1989). *Intuiting the future: A new age vision of the 1990s.* San Francisco: Harper and Row.

Keel, John A. (1970). *UFOs: Operation Trojan Horse.* New York: G. P. Putnam's Sons.

Kelsey, Morton. (1964). *Tongue speaking.* Garden City, NY: Doubleday.

Kelsey, Morton. (1978). *Discernment: A study in ecstasy and evil.* New York: Paulist Press.

Kerr, Howard. (1972). *Mediums, and spirit-rappers, and roaring radicals: Spiritualism in American literature, 1850–1900.* Urbana: Univ. of Illinois.

Klimo, Jon. (1987). *Channeling: Investigations on receiving information from paranormal sources.* Los Angeles: Tarcher.

Knight, Carol Bell. (1981). *Passing the torch: The way of the avatar.* Walpole, NH: Stillpoint.

Knight, David C. (1969). *The ESP reader.* New York: Grosset and Dunlap.

Krippner, Stanley. (1980). *Human possibilities.* New York: Anchor Doubleday.

The law of one, bk. II (Carla Rueckert, Chan.). (1982a). Louisville, KY: L/L Research. (See Elkins, et al., 1984, for book I.)

The law of one, bk. III (Carla Rueckert, Chan.). (1982b). Louisville, KY: L/L Research.

The law of one, bk. IV (Carla Rueckert, Chan.). (1983). Louisville, KY: L/L Research.

LeShan, Lawrence. (1966). *The medium, the mystic, and the physicist.* New York: Ballantine.

LeShan, Lawrence. (1976). *Alternate realities: The search for the full human being.* New York: Ballantine Books.

Lilly, John C. (1972). *The center of the cyclone.* New York: Julian.

Lilly, John C. & Hart, Joseph E. (1975). The Arica training. In Charles T. Tart (Ed.), *Transpersonal psychologies* (pp. 329–351). New York: Harper and Row. Reprinted 1983, Psychological Processes, El Cerrito, CA.

Lincoln, Robert. (1983). *The relationship between depth psychology and protoanalysis.* Unpublished Ph.D. dissertation. Institute of Transpersonal Psychology, Menlo Park, CA.

Litvag, Irving. (1972). *Singer in the shadows: The strange story of Patience Worth.* New York: Macmillan.

Long, Donna Wilson. (1986). The discarnate masters of Luiz Gasparetto. *Shaman's Drum,* No. 5 (Summer), 32–37.

Maslow, Abraham. (1964). *Religions, values and peak experiences.* Columbus: University of Ohio.

Masters, Robert, & Houston, Jean. (1972). *Mind games: The guide to inner space.* New York: Dell.

McGarey, William A. (1970). *Edgar Cayce and the palma cristi.* Virginia Beach, VA: Edgar Cayce Foundation.

McGarey, William A. (1983). *The Edgar Cayce remedies.* New York: Bantam.

McLaughlin, Corrine. (1987). Tuning in the best channel. *New Realities,* 7(6), 37–42.

Mentor (Meredith Lady Young, Chan.) (1985). Mentor: On the rest of the century. *Metapsychology: The Journal of Discarnate Intelligence,* 1(1), 23–24.

Merrill, James. (1982). *The changing light at Sandover.* New York: Atheneum.

Metapsychology: The Journal of Discarnate Intelligence. (1985–1987). Vols. 1–2.

Metzger, W. (1989). The Psi-Cops convene in Chicago. *The Quest,* 2(1), 87–89.

Metzner, Ralph. (1979). *Know your type.* New York: Anchor Doubleday.

Millar, Charles R. (1990). A descriptive analysis of psychic opening. Unpublished doctoral dissertation, California Institute of Integral Studies, San Francisco.

Mossman, Tam. (1986). Editorial realities. *Metapsychology: The Journal of Discarnate Intelligence,* 2(1), 13–14.

Muhl, Anita. (1963). *Automatic writing: An approach to the unconscious.* New York: Helix Press. (Original work published 1930.)

Murphy, Gardner. (1961). *Challenge of psychical research: A primer of parapsychology.* New York: Harper and Brothers.

Murphy, Gardner, & Ballou, Robert O. (Eds.). (1960). *William James on psychical research.* New York: Viking.

Myers, F.W.H. (1903). *Human personality and its survival of bodily death* (Two vols.). New York: Longmans, Green.

Naranjo, Claudio. (1985). The Quadrinity process: A new synthesis. Article published by Hoffman Institute, Oakland, CA.

Norman, Ruth E., & Spaegel, Charles. (1987). *Principles and practice of past life therapy.* El Cajon, CA: Unarius.

Oahspe: A new bible in the words of Jehovih and his angel ambassadors (John Ballou Newbrough, Chan.). (1960). Amherst, WI: Amherst Press. (Original work published 1882.)

Oesterreich, Traugott K. (1974). *Possession and exorcism* (D. Ibberson, Trans.). New York: Causeway. (Original work published 1921, as *Possession: Demoniacal and other.)*

Ostrander, Sheila, & Schroeder, Lynn. (1970). *Psychic discoveries behind the iron curtain.* Englewood Cliffs, NJ: Prentice-Hall.

Palmer, Helen. (1988). *The enneagram.* San Francisco: Harper and Row.

Parke, H. W., & Wormell, D.E.W. (1956). *The Delphic oracle* (Two vols.). Oxford: Basil Blackwell.

Parrott, Ian. (1978). *The music of Rosemary Brown.* London: Regency Press.

Peck, M. Scott. (1978). *The road less traveled: A new psychology of love, traditional values, and spiritual growth.* New York: Simon and Schuster.

Perry, Michael. (1990). Possession. *Parapsychology Review, 21*(2), 1–4.

Pickthall, Mohammed Marmaduke (Trans.). (n.d.). *The meaning of the glorious Koran.* New York: Mentor.

Pope, Joya. (1987). *The world according to Michael.* San Mateo, CA: Sage.

Popenoe, Chris, & Popenoe, Oliver. (1984). *Seeds of tomorrow: New age communities that work.* New York: Harper and Row.

Prince, Walter Franklin. (1927). *The case of Patience Worth: A critical study of certain unusual phenomena* (Second edition). Boston: Boston Society for Psychical Research.

Progoff, Ira. (1964). *The image of an oracle; A report on research into the mediumship of Eileen J. Garrett.* New York: Helix.

Progoff, Ira. (1974). *At a journal workshop.* New York: Dialogue House.

Prophet, Elizabeth Clare. (1976). *The great white brotherhood in the culture, history, and religion of America.* Malibu, CA: Summit Lighthouse.

Psychotherapy: Purpose, process and practice (Helen Schucman, Chan.). (1976). Tiburon, CA: Foundation for Inner Peace.

Puharich, Andrija. (1974). *Uri: A journal of the mystery of Uri Geller.* New York: Doubleday Anchor.

Radha, Sivananda. (1978). *Kundalini yoga for the West.* Palo Alto, CA: Timeless Books.

Ramtha (J. Z. Knight, Chan.) (Steven L. Weinberg, Ed.). (1986). Eastsound, WA: Sovereignty.

Randi, James. (1982). *Flim-flam.* Buffalo, NY: Prometheus.

Rawcliffe, D. H. (1959). *Illusions and delusions of the supernatural and the occult.* New York: Dover.

Reality Change: A Magazine for People Who Want to Change Their Lives. (1980– to date). Vols. 1–.

Reed, Henry. (1989). *Edgar Cayce on channeling your higher self.* New York: Warner.

Rhine, J. B. (1934). Telepathy and clairvoyance in the normal and trance states of a "medium". *Character and Personality, 3,* 91–111.

Rhine, J. B. (1937). *New frontiers of the mind: The story of the Duke experiments.* New York: Farrar & Rinehart.

Richards, Douglas. (1990). Dissociation and transformation. *Journal of Humanistic Psychology, 30*(3), 54–83.

Ridall, Kathryn. (1988). *Channeling: How to reach out to your spirit guides.* New York: Bantam.

Ridall, Kathryn. (1990). The Hoffman Quadrinity process. *New Realities, 10*(3), 35–39.

Rilke, Rainer Maria. (1939). *Duino elegies* (J. B. Leishman and S. Spender, Trans.). New York: W. W. Norton.

Riso, Don Richard. (1987). *Personality types: Using the enneagram for self-discovery.* Boston: Houghton Mifflin.

Roberts, Jane. (1970). *The Seth material.* Englewood Cliffs, NJ: Prentice-Hall.

Roberts, Jane. (1972). *Seth speaks: The eternal validity of the soul.* Englewood Cliffs, NJ: Prentice-Hall.

Roberts, Jane. (1973). *The education of Oversoul 7.* Englewood Cliffs, NJ: Prentice-Hall.

Roberts, Jane. (1974). *The nature of personal reality: A Seth book.* Englewood Cliffs, NJ: Prentice-Hall.

Roberts, Jane. (1975). *Adventures in consciousness: An introduction to aspect psychology.* Englewood Cliffs, NJ: Prentice-Hall.

Roberts, Jane. (1976). *The coming of Seth.* New York: Pocket Books. (Original work published 1966 as *How to develop your ESP power.*)

Roberts, Jane. (1978). *The afterdeath journal of an American philosopher: The world view of William James.* Englewood Cliffs, NJ: Prentice-Hall.

Rodegast, Pat, & Stanton, Judith. (1985). *Emmanuel's book: A manual for living comfortably in the cosmos.* Weston, CT: Friend's Press.

Roman, Sanaya & Packer, Duane. (1987). *Opening to channel: How to connect with your spirit guide.* Tiburon, CA: H. J. Kramer.

Rueckert, Carla L. (1987). *A channeling handbook.* Louisville, KY: L/L Research.

Ryerson, Kevin, & Purcell, Jack. (1987). Address made to the Whole Life Exposition, Pasadena, CA (tape recording). Conference Recording Service, Berkeley, CA.

Schucman, Helen. (1973). *Autobiography.* Unpublished manuscript.

Schwarz, Jack. (1980). *Human energy systems.* New York: Dutton.

Shaw, George Bernard. (1958). *Seven plays.* New York: Dodd, Mead.

Shealy, C. Norman, & Myss, Caroline M. (1988). *The creation of health: Merging traditional medicine with intuitive diagnosis.* Walpole, NH: Stillpoint.

Shepherd, Leslie (Ed.). (1984). *Encyclopedia of occultism and parapsychology* (2nd Ed.). Detroit, MI: Gale Research.

Sinclair, John R. (1984). *The Alice Bailey inheritance.* Wellingborough, England: Turnstone Press.

Singer, June. (1973). *Boundaries of the soul: The practice of Jung's psychology.* New York: Doubleday Anchor.

Skutch, Robert. (1984). *Journey without distance: The story behind* A Course in Miracles. Berkeley, CA: Celestial Arts.

Smith, Huston. (1958). *The religions of man.* New York: Harper and Row.

Smith, Susy. (1974). *The book of James: Conversations from beyond.* New York: G. P. Putnam's Sons.

Smoley, Richard. (1987). Pitfalls of *A Course in Miracles.* Gnosis, No. 5, 17–19.

Sommerlott, Robert. (1971). *Here Mr. Splitfoot: An informal exploration into modern occultism.* New York: Viking.

The song of prayer (Helen Schucman, Chan.,). (1974). Tiburon, CA: Foundation for Inner Peace.

Spangler, David. (1976). *Revelation: The birth of a new age.* Middleton, WI: Lorian Press.

St. Clair, David. (1974). *Psychic healers.* New York: Doubleday.

Stearn, Jess. (1967). *Edgar Cayce: The sleeping prophet.* Garden City, NY: Doubleday.

Steiger, Brad (1973). *Revelation: The divine fire.* Englewood Cliffs, NJ: Prentice-Hall.

Steiger, Brad. (1988). *The fellowship: Spiritual contact between humans and outer space beings.* New York: Ivy.

Stevens, Jose, & Warwick-Smith, Simon. (1986). *The Michael handbook, vol. one: Essence and personality.* Orinda, CA: Warwick Press.

Stevenson, Ian. (1974). *Twenty cases suggestive of reincarnation.* Charlottesville: University of Virginia.

Stevenson, Ian. (1974). Some comments on automatic writing. *Journal of the American Society for Psychical Research, 72,* 315–352.

Stillings, Dennis. (1986). Strip mining the psyche. *Artifex, 5*(5), 1–5.

Stone, Hal, & Winkelman, Sidra. (1989). *Embracing our selves.* San Rafael: New World Library.

The story of A Course in Miracles (video). (1987). Tiburon, CA: Foundation for Inner Peace.

Sugrue, Thomas. (1945). *There is a river: The story of Edgar Cayce.* New York: Dell.

Swedenborg, Emanuel. (1852). *Heaven and hell: From things heard and seen.* New York: Swedenborg Foundation.

Swedenborg, Emanuel. (1875). *A compendium of Swedenborg's theological writings* (Compiled by Samuel M. Warren). New York: Swedenborg Foundation.

Targ, Russell; Hastings, Arthur; & Harary, Keith. (1987). Psychological impact of psychic abilities. *Psychological Perspectives, 18*(1), 38–51.

Tart, Charles T. (1975). *States of consciousness.* New York: Dutton.

Tart, Charles T. (1983) *Transpersonal psychologies.* El Cerrito, CA: Psychological Processes.

Tart, Charles T. (1989). *Open mind, discriminating mind: Reflections on human possibilities.* San Francisco: Harper and Row.

Tate, David A. (1989). *Health, hope and healing.* New York: M. Evans.

Thomason, Sarah. (1989). Entities in the linguistic mine field. *Skeptical Inquirer, 13,* 391–396.

Thondrup, Tulku, Rinpoche. (1986). *Hidden teachings of Tibet: An explanation of the terma tradition of the Nyingma school of Buddhism.* London: Wisdom.

Tuttle, Paul Norman. (1985). *You are the answer.* Seattle, WA: Kairos.

The Urantia book. (1955). Chicago: Urantia Foundation.

Vallee, Jacques. (1975). *The invisible college: What a group of scientists has discovered about UFO influences on the human race.* New York: E. P. Dutton.

Vallee, Jacques. (1979). *Messengers of deception: UFO contacts and cults.* New York: Bantam.

Vandenberg, Philip. (1982). *The mystery of the oracles.* New York: Macmillan.

Van Dusen, Wilson. (1972). *The natural depth in man.* New York: Harper and Row.

Van Dusen, Wilson. (1973). The presence of spirits in madness. In James Fadiman & Donald Kewman (Eds.), *Exploring madness: Experience, theory, research* (pp. 118–134). Monterey, CA: Brooks/Cole.

Vargiu, James G. (1974). Subpersonalities. *Synthesis, 1,* 52–90.

Vaughan, Frances. (1979). *Awakening intuition.* New York: Anchor Doubleday.

Vaughan, Frances. (1986). *The inward arc: Healing and wholeness in psychotherapy and spirituality.* Boston: Shambhala.

Wallace, Anthony F. C. (1961). *Culture and personality.* New York: Random House.

Wallace, Irving; Wallechinsky, D.; Wallace, A.; & Wallace, S. (1980). *The book of lists #2.* New York: William Morrow.

Walsh, Roger N. (1984). *Staying alive: Survival in the nuclear age.* Boston: Shambhala.

Walsh, Roger N. (1989). The perennial wisdom of A Course in Miracles. *Common Boundary, 7*(1), 10–17.

Walsh, Roger N. (1990). *The spirit of shamanism.* Los Angeles: Tarcher.

Walsh, Roger N., & Vaughan, Frances (Eds.). (1980). *Beyond ego: Transpersonal dimensions in psychology.* Los Angeles: Tarcher.

Walters, J. Donald. (1987). *How to be a channel.* Nevada City, CA: Crystal Clarity.

Wapnick, Kenneth. (1978). *Christian psychology in* A Course in Miracles. Available from Foundation for Inner Peace, Glen Ellen, CA.

Wapnick, Kenneth. (1982). *Glossary-Index for* A Course in Miracles. (2nd Ed., Enlarged). Crompond, NY: Foundation for "A Course in Miracles."

Wapnick, Kenneth. (1983). *Forgiveness and Jesus: The meeting place of* A Course in Miracles *and Christianity.* Crompond, NY: Foundation for "A Course in Miracles."

Wapnick, Kenneth. (1985). *The fifty miracles principles of* A Course in Miracles. Crompond, NY: Foundation for "A Course in Miracles".

Watkins, Mary. (1986). *Invisible guests: The development of imaginal dialogues.* Hillsdale, NJ: Analytic Press.

Watkins, Susan M. (1980). *Conversations with Seth: The story of Jane Roberts's ESP class, vol. 1.* Englewood Cliffs, NJ: Prentice-Hall.

Watkins, Susan M. (1981). *Conversations with Seth: The story of Jane Roberts's ESP class, vol. 2.* Englewood Cliffs, NJ: Prentice-Hall.

Westen, Robin. (1988). *Channelers: A new age directory.* New York: Perigee/Putnam.

Wheatley, James M. O., & Edge, Hoyt L. (Eds.) (1976). *Philosophical dimensions of parapsychology.* Springfield, IL: C. C. Thomas.

White, Ruth, & Swainson, Mary. (1971). *Gildas communicates: The story and the scripts.* London: Neville Spearman.

White, Stewart Edward (1940). *The unobstructed universe.* New York: E. P. Dutton.

Wickland, Carl A. (1974). *Thirty years among the dead.* Van Nuys, CA: Newcastle.

Wilber, Ken. (1980). *The Atman project.* Wheaton, IL: Theosophical Publishing House.

Williams, B.A.O. (1964). Personal identity and individuation. In D. F. Gustafson (Ed.), *Philosophical psychology* (pp. 324–345). New York: Anchor Doubleday.

Wilson, Mona. (1971). *The life of William Blake.* Oxford: Oxford University Press.

The work of the master Djwhal Khul with Alice A. Bailey. (1967). Tunbridge Wells, Kent, England: Sundial House.

Worth, Patience. (1913–1937). *Patience Worth papers.* Unpublished manuscript vols. 1–29, and documents. Archives of the Missouri Historical Society, St. Louis.

Yamada, Helen Washburn. (1986–1987). Our intergalactic connections. *Metapsychology: The Journal of Discarnate Intelligence, 2*(4), 53–50.

Yarbro, Chelsea Quinn. (1979). *Messages from Michael.* New York: Playboy Books.

Yarbro, Chelsea Quinn. (1986). *More messages from Michael.* New York: Berkley Books.

Yeats, W. B. (1938). *A vision.* New York: Collier.

Young, Peggy S. J. (1986). *A study of the experience of channeling.* Unpublished doctoral dissertation. Sierra University, Santa Monica, CA.

APPENDIX

Resources for Further Investigation

For those who wish to further investigate the world of channels and channeling, the research and perspectives, here is a selective list of resources available when this book was published. Publication data for books will be found in the references.

STUDIES OF CHANNELING

The most comprehensive account of the phenomena of channeling is *Channeling: Investigations on Receiving Information from Paranormal Sources* (1987), by Jon Klimo. This book is an excellent survey of many channels, present and past, their messages and theories of explanation. Brad Steiger's *Revelation* (1988) points out the similarities of spiritual messages from many sources, including mystical experiences, and suggests the presence of an outside intelligence. Various viewpoints are represented by Eyer (1987), Houston (in Carey, 1985), Kautz and Branon (1987), and Anderson (1989).

C. G. Jung's studies of mediumship and spirits are collected in *Psychology and the Occult* (1977). He tells his personal experiences with inner guides and the spirits who inspired his seven sermons in *Memories, Dreams, Reflections* (1973). Ira Progoff, a pioneering transpersonal psychologist who developed the Intensive Journal method, discusses his in-depth interviews with Eileen J. Garrett and her spirit guides in *Image of an Oracle* (1964). The interview transcripts are included.

Automatic Writing, by Anita Muhl (1963), emphasizes the unconscious and pathological sources of the material. *Divided Consciousness*, by eminent psychologist Ernest Hilgard (1986), presents a model of dissociation that is relevant to channeling, multiple personality, and hypnosis. Julian Jaynes' (1976) *The Origin of Consciousness in the Breakdown of the Bicameral Mind* traces verbal channeling phenomena back to prehistory as a form of communication from one part of the brain to another.

The research on spirit mediums can barely be touched here. Alan Gauld's (1977) chapter in Wolman's *Handbook of Parapsychology* is a review of survival evidence. The classic *Human Personality and its Survival of Bodily Death*, by F. W. H. Myers (1903) includes examples, analysis, and seminal thinking on many phenomena that are similar to current channeling. Much important research on mediumship was published in early issues of the *Journal of the Society for Psychical Research* and the *Journal of the American Society for Psychical Research*.

Two reference sources on psychical research and the spiritualist traditions are Nandor Fodor (1966), *Encyclopædia of Psychic Science*, and Leslie Shepherd (1984), *Encyclopedia of Occultism and Parapsychology*.

UFOS AND CHANNELING

Messages coming from entities claiming to be UFO occupants or extraterrestrials have a literature of their own. An excellent compilation of selections from contactees (usually received telepathically) with a thoughtful unorthodox perspective is in *Secrets of the UFO*, by Don Elkins and Carla Rueckert (1977). John Keel (1970) draws specific parallels to channeled communication in *UFOs: Operation Trojan Horse* (1970). Jacques Vallee (1975; 1979) reports on UFO groups, channeled messages, and effects on contactees in *The Invisible College* and *Messengers of Deception: UFO Contacts and Cults*. A classic social psychology report, *When Prophecy Fails*, by Leon Festinger, et al., (1956) is a study of a group that was deceived by automatic writing purporting to come from a UFO crew. The archetypal nature of UFO imagery and communications is discussed by C. G. Jung (1959) in *Flying Saucers: A Modern Myth of Things Seen in the Skies*. Hilary Evans (1984) draws parallels between UFOs and other hallucinatory phenomena in *Visions, Apparitions, Alien Visitors*, and postulates that the unconscious is producing them to influence the conscious mind.

LISTINGS OF CHANNELS

Specific channels are named, addresses given, and their work described in Robin Westen's (1988) *Channelers: A New Age Directory*, and William Kautz and Melanie Branon, (1987) *Channeling: The Intuitive Connection*. Channels who have publications can usually be reached with a letter in care of their publisher.

CHANNELED MATERIALS

Several periodicals print channeled material, including *Body, Mind, Spirit*, P.O. Box 7377, Johnston, RI 02919, and *Connecting Link*, P.O. Box 891, Grand Rapids, MI 49518. Although it is no longer published, the journal *Metapsychology* is a valuable collection of channeled communications. *Venture Inward*, directed toward Cayce's work, is published by the Association for Research and Enlightenment. *Reality Change*, directed toward Seth's teachings, is published by the Austin Seth Center (see below).

RECORDINGS

Cassette recordings of many contemporary channels, from the 1970s to the present, are available from the Conference Recording Service, 1308 Gilman St., Berkeley, CA 94702. (415) 527-3600.

ORGANIZATIONS

The following organizations are associated with specific channeled material:

A Course in Miracles.
Foundation for Inner Peace.
P.O. Box 1104, Glen Ellen, CA, 95442. (707) 939-0200.

Edgar Cayce.
Association for Research and Enlightenment.
67th Street and Atlantic Avenue, or P.O. Box 595,
Virginia Beach, VA 23451.

Alice A. Bailey.
Meditation Group for the New Age.
P.O. Box 566,
Ojai, CA 93023.

Lucis Trust and Arcane School (U.S.),
866 United Nations Plaza, Suite 566–7
New York, NY 10017
Lucis Trust and Arcane School (U.K.)
3 Whitehall Court, Suite 54. London, SW1A 2EF

Jane Roberts and Seth.
Austin Seth Center,
Dr. Maude Carwell, Director.
P.O. Box 7786,
Austin TX 78713-7786.

Center for Applied Intuition.
Dr. William Kautz, Director
Kevin Ryerson, Jon Fox, and other channels.
P.O. Box 218
Fairfax, CA 94930.
(415) 453-2130.

LEARNING TO CHANNEL

For suggestions on how to learn channeling, several books give methods of preparation, techniques, and precautions: *A Channeling Handbook,* by Carla Rueckert (1987); *How to Channel,* by J. Donald Walters (1987); *Opening to Channel,* by Sanaya Roman and Duane Packer (1987); *Edgar Cayce on Channeling Your Higher Self,* by Henry Reed (1989); and *Channeling: How to Reach Out to Your Spirit Guides,* by Kathryn Ridall (1988). Chapters 12 and 13 in this book should be noted, and there is useful information in the volumes by Kautz and Branon (1987) and Klimo (1987).

THERAPISTS

Therapists working with clients who have unexpected or distressing channeling experiences may find these articles useful: "A Counseling Approach to Parapsychological Experience" (Hastings, 1983) and "Psychological Impact of Psychic Abilities" (Targ, Hastings, and Harary, 1987). The chapter by Anne Armstrong, "The Challenges of Psychic Opening," in *Spiritual Emergency,* by Stanislav and Christina Grof (1989), is a first-person account of psychic and channeling experiences. The Grofs' book offers valuable perspectives on several kinds of spiritual crises that are relevant to the psychology of channeling.

CONSULTING A CHANNEL

Those who wish to consult channels (and psychics) for information, advice, and personal growth will find suggestions for preparation and evaluation in these sources. Chapter 10, "How to Use a Psychic Reading," in *Open Mind, Discriminating Mind,* by Charles T. Tart (1989); *Channeling: The Intuitive Connection,* by William Kautz and Melanie Branon (1987); "Tuning in the Best Channel," by Corrine McLaughlin (1987); and my article, "A Counseling Approach to Parapsychological Experience" (Hastings, 1983).

INDEX

Note: (s) indicates a channeled source, e.g., an entity, deity, spirit, and so on, communicating through a channel.

PHOTO AND ILLUSTRATION CREDITS

About the Author

Arthur Hastings is a professor at the Institute of Transpersonal Psychology, Menlo Park, California. The institute offers educational programs and graduate degrees in transpersonal psychology, which is the study of the integrated development of body, mind, emotions, and spiritual aspects of the self. Dr. Hastings has taught at ITP, where he has also been Dean of Faculty and President, since 1975. He is a former president of the Association for Transpersonal Psychology.

He received a B.A. from Tulane University. His doctoral work was performed at Northwestern University, where he received a Ph.D. in public address and small group communication. He studied with F. S. Perls in Gestalt therapy and Milton H. Erickson in hypnosis.

Dr. Hastings has conducted research in parapsychology, computer communication, health, and consciousness studies. He is a member of the professional Parapsychological Association. He is also a magician and uses his knowledge of conjuring techniques in evaluating possible psychic abilities.

Dr. Hastings was senior editor of *Health for the Whole Person,* an award-winning book on holistic medicine sponsored by the Institute of Noetic Sciences. He has co-authored (with Russel Windes) a book on debate, *Argumentation and Advocacy,* co-authored *Changing Images of Man* (Ed. by Willis Harman and O. W. Markley), and has written on communication, semantics, health, parapsychology, hypnosis, counseling, and transpersonal psychology.

During his career, he has held faculty appointments at the University of Nevada at Reno, Stanford University, San Jose State University, and the University of California, Santa Barbara. He has been a consultant to SRI International and the Institute for the Study of the Future.

Dr. Hastings lives in California with his wife Sandy and son Michael.

THE INSTITUTE OF NOETIC SCIENCES

Astronaut Edgar Mitchell founded this nonprofit membership organization in 1973 to expand knowledge of the nature and potentials of the mind and spirit and to apply that knowledge to advance health and well-being for humankind and our planet. The word *noetic* comes from the Greek "nous," meaning mind, intelligence and understanding; the "noetic sciences," then, are those that *encompass diverse ways of knowing:* the reasoning processes of the intellect, the perceptions of the physical senses, and the intuitive, spiritual, inner ways of knowing.

The Institute funds scientific research; brings top-level scientists and scholars together to share their methods, perspectives and knowledge; and, in publications to its members, discusses new developments in consciousness research.

THE EXCEPTIONAL ABILITIES PROGRAM

The Institute seeks to foster a vital, contemporary vision of constructive human potentials—a vision that incorporates all that is known about the farther and higher reaches of human nature. By encouraging the study of people with outstanding and extraordinary capacities—such as exceptional creativity, peak physical performance, unusual mental ability, or, as in this case, the ability to employ channeling—the Institute hopes to learn how individuals can realize and expand their unique abilities and, with them, create a world that better supports human fulfillment. The Institute sponsored Dr. Hastings' inquiry and the publication of *With the Tongues of Men and Angels* in this spirit, both to learn more about the likely mechanisms of this unusual ability, and to more fully understand its psychological, transpersonal, sociological, and historical significance.

THE ALTRUISTIC SPIRIT PROGRAM

In the Altruistic Spirit Program, the Institute studies the human capacity for unselfish love and creatively altruistic behavior. The Institute hopes to discover the conditions that foster or suppress creative altruism and encourage its presence in everyday life.

THE INNER MECHANISMS OF THE HEALING RESPONSE PROGRAM

One of the fundamental goals of the Institute has been to create a scientific understanding of the mind-body relationship. The Institute's Inner Mechanisms Program is devoted to studying *how* the healing response functions. This Program asks: What are the innate processes within us that stimulate recovery and natural self-repair? Is there an unknown healing system that promotes remission from normally fatal illnesses? The Institute supports proposals from selected researchers and supports targeted interdisciplinary working conferences on the mechanisms of healing in areas such as psychoneuroimmunology, energy medicine, spontaneous remission, and spiritual healing.

EMERGING PARADIGMS IN SCIENCE AND SOCIETY PROGRAM

This Program explores the relationship between consciousness—particularly values and beliefs—and global issues, and the premise that *a fundamental change of mind* may be occurring worldwide, for example, in areas such as global peace and common security. In its newest project, "Expanding the Foundations of Science," the Institute is attempting to identify and illuminate what the Institute sees as the changing *foundations* of science—evident in the exciting new developments in physics, biology, the neurosciences, systems theory, and other fields. These developments provide startling insights into understanding the basic processes of health and healing, psychology, parapsychology, sociology, and international relations. In fact, the Institute believes these changes in the very foundations of science will generate a "global mind change" every bit as sweeping as the dramatic change in worldview accompanying the scientific revolution in the seventeenth century. The New Paradigms Program also explores the role of business in a positive global future.

The Institute's pioneering research and educational programs are financed completely by donations from members and other sources of private support. Institute members receive a quarterly journal, the *Noetic Sciences Review*, which offers serious discussion of emerging concepts in consciousness research, the mind-body connection and healing, and our changing global reality. Members also receive occasional *Special Reports*, which provide a deeper look into specific issues within these areas; the quarterly *Noetic*

Sciences Bulletin, with reports on continuing Institute projects, member activities, and upcoming conferences and lectures; and *An Intelligent Guide*, a comprehensive catalog of the many books, audiotapes, and videotapes in this field, which are available to members at a discount.

The Institute of Noetic Sciences
475 Gate Five Road, Suite 300
Sausalito, California 94965-0909
(415) 331-5650